Hiking through History
New England

Exploring the Region's Past by Trail

Johnny Molloy

GUILFORD, CONNECTICUT
HELENA, MONTANA

FALCONGUIDES®

An imprint of Rowman & Littlefield
Falcon, FalconGuides, and Outfit Your Mind are registered trademarks of Rowman & Littlefield.

Distributed by NATIONAL BOOK NETWORK

Copyright © 2015 by Rowman & Littlefield
Photos: Johnny Molloy
Maps: Designmaps Inc. © Rowman & Littlefield

British Library Cataloguing-in-Publication Information available

Library of Congress Cataloging-in-Publication Data available

ISBN 978-1-4930-0146-0 (paperback)
ISBN 978-1-4930-1441-5 (electronic)

∞™ The paper used in this publication meets the minimum requirements of American National Standard for Information Sciences—Permanence of Paper for Printed Library Materials, ANSI/NISO Z39.48-1992.

This book is for the woman who lives in the moment—Keri Anne Molloy.

HELP US KEEP THIS GUIDE UP TO DATE

Every effort has been made by the author and editors to make this guide as accurate and useful as possible. However, many things can change after a guide is published—trails are rerouted, regulations change, facilities come under new management, and so forth.

We welcome your comments concerning your experiences with this guide and how you feel it could be improved and kept up to date. While we may not be able to respond to all comments and suggestions, we'll take them to heart, and we'll also make certain to share them with the author. Please send your comments and suggestions to the following address:

FalconGuides
Reader Response/Editorial Department
246 Goose Lane
Guilford, CT 06437

Or you may e-mail us at: editorial@falcon.com

Thanks for your input, and happy trails!

Contents

The Hikes

Overview

Montreal

QUEBEC

MAINE

CANADA
UNITED STATES

VERMONT

5

3

2

Burlington   South Burlington

89   27

Whitefield   33   34   Gorham

28   302   302   32

Montpelier

Barre   91   30

31

Lincoln

7   93

GREEN
MOUNTAIN
NATIONAL
FOREST

302

25   Woodstock   WHITE
MOUNTAINS
NATIONAL
FOREST

Portland

4   Rutland   26   4

202

89

GREEN
MOUNTAIN
NATIONAL
FOREST

NEW HAMPSHIRE

35

24   Jamaica   202

Concord   4

NY   95

23   30

Bennington   Manchester

93

22   Williamstown   3

7   Lawrence   16

Lowell   128

MASSACHUSETTS   15

7   68

90   91   19   190   14

20   495   Cambridge   Boston

21   Worcester   Newton   13

20   202   Quincy   12

Springfield   90   1

18   17   Brockton   3A

146

44   84   44   395   9   Pawtucket

6   Hartford   6   Cranston   Providence   44

1   New Britain   Warwick   495

202   RI   Fall River

2   Waterbury   91   195   Cape Co

84   9   8

4-5   7

New Haven   95

3   95   1

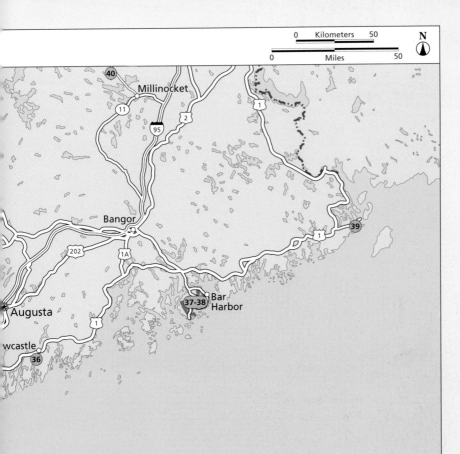

0 Kilometers 50

0 Miles 50

N

Millinocket

40

11

95

2

1

Bangor

202

1A

39

1

37-38 Bar
Harbor

Augusta

1

wcastle

36

*ATLANTIC
OCEAN*

Acknowledgments

Thanks to all the people who preserved history before we ever got here. Thanks to DeLorme for the fine GPS that helped create the maps for this book. Thanks to Kelty for providing me with great tents, sleeping bags, and clothing for the outdoors. Thanks also to the folks at FalconGuides, especially that Connecticuter Katie Benoit. Thanks to Scott and Rina Grierson for their Maine hospitality, to Eric and Sally Mullins for making us feel at home, and to Ken Ashley and Anne Leeds for their friendship. And thanks to Eve Sherwood for holding down the fort.

Leftover steps from the quarry operation are now incorporated into the trail (hike 5).

Introduction

What a pleasure it has been to pen this guide to New England's historic hikes! The meshing of mental and physical exertion while completing this book reflects the book itself, which meshes hiking and historic interest. Using New England's rich past as a backdrop, I have selected forty hikes scattered throughout the six states composing New England—Connecticut, Rhode Island, Massachusetts, Vermont, New Hampshire, and Maine—taking you to the most fascinating places where New England's past can be experienced by trail. These historic hiking destinations include Connecticut's Mine Hill, a huge ore-smelting complex from yesteryear; Rhode Island's Blackstone Canal, with its waterside canal towpath; Massachusetts's Great Brook Farm, a living history farm awash in trails; and Vermont's Stone House of Robert Frost, where he penned his famous poem "Stopping by Woods on a Snowy Evening."

And there is more—hiking to see relics of the Civilian Conservation Corps at New Hampshire's Moose Brook State Park, or strolling around historic Jordan Pond at Acadia National Park in Maine. The book includes trails of varied lengths and difficulties, as well as different types of destinations, from sites where wealthy magnates built mountaintop mansions; to places like Lincoln Woods, where loggers left their mark; to Mount Katahdin, the northern terminus of America's most notable footpath, the Appalachian Trail.

Being part of the original thirteen states—or the fourteenth as is the case with Vermont and twentieth for latecomer Maine—makes New England crammed with history. The United States was settled east to west, with many of New England's villages and townships established well before the United States even came to be. Being a writer of outdoor guidebooks and a student of American history, I excitedly tackled this project. When preparing this book, I realized that readers, even those going on historic hikes, want to know the basics: how to get to the trailhead, how far the hike is, hike difficulty, when to go, what they are going to see along the way, and where they are within reason at any given moment of the hike. This book covers those essentials, yet it differentiates itself from other hiking guides by emphasizing trailside history.

Let's face it: In our rush-rush electronic world, we are looking for fast info, maybe an authority, "someone who knows," to lead us as we pursue our goal of hiking through New England's history. This is my approach: Imagine you and I are relaxing around a campfire. You ask about the best historic hikes in New England and I tell you as one friend would to another, in story fashion rather than simply reciting information like a dry, dull textbook. New England's history is too fascinating for that! This guide conveys concise, organized information to help busy people make the most of their limited and precious outdoor recreation time and provides an opportunity to experience the mosaic of history that can be found in the Northeast.

While contemplating the historical hikes in this guide, Cape Cod comes to mind first. After all, this is where the Pilgrims landed and then established the Mayflower

Deer Island sports a fine view of the Boston Skyline (hike 13).

Compact, arguably the first civil democratic framework in what became the United States. You can hike through the former community of Nauset, seeing where the Pilgrims lived and worked, along with relics from the Wampanoag Indians, who helped them survive. Another hike on Cape Cod visits Wellfleet Harbor and the site of an old whaler's tavern then looks out on islands once occupied by colonial settlers.

Cape Cod pulses with New England's past, yet many other historic hiking locales are scattered throughout the six states. Weir Farm National Historic Site is the only national park dedicated to American painting. Contemplative reflections can be found while hiking around Walden Pond, where Henry David Thoreau solidified his theses on nature and man. Aboriginal New Englanders are represented at Salt Bay Preserve, where a 2,400-year-old shell midden provides clues left by ancient Mainers. The Dalley Loop at Vermont's Little River State Park takes you through a whole community of homesites on the slopes of Ricker Mountain, providing a snapshot of rural New England life in the 1800s.

And then there is the evolution of outdoor tourism and how popular natural destinations led to preservation that we can enjoy today. New Hampshire's Flume Gorge is a great example of that. You can hike where tourists did 150 years ago—to see where water and rock morphed the mountains into a sight to behold. Other places like Newport's Cliff Walk and Ogunquit, Maine's Marginal Way let us humble folk walk along majestic oceanside cliffs near multimillion-dollar historic mansions.

Massachusetts's Mount Holyoke was second only to Niagara Falls as an American tourist destination of the early 1800s. Today you can scale its heights, learn about the hotel at the top, and walk the adjacent land, forever preserved.

Then there are places that combine history with superlative beauty. On New Hampshire's Pondicherry Trail, you can walk a railroad grade from yesteryear and reach one of the finest birding locales in New England. Climb to the top of Maine's Cadillac Mountain and see the reason the land around you was the first national park east of the Mississippi River. Halibut Point State Park in Massachusetts explores an old granite quarry while providing incredible panoramas of the Atlantic Ocean. The Willey House Loop at New Hampshire's Crawford Notch State Park tells the story of a deadly but mysterious landslide and offers a fantastic waterfall and mountain panoramas high and low. Visit Maine's West Quoddy Head Lighthouse, perched on the easternmost point in the contiguous United States, overlooking magnificent cliffs pounded by the salty sea.

How fortunate we are to have lands laced with trails that preserve New England's past! In Massachusetts we can see mining history and great views at Chester-Blandford State Forest or view an old mill village turned country estate at Moore State Park. In Connecticut you can walk through Bulls Bridge, a covered bridge, then head through forgotten farmland to reach a mountain vista. The West River Trail at Vermont's Jamaica State Park traces a short-lived railroad line through a highland gorge and then follows an old wagon trail to a free-falling cataract.

The foresight of creating history-laden parks and building trails within them benefits us greatly, providing a tangible link to what has transpired. These destinations also harbor some of the natural beauty for which New England is known, from the mountains to the sea. May the hikes presented in this book help you explore, understand, and appreciate the natural and human history of New England. Enjoy.

Weather

New England's weather offers as much variety as its terrain and elevation imply, from 6,278 feet atop Mount Washington to sea level along the Atlantic, from Mount Katahdin in the north of Maine to the lowlands of Connecticut in southern New England. All four seasons lay their hand on New England, with more winter than summer in the northern states. Given New England's varied elevations, the area could be experiencing them all at the same time!

Summer is mostly mild, with sporadic hot spells in the lowlands. The mountains will be cooler, as will the coastline. Morning hikers can avoid heat and the occasional afternoon thunderstorms. A smart phone connected to the Internet allows hikers to monitor storms as they arise.

Hikers are drawn outdoors in increasing numbers when the first northerly fronts of fall sweep cool air across the Northeast. Crisp mornings, great for vigorous treks, give way to warm afternoons more conducive to family strolls. Fall is drier than summer.

Winter will bring many subfreezing days, chilling rains, and heavy snows, even more so in the mountains. Lots of parks close or severely curtail their facilities for the long cold season. There are also far fewer hours of daylight. However, a brisk hiking pace and smart time management will keep you warm and walking while the sun is still above the horizon. Each cold month has a few days of mild weather. Make the most of them.

Spring will be more variable. A warm day can be followed by a cold one. Extensive spring rains and falling then melting snows bring regrowth but also keep most hikers indoors. However, avid hikers will find more good hiking days than they will have time to hike in spring—and every other season.

A smart way to plan your hiking is to check monthly averages of high and low temperatures and rainfall near your chosen destination. Elevation and specific location will lead to different exact temperatures.

Flora and Fauna

The natural landscape of New England, inextricably intertwined with its human history, offers everything—a maze of islands and waters along the Atlantic coast to mile-high mountains of the Appalachians. A wide variety of wildlife calls these dissimilar landscapes home.

Even unicyclists enjoy the Farmington Canal Trail (hike 4).

Deer are the land animal you're most likely to see as you hike New England's historic trails. They can be found throughout the land, save for the most urbanized locations. Deer in some of the parks are remarkably tame and may linger on or close to the trail as you approach. A quiet hiker may also see moose, bears, turkeys, porcupines, raccoons, or even a coyote. Bears can be found in most of New England these days; again, urban areas excepted. They occur in greatest numbers in the remote mountains of New England and Maine in general. Moose range from northwestern Connecticut and western Massachusetts up through Vermont, New Hampshire, and into Maine. Do not be surprised if you observe beaver along streams and lakes. If you feel uncomfortable when encountering any critter, keep your distance and they will generally keep theirs.

Overhead, many raptors, including hawks, falcons, and owls, will be plying the skies for food. Maine's Cadillac Mountain is known as a hawk migration flyover. Depending upon where you are, other birds you may spot include kingfishers and woodpeckers. Look for waterfowl in lakes and tidal waters. Songbirds are abundant throughout the area.

The flora offers just as much variety, especially with such a variety of elevation and transitioning aquatic environments from mountain streams to saltwater seas. Atop the highest mountains of New Hampshire and Maine, there is a tree line where arctic vegetation persists. Along the trails you will find evergreen forests of spruce and balsam, hardwoods coloring autumn's landscapes, even spartan beach environments along the coast. Wildflowers will be found in spring, summer, and fall throughout New England.

Wilderness/Land Use Restrictions/Regulations

New England's historic hikes are primarily in city, state, and federal parks, as well as national forests and wildlife refuges. Each operates with its own system of rules. We are responsible for knowing them. Since these hikes travel to historical destinations, a layer of New England's past overlays each park. For example, though the Robert Frost Trail uses town land and affords multiple forms of outdoor recreation from swimming to boating, the preserved home of Robert Frost to which you hike is managed by an entirely different entity. National parks often have a mix of preservation and recreation. At the Jordan Pond House at Acadia National Park, historical, recreation, and nature trails are all interconnected with facilities that include a visitor center, gift shop, and restaurant. At Weir Farm National Historic Site, emphasis is on history first. So in the end, it depends on the managing body and the mission of the park how the preserved past is treated.

No matter where you go to hike through New England's past, consider adding other recreational opportunities while you are there, whether you strap on a backpack and overnight in the back of beyond, stay in a nearby campground, take a guided tour, go on a bike ride, or spend the night in a cozy cabin. The important thing is to get out there and connect with history on your own terms.

How to Use This Guide

This guide contains just about everything you'll ever need to choose, plan for, enjoy, and survive a historical hike in New England. Stuffed with useful area information, *Hiking through History: New England* features forty mapped and cued hikes. Here's an outline of the book's major components:

Each hike starts with a short **summary** of the hike's highlights. These quick overviews give you a taste of the hiking adventures and the history contained within. You'll learn about the trail terrain and what surprises each route has to offer. Following the overview, you'll find the **hike specs:** quick, nitty-gritty details of the hike. Most are self-explanatory, but here are a few details:

Distance: The total distance of the recommended route—one-way for loop hikes, the round-trip on an out-and-back or lollipop hike, point-to-point for a shuttle. Options are additional.

Hiking time: The average time it will take to cover the route. It is based on the total distance, elevation gain, and condition and difficulty of the trail. Your fitness level will also affect your time.

Difficulty: Each hike has been assigned a level of difficulty. The rating system was developed from several sources and personal experience. These levels are meant to be a guideline only and may prove easier or harder for different people depending on ability and physical fitness.

> Easy—Five miles or less total trip distance in one day, minimal elevation gain, and paved or smooth-surfaced dirt trail.
>
> Moderate—Up to 8 miles total trip distance in one day, moderate elevation gain, and potentially rough terrain.
>
> Difficult—More than 8 miles total trip distance in one day, strenuous elevation gains, and rough and/or rocky terrain.

Trail surface: General information about what to expect underfoot.

Best season: General information on the best time of year to hike.

Other trail users: Equestrians, mountain bikers, inline skaters, joggers, etc.

Canine compatibility: Know the trail regulations before you take your dog hiking with you. Dogs are not allowed on several trails in this book.

Land status: City park, state park, national park or forest, etc.

Fees and permits: Whether you need to carry any money with you for park entrance fees and permits.

Schedule: When the park or trail is open to the public.

Maps: Other maps to supplement the maps in this book. US Geological Survey (USGS) maps are the best source for accurate topographical information, but the local park map may show more recent trails. Use both.

Trail contact: This is the location, phone number, and website URL for the local land manager(s) in charge of all the trails within the selected hike. Before you head out, get trail access information; or contact the land manager after your visit if you see problems with trail erosion, damage, or misuse.

Finding the trailhead gives you dependable driving directions to where you'll want to park.

The Hike is the meat of the chapter. Detailed and honest, it is a carefully researched impression of the trail and the history along the way, both natural and human.

Under **Miles and Directions,** mileage cues identify all turns and trail name changes, as well as points of interest. Options are also given for some hikes to make your journey shorter or longer, depending on the amount of time you have. Do not feel restricted to the routes and trails that are mapped here. Be adventurous; use this guide as a platform to discover new routes for yourself.

Interspersed throughout this guide you'll find quick and often fascinating facts about the locales. Some hikes include a **sidebar** that expounds on a particular aspect of the area's past or suggests better ways to enjoy your historical hiking experience. These sidebars may pique your interest to research beyond the history given here. Enjoy your outdoor exploration of New England's past—and remember to pack out what you pack in.

How to Use the Maps

Overview map: This map shows the location of each hike in the area by hike number.

Route map: This is your primary guide to each hike. It shows all the accessible roads and trails, historical points of interest, water, landmarks, and geographical features. It also distinguishes trails from roads, paved roads from unpaved roads. The selected route is highlighted, and directional arrows point the way.

Trail Finder

#	Hike Name	Best Hikes for Stories of People	Best Hikes for Ocean Lovers	Best Hikes for Industrial History	Best Hikes for History Loving Dogs	Best Hikes for History Loving Children	Best Hikes for History Lovers who also Love Mountains	Best Hikes for Backpacking History Buffs
1	Bulls Bridge						●	●
2	Mine Hill Preserve	●		●	●			
3	Weir Farm National Historic Site	●				●		
4	Lock 12 Historical Park	●		●		●		
5	The Tower of the Sleeping Giant	●		●	●		●	
6	Talcott Mountain	●					●	
7	Gillette Castle	●						
8	Newport Cliff Walk	●	●			●		
9	Blackstone River Valley	●		●		●		
10	Fort Hill Trail at Cape Cod	●	●			●		
11	Great Island Trail at Cape Cod	●	●					
12	World's End	●	●					
13	Deer Island		●	●		●		

	Hike Name	Best Hikes for Stories of People	Best Hikes for Ocean Lovers	Best Hikes for Industrial History	Best Hikes for History Loving Dogs	Best Hikes for History Loving Children	Best Hikes for History Lovers who also Love Mountains	Best Hikes for Backpacking History Buffs
14	Walden Pond	●				●		
15	Great Brook Farm				●	●		
16	Halibut Point State Park		●	●		●		
17	Borderland State Park	●				●		
18	Blackstone Canal at Uxbridge			●	●	●		
19	Moore State Park	●		●	●			
20	Summit House at Skinner State Park	●					●	
21	Chester-Blandford State Forest			●	●		●	
22	Mount Greylock						●	●
23	The Stone House of Robert Frost	●				●		
24	West River Trail			●			●	
25	Deer Leap Loop						●	●

	Hike Name	Best Hikes for Stories of People	Best Hikes for Ocean Lovers	Best Hikes for Industrial History	Best Hikes for History Loving Dogs	Best Hikes for History Loving Children	Best Hikes for History Lovers who also Love Mountains	Best Hikes for Backpacking History Buffs
26	Mount Tom	●				●	●	
27	Dalley Loop	●			●		●	
28	Groton Forest Hike			●			●	●
29	Smarts Mountain						●	●
30	The Flume	●				●	●	
31	Lincoln Woods Trail			●	●		●	
32	Willey House Loop	●					●	
33	Pondicherry Trail			●		●	●	
34	CCC Perimeter Path	●			●	●	●	
35	Marginal Way		●			●		
36	Salt Bay Preserve	●	●			●		
37	Cadillac Mountain	●					●	
38	Jordan Pond House	●				●	●	
39	West Quoddy Head Lighthouse	●	●					
40	Katahdin	●					●	

Map Legend

Municipal

84	Interstate Highway
202	US Highway
100	State Road
	Local/County Road
	Unpaved Road
	Carriage Road
	Railroad
	State Boundary

Trails

	Featured Trail
	Trail
	Paved Trail

Water Features

	Body of Water
	Marsh
	River/Creek
	Intermittent Stream
	Waterfall

Land Management

	National Park/Forest
	National Monument/Wilderness Area
	State/County Park
	Parking Lot

Symbols

	Bridge
▲	Backcountry Campground
	Boardwalk/Steps
	Boat Launch
■	Building/Point of Interest
Λ	Campground
∧	Cave/Cavern
	Gate
×	Elevation
	Inn/Lodging
	Lighthouse
P	Parking
▲	Peak
	Picnic Area
	Ranger Station/Park Office
	Restroom
	Scenic View
	Telephone
	Tower
○	Town
20	Trailhead
	Tunnel
?	Visitor/Information Center

Connecticut

Hiking through history matches up hikes into amazing scenery with fascinating historical exhibits indoors—like this interior of the largely intact Weir Studio (hike 3).

1 Bulls Bridge

This hike treks along the wild Housatonic River, first spanning it via a historic covered bridge. Next join the Appalachian Trail, wandering by whitewater rapids amid former farmland, replete with stone fences. The hike then stops by an AT shelter, where old agricultural implements can be found. Leave the enticing water and then climb to Ten Mile Hill for a view. A mini-loop at hike's end leads by old chimneys from a forgotten homesite.

Start: Bulls Bridge parking area
Distance: 4.7 miles out and back with a mini-loop on return
Hiking time: 3–3.5 hours
Difficulty: Moderate due to 700-foot climb
Trail surface: Natural
Best season: Summer for aquatic fun
Other trail users: None
Canine compatibility: Dogs allowed
Land status: First Light Power Generating Company, National Park Service

Fees and permits: No fees or permits required
Schedule: Open 24 hours a day year-round; no trailhead parking allowed between sunset and sunrise
Maps: Appalachian Trail, Kent to CT 55 section
Trail contact: National Park Service, Appalachian Trail Park Office, PO Box 50, Harpers Ferry, WV 25425; (304) 535-6278; nps.gov/appa

Finding the trailhead: From the intersection of CT 7 and US 202 in New Milford, Connecticut, take CT 7 north 9 miles to the hamlet of Bulls Bridge. Turn left onto Bulls Bridge Road at a traffic light and follow it just a few feet; turn left into a parking area just before driving through Bulls Bridge. **Trailhead GPS:** N41 40.539'/W73 30.494'

The Hike

The community of Bulls Bridge, in western Connecticut near the New York border, is named for the covered bridge located here. The one-lane bridge, part of this hike, spans a channel of the Housatonic River. As we all know, George Washington got around in his day, and it is said that the general lost his favored horse while crossing the Housatonic at the bridge site and had to pay a hefty bill of $212 to get it retrieved from the rapids. The 109-foot covered bridge was built in 1842, long after Washington's day.

Enjoy both human history and natural beauty on this trek. After crossing the power generation canal dug by First Light Power Generating Company, you stroll through Bulls Bridge, which is open to cars but regularly walked through by tourists and hikers alike. In fact, to get from the trailhead parking to the trail itself, you must hike through the dim wooden structure rising above frothing torrents of the Housatonic River. Ahead, trails spur off, including a portage trail whereby Housatonic paddlers tote their boats around the power station. On your way to the AT connector

Walking through Bulls Bridge covered bridge

trail, look for the short loop path leading to an overlook of the convergence of two channels of the Housatonic. Observe the whitewater extravaganza as daring boaters ply their craft, while others head for riverside rocks to fish or soak in the atmosphere. No swimming is allowed hereabouts.

You then pick up a connector to meet the Appalachian Trail. Your southbound hike leads along the Housatonic River gorge, an impressive mix of motionless stone and frenetic aqua. See more watery wonders in the form of Ten Mile River, which you cross on an impressive iron span. The sandy confluence of the Ten Mile and Housatonic Rivers beckons you to linger. AT thru-hikers camp here and at the nearby Ten Mile trail shelter. The structure faces a field and offers a perspective of what this area looked like before reforestation shaded the amazing number of stone fence–lined fields. Scan for old farm implements near the shelter, further evidence of a previously peopled past.

▶ The first section of the Appalachian Trail in Connecticut was constructed in 1930 by Ned Anderson. He and his Boy Scout troop maintained the Connecticut AT for the next eighteen years.

After exploring the shelter/camping area, continue on the Appalachian Trail to the crest of Ten Mile Hill. En route, the path leads through deep towering hardwoods shading a mossy, ferny, and stony forest floor. Switchbacks ease the climb. A short spur at the top of the 1,000-foot peak leads to a stone outcrop amid sturdy oaks and hickories. Here, peer northwest into the Ten Mile River valley and the state of New York. From this vantage, make the descent back to the Housatonic–Ten Mile River confluence, crossing the iron span again. This time, an alternate loop leads up a low hill on a time-worn farm road. Here, more stone fences appear; a keen eye will spot a pair of standing chimneys, one brick and one stone, all that remains of a Housatonic valley farm. Before reaching the trailhead, you get one more chance to walk through Bulls Bridge, with its undersize windows letting in just enough light for you to make your way.

Miles and Directions

0.0   Start from the Bulls Bridge parking area and walk east on Bulls Bridge Road. Cross an outflow canal of the power plant, visible just upstream. Dip to enter historic Bulls Bridge covered bridge. Watch for cars. Beyond Bulls Bridge, trails lead right, but stay with Bulls Bridge Road, coming to a gated parking area. (**Option:** Just past the gated parking area, look left for a little loop leading to an observation deck overlooking the Housatonic.) Continue along Bulls Bridge Road.

0.2   Reach a trailhead kiosk on the left. Leave Bulls Bridge Road and head left on a wide blue-blazed trail, a former farm road, entering the forest. Cruise downstream with the waterfall-laden Housatonic River to your left and hilly terrain rising to your right. Soon pass the first of numerous rock walls lacing now-forested former fields. User-created spur trails lead to the Housatonic.

0.4   Meet the white-blazed Appalachian Trail. Head left, southbound and uphill, still on a wide old roadbed. Rise to a bluff overlooking the wild waterway. Good views can be had from this perch.

0.5   Come to another trail intersection. Here the wide road leaves right as a blazed trail. This will be your return route. For now stay left with the AT, negotiating rugged terrain along the river gorge. Amazingly, walk beside more stone fences in this inhospitable terrain.

1.0   Pass a spur leading left to a river beach. Descend under a power line.

1.1   Reach Ten Mile River, an iron span, and a blazed trail leading right. Keep straight, crossing Ten Mile River on the arched iron span. Immediately enter an AT hiker camping area (no fires allowed) in a flat at the confluence of the Ten Mile and Housatonic Rivers. Turn right with the AT, heading upstream along the Ten Mile River, flowing to your right. Look for rock and metal fences in this former farm area.

1.3   Follow the blue-blazed trail leading left and uphill toward the Ten Mile trail shelter. Look for old metal farm implements. The shelter overlooks a field and gives a visual hint as to what this wooded land once resembled. Backtrack to the AT and continue southbound (upstream) along the Ten Mile River.

1.6   Leave the Ten Mile River and begin ascending Ten Mile Hill. It is a 700-foot climb through rocky topography.

1.9   The AT makes a switchback to the left after passing a spring. Keep working up an incline, aided by occasional stone steps, in deep woods.

2.2   Make a sharp switchback to the right on the shoulder of Ten Mile Hill. The incline moderates.

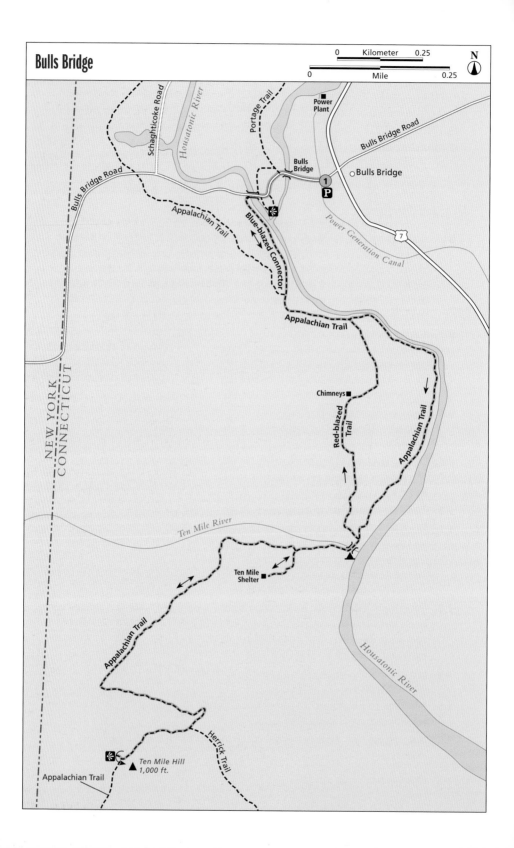

Bulls Bridge

| 0 | Kilometer | 0.25 |
| 0 | Mile | 0.25 |

N

Schaghticoke Road

Housatonic River

Portage Trail

Power Plant

Bulls Bridge

Bulls Bridge

Bulls Bridge Road

Bulls Bridge Road

1

P

Appalachian Trail

Blue-blazed Connector

7

Power Generation Canal

Appalachian Trail

Chimneys

Red-blazed Trail

Appalachian Trail

NEW YORK

CONNECTICUT

Ten Mile River

Ten Mile Shelter

Housatonic River

Appalachian Trail

Herrick Trail

Ten Mile Hill
1,000 ft.

Appalachian Trail

2.3 Reach a trail intersection. Here the lesser-used Herrick Trail heads left. Stay straight on the AT, making a final push up Ten Mile Hill, entering oak woods.

2.4 Reach a sign indicating the peak of Ten Mile Hill. A short spur leads right to emergent rocks and a northwest view into the Ten Mile River valley in New York. Backtrack on the AT.

3.7 Return to the Ten Mile River. Cross back over the iron bridge and then leave the AT, heading left on the red-blazed trail. Briefly head up along the right bank of Ten Mile River then turn from the waterway, tracing an old farm road through former fields, where cedar and tulips trees now dominate the woodscape.

4.0 Pass stone and brick chimneys on trail left, all that remains of a farmhouse. Look for other signs of the past.

4.2 Rejoin the AT, heading left (northbound). The Housatonic noisily falls to your right.

4.3 Leave right from the AT on the connector path, backtracking along the Housatonic.

4.5 Return to Bulls Bridge Road, backtracking right to once again pass through Bulls Bridge.

4.7 Arrive back at the trailhead.

2 | Mine Hill Preserve

This fun hike explores a mine and ore-processing site listed on the National Register of Historic Places. View a smelting complex where ore was turned into iron. Explore the well-preserved remains, including an intact blast furnace, roasting ovens, and more. From here take the Donkey Trail past mine entrances and air shafts where iron ore was dug, as well as granite quarries. Leave the rocky hillside to join the old Hodge Road. Walk the Shepaug River valley, returning to the furnace site. Explore more of the complex before the short finale back to the trailhead.

Start: Mine Hill Preserve parking area
Distance: 3.6-mile loop
Hiking time: 3–3.5 hours, including exploration of furnace complex
Difficulty: Moderate
Trail surface: Natural
Best season: Spring through fall
Other trail users: None
Canine compatibility: Dogs allowed

Land status: Land trust
Fees and permits: No fees or permits required
Schedule: Open year-round
Maps: Mine Hill Preserve/Carter Preserve Trail Map
Trail contact: Roxbury Land Trust, 7 South St., Roxbury, CT 06783; (860) 350-4148; http://roxburylandtrust.org

Finding the trailhead: From the intersection of CT 67 and CT 202 in New Milford, Connecticut, take CT 67 east toward Roxbury. Drive 5.8 miles and turn left onto Mine Hill Road. Mine Hill Road shortly turns to gravel as it ascends. Turn right into the Mine Hill Preserve parking area at 0.3 mile and quickly reach the trailhead. **Trailhead GPS:** N41 33.584' / W73 20.238'

The Hike

It is no wonder this area was called Mine Hill. Yankee farmers first rejected the place as too rocky for even them. And from the early 1800s, the place was known as a reservoir of fine granite. You will visit a pair of stone quarries on your hike. However, it was the iron industry of Mine Hill that spectacularly rose and fell. Its remnants will amaze on this hike. Back in the 1860s, the mountain's rich ore deposits attracted investors to create an iron and steel forge at its base. Hundreds of thousands of dollars and hundreds of men poured into this hilly backwoods. The smelting complex went up and fired into action—the mines to extract the ore, trails to move the ore from mine to processing area, and an impressive blast furnace where the ore was smelted and turned to iron.

A community by the name of Chalybes developed around the furnace. Even the railroad came to this former non-place. Even more eager workers descended on the community to serve the employees of the iron-processing operation, which underwent several company names during its seven-year run. At its height, the locale was

The furnace at Mine Hill rises proudly amid the forest.

producing 10 tons of pig iron per day. However, the steelmaking operation was a failure from the get-go, despite extensive planning.

The town of Chalybes, with its rail spur leading to the smelting operation to ship the ore, thrived. At one point there was even a cigar-rolling shop in town! Then fortunes turned for the worse at the mine. The company just couldn't get the processing down right, especially the steel smelting part. The investors backed out and the operation shut down. Chalybes went on life support, reduced to a railroad stop, and eventually changed its name to Roxbury Station. A few of the buildings of Chalybes remain, and you can see them on your drive to the trailhead. They have been turned into private residences.

The fine granite found on Mine Hill had always been there. By the early 1800s this gray stone was being extracted on a limited basis. You will hike past a granite quarry opened in 1850. The stone was initially used only locally. Later, when the railroad came, this fine stone was shipped as far away as New York City before the quarry went silent in 1905.

Toward the end of your hike, you will pass a second quarry, Rockside Quarry, opened before the Civil War as well. Extraction continued into the 1930s, then both quarries were reopened in the 1950s for one final run. Around these two quarries you will see broken stone galore.

The sounds of industry have now gone silent, yet you can visit the extensive operations that once belched smoke and fire upon this land. The intact blast furnace alone is worth the visit. You will walk atop the Donkey Trail, an elevated path once topped with rails that used gravity-driven carts to bring the ore to the smelting site from mines nearly a mile away. Brakemen rode these ore-laden carts, then donkeys pulled the empty carts back from the smelting site up to the mines. You will visit these mines, as well as pass airshafts venting the mines. All holes have been barred for safety and now attract bats. You will also visit both quarry sites, but the clear highlight will be the main smelting operation, where relics of Connecticut's industrial past are concentrated.

▶ A miner bet he could ride an ore cart from the mine downhill to the smelting area without using the brakes. He lost the bet—and his life.

Miles and Directions

0.0 Start from the Mine Hill Preserve parking area. Descend on a gravel path, reach a creek and step over it. Continue forward in lush woods.

0.1 Meet the Donkey Trail. It leads left toward the mines. Keep straight toward the smelting area. Descend on a path of broken rock, gravel, and bricks into the smelting area. Begin to pass elaborate rock support walls and signs indicating building sites. Follow the trail toward the lower level of the smelting site and then turn left toward the blast furnace.

0.2 Reach the imposing stone-and-brick blast furnace. Take time to explore the area, reading the informative interpretive signage that describes this once-thriving industrial area. After exploring, head up toward the roasting ovens, where iron ore was cooked down before being put into the blast furnace. The roasting ovens are the second most intact parts of the operation. From there, keep uphill to reach the Donkey Trail, which is just above the roasting ovens. Turn right on the blazed Donkey Trail.

0.4 Meet the Reservoir Trail after walking the elevated Donkey Trail, where rail cars full of ore once ran and donkeys pulled the cars back to the mine. The Reservoir Trail makes a 0.3-mile loop and then rejoins the Donkey Trail. Keep straight on the Donkey Trail.

0.6 Pass the other end of the Reservoir Trail. Keep straight on the gently rising Donkey Trail.

0.8 Come to the primary mine shaft. It has an arched entryway and emits water. The blazed trail splits then comes together just uphill. Keep with the main path (northbound), still following the paint blazes. The path becomes slow and rough as you work uphill among slag piles and rocky areas.

1.1 Come to three metal-enclosed air shafts, where you can peer down into the mine. These are now significant bat habitats. The path is rocky here. Enter oak and laurel dominated woods.

1.2 Reach a high point and trail junction. Here a user-created trail keeps straight for terrain outside the 360-acre preserve. The official trail makes a hard right downhill on a stony path and quickly comes to a covered airshaft. The trail then turns left and begins running alongside a rock escarpment on a very rough and slow-going track, often going where you don't think it will or should go. Stay with the paint blazes.

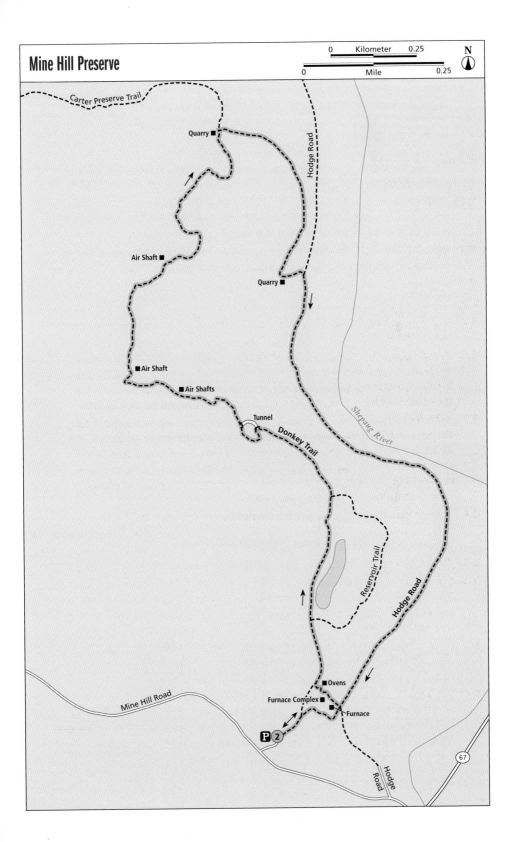

Mine Hill Preserve

Carter Preserve Trail

Hodge Road

Quarry ■

↗

Air Shaft ■

Quarry ■

↓

■ Air Shaft

■ Air Shafts

Tunnel

Donkey Trail

Shepaug River

Reservoir Trail

↑

Hodge Road

↑

↓

■ Ovens

Furnace Complex ■

↕

■ Furnace

P 2

Mine Hill Road

Hodge Road

67

0   Kilometer   0.25

0   Mile   0.25

N

1.4 Pass another air shaft. You are descending now, heading northeast along the east slope of Mine Hill. At times the path seems a boulder maze.

1.9 Reach the upper quarry and trail junction at the quarry bridge. Here a granite wall rises to your left. The 2.0-mile loop trail to the Carter Preserve keeps straight, crossing a stone bridge over the creek. This hike turns acutely right, descending on an old mining track toward Hodge Road and the Shepaug River.

2.3 Come to the lower quarry area, with literally tons of rubble where Mine Hill meets the level Shepaug River valley. Ahead, meet Hodge Road and turn right on the grass and dirt track, used to access the fields of the river valley. Keep southbound.

2.6 Reach an elevated point overlooking the Shepaug River. The trail soon dips to valley level again as the river curves away. The walking where the valley and Mine Hill meet is as swift and smooth as the earlier trail was slow and irregular.

3.4 Return to the smelting area. Here a short path leads uphill from old Hodge Road. Explore the smelting area one last time then backtrack toward the trailhead.

3.6 Arrive back at the trailhead.

3 Weir Farm National Historic Site

This hike explores the only national park in Connecticut, as well as the only national park in the country dedicated to American painting. First tour the historic site, where thousands of works of art were produced—its homes, art studios, and farm buildings. The hike then takes off through woods replete with rock walls from early American farms before reaching Weir Pond. From there visit a little waterfall and then make an elongated loop through rocky woods. Circle around the rest of Weir Pond before backtracking to Weir Farm for an encore visit. Additional hiking trails are available.

Start: Weir Farm NHS parking area
Distance: 2.3-mile lollipop
Hiking time: 1.5–2.5 hours, including farm exploration
Difficulty: Easy
Trail surface: Mostly natural surface
Best season: Summer weekends when home and studios are open for visitation
Other trail users: None
Canine compatibility: Leashed dogs allowed at historic site but not on Weir Preserve

Land status: National park
Fees and permits: No fees or permits required
Schedule: Grounds open year-round dawn to dusk
Maps: Weir Farm National Historic Site & Nod Hill Refuge
Trail contact: Weir Farm National Historic Site, 735 Nod Hill Rd., Wilton, CT 06897; (203) 834-1896; nps.gov/wefa

Finding the trailhead: From exit 3 on I-84 in Danbury, Connecticut, take US 7 south for 8 miles to CT 102. Turn right onto CT 102 west and follow it for 0.3 mile, then turn left on Old Branchville Road. Follow Old Branchville Road for 0.5 mile and turn left onto Nod Hill Road; follow it just a short distance to the parking area on your left, across from the visitor center. **Trailhead GPS:** N41 15.390' / W73 27.367'

The Hike

Have you ever wondered how acclaimed (and non-acclaimed) artists get their inspiration? At Weir Farm you can visit a place that stimulated generations of artists. Back in June 1882, when the New England spring was in full blossom, Julian Weir made his way to this quiet farm on Nod Hill. Weir, one of the founding American Impressionists, had brought his paints with him and created a postcard-size masterpiece inspired by this Connecticut farm scene. An inspiration was born, and from that day for more than a century, artists have resided here, using the farm and adjacent woods to jump-start their id. Julian Weir lived here until his death in 1919, when his daughter and her sculptor husband inherited the farm, creating art for decades. The last full-time owner/artists here were Sperry and Doris Andrews.

The Weir Farm house stands against a brilliant blue sky.

In 1990 the Weir Farm was established as a national historic site. The park preserves and interprets the property—including two art studios—as well as the natural terrain that is portrayed in so much of Weir's art. Luckily for us hikers, the Weir Farm National Historic Site also includes trails that explore the farm, including Weir Pond. Even better, an adjacent State of Connecticut open space—Nod Hill Refuge—offers connecting trails that make a loop through rocky woods centered by a little stream. And if that isn't enough, there is yet another adjacent area with trails—the 110-acre Weir Preserve. These paths also link up to the historic site, so if the loop described below isn't long enough for you, just hit the trails at the Weir Preserve. A Weir Preserve trail map is available at the national historic site visitor center. By the way, this visitor center is not some ordinary add-on building but a historic home known as the Burlingame House. Some of the original artworks created at the farm are on display at the visitor center and studios. The studios and their furnishings are almost all original.

▶ Weir Farm National Historic Site was established in 1990.

Our hike starts out slow. It has to be in order to visit all the interesting buildings of the farm. Call ahead to find out when the studios and other buildings are open to visitors. Guided tours of the Weir House are available as well, but reservations must be made in advance. After checking out the visitor center and buildings around it, cross

It Runs in the Family

It seems the Weir family just had that artistic touch. Julian Weir's father, Robert Walter Weir, was appointed Instructor of Drawing at West Point in 1834. He maintained this position for over forty years, teaching drawing to US Army cadets to use as mapmakers, surveyors, or engineers. You might call this practical art. Not only did his son Julian come through his father's class, but so did Civil War titans Robert E. Lee, Stonewall Jackson, William Tecumseh Sherman, and Ulysses S Grant.

Farther down the Weir family lineage, Julian's daughter Dorothy was an accomplished painter. She resided at Weir Farm with her sculptor husband, Mahonri Young.

Pelham Lane to see the Weir House. The Weir Studio and Young Studio both have north-facing windows for the best light.

Stop by the barn, subject of many a painting, as well as the secret garden, the orchard, and the icehouse before crossing Nod Hill Road and taking the trail to Weir Pond. Traverse bouldery woods to reach the still water. The hike then turns away from the pond to trace a stream downhill past an ambitiously named waterfall—more of a small, sloped cascade. Keep north and wander through a narrow vale, a linear rock garden. The final part of the hike takes you back to Weir Pond. From there it's a backtrack to the Weir Farm. The trails of Nod Hill Refuge are marked with paint blazes and signs.

Miles and Directions

0.0   Start by crossing Nod Hill Road to reach the visitor center/Burlingame House. Grab trail maps and soak in the interpretive information. The trail to Weir Preserve keeps straight toward the Burlingame barn, but our hike turns right from the visitor center toward the Weir House on a pea gravel path.

0.1   Cross Pelham Lane and immediately reach the Weir House. Tour the grounds, including the two art studios, as well as the barn and gardens. Eventually make your way toward the icehouse, then cross Nod Hill Road to join a wide grassy path heading east toward Weir Pond.

0.2   A spur trail leads right through a low swale then up steps, back to the front of the Weir House. Keep straight on the trail to Weir Pond and shortly enter woods crisscrossed with stone fences. Cross a small creek on a bridge.

0.5   Come to a trail intersection just as Weir Pond appears. Begin curving along the wooded shoreline. Rock-hop a small feeder stream and keep circling around the pond. Step over the pond outflow then walk along the dam.

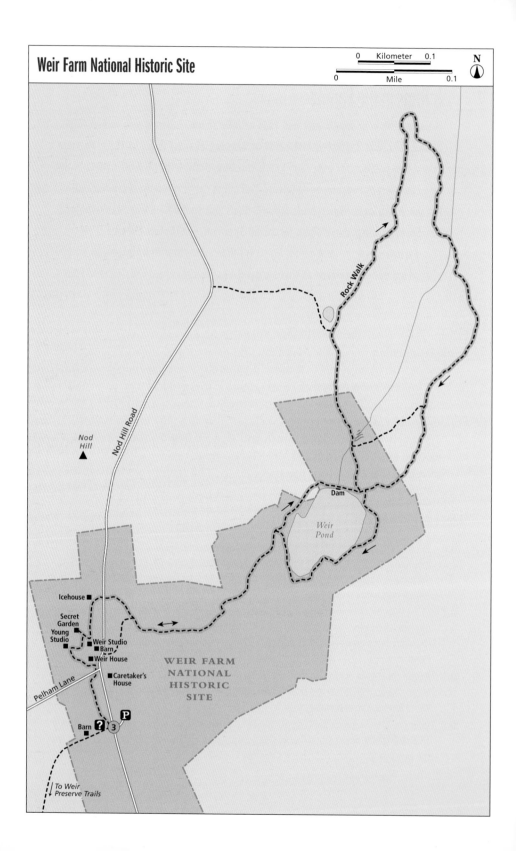

Weir Farm National Historic Site

0 Kilometer 0.1

0 Mile 0.1

N

Rock Walk

Nod Hill Road

Nod Hill ▲

Dam

Weir Pond

Icehouse ■

Secret Garden ■
Young Studio ■
Weir Studio ■
Barn ■
Weir House ■

Caretaker's House ■

Pelham Lane

Barn ■

WEIR FARM NATIONAL HISTORIC SITE

? ③ P

To Weir Preserve Trails

0.6 Reach a trail intersection and Nod Hill Refuge trails. Head left toward the waterfall on a paint-blazed path. Pass through and around rock walls on rocky land bordered by rock outcrops. This is one rocky place, but it does have ample trail-shading hardwoods.

0.7 Reach the "waterfall." It is more of a small sloping cascade that runs over a rock face. A spur trail leads right; keep straight, wandering through forest.

0.8 A spur trail leads left to Nod Hill Road. This hike stays right on the Rock Walk. Pass a little pond. This segment becomes rocky to the extreme as you descend through a boulder garden bordered by a wetland.

1.1 The trail turns right, back toward Weir Pond. Cross a stream and hike through woods. Neighborhood houses are visible outside the refuge.

1.4 Reach the spur trail heading right, back toward the waterfall. Keep straight toward Weir Pond.

1.5 Pass through a narrow break in a rock wall just before returning to Weir Pond and the trail intersection where you were earlier. Stay left and finish circling Weir Pond.

1.8 Reach a trail intersection after circumnavigating Weir Pond. Backtrack toward the trailhead.

2.3 Arrive back at the trailhead.

4 Lock 12 Historical Park

This hike traverses a special section of a restored canal towpath from the 1830s, now known as the Farmington Canal Trail. Start your walk at Lock 12 Historical Park. First visit Lock 12, the only restored lock on the entire former canal, along with the lock tender's house. Peer inside the Lock 12 Museum. From there head southbound, passing open wetlands, thick woods, and an additional canal lock, albeit unrestored. Walk to Mount Carmel Center then backtrack, enjoying more of this transportation corridor.

Start: Lock 12 Historical Park
Distance: 6.0 miles out and back
Hiking time: About 3 hours
Difficulty: Moderate
Trail surface: Asphalt, gravel
Best season: Year-round
Other trail users: Bicyclers, runners, inline skaters

Canine compatibility: Dogs allowed
Land status: Railroad right-of-way
Fees and permits: No fees or permits required
Schedule: Open sunrise to sunset
Maps: Farmington Canal, Cheshire Section
Trail contact: The Farmington Canal Rail-to-Trail Association, 940 Whitney Ave., Hamden, CT 06517; http://farmingtoncanal.org

Finding the trailhead: From exit 26 on I-84, take CT 70 south for 2.4 miles. Turn right onto Mountain Road and continue for 2.7 miles to a T intersection and CT 42. Turn left onto CT 42 east. Drive for 0.3 mile and turn right to enter Lock 12 Historical Park. **Trailhead GPS:** N41 28.683' / W72 55.287'

The Hike

If you think getting around New England is not easy today, you should have seen it back in the early 1800s. The few public roads were rocky, or dusty, or muddy—or snow covered. Toll roads charged confiscatory rates. Moving people and goods overland was a challenge. Going by sea was easier, but settlers were moving deeper into the hinterlands, away from the coast, and you just could not get a sailing ship through the woods! Thus the idea for shipping goods through the interior via canals was born. It had been done back in the Old World for centuries, but we Americans would build canals and make them better and more efficient.

Here is how the shipping canals worked: The canals were dug, a parallel towpath was made, and locks were built to compensate for the changing elevation of the land. Boats were loaded with goods and/or passengers and then towed by mules along the canal. Upon reaching a lock, the boat or barge entered the lock, the gates were closed, water was let in or out, depending on whether the next stage of the canal was higher or lower in elevation, and the vessel moved on down the line. Just think—this was the new fast means of freight transportation!

Preserved Lock #12 displays how canal locks worked.

In 1822 the Farmington Canal Company was chartered to build a shipping canal from the port of New Haven, Connecticut, north to Southwick, Massachusetts. It was to be the longest canal ever constructed in New England. A route was surveyed and money raised. Irish immigrants were hired for the work. They dug the 78-mile canal by hand! Other finishing work, such as building the twenty-eight locks and

What Were the Shipping Costs?

All sorts of goods moved up and down the Farmington Canal during its twenty-year existence. A sample "Rates of Toll" notice from 1835 established specific billing rates per mile shipped for specific goods. Average shipping charges ran around 1 to 1.5 cents per ton per mile.

Here are some of the listed products you may recognize: beef, butter, stone, charcoal, domestic spirits, and shingles. Some others are not so recognizable these days: brimstone, saltpeter, corn brooms, copperas, and staves.

If the goods shipped on the canal were not specifically listed, there was the catchall bill: "Items not enumerated, and passing from tide water on northward on the canal, 2 cents per ton, per mile."

People were the most expensive toll on the sheet: 6 cents per mile.

incorporating adjacent streams into the canal, was undertaken. The canal was generally unlined, with earthen walls. However, stone lining was used when necessary to prevent collapse. Most of the locks were stone lined, though some were lined with wood. To fit through the canals, boats could be no longer than 74 feet and no wider than 11 feet. A full boat could hold about 25 tons of freight. By 1827 the Farmington Canal was mostly completed. However, seed money was running out, and fares needed to be generated.

It was not until the end of 1828 that boats started moving up and down the canal. Problem was, the canal was already failing in places, and little money was available to repair it. Yet the tide was turning. The city of New Haven bought $100,000 worth of company stock, and the canal established continuing business. By 1835 the water route was linked to the Connecticut River in Massachusetts.

No matter what, the death knell of the Farmington Canal was coming, arriving on steel tracks as the newfangled railroad spread it tentacles throughout the Northeast. The rail line's efficiency was making the mule-pulled boat canal system laughingly obsolete. By 1838 a rail line between New Haven and Hartford had opened. However, the canal's demise was slow, as inland product transportation corridors were still limited. Eventually the Farmington Canal was linked with other aquatic transportation systems from New York City to Brattleboro, Vermont, extending the life of the waterway. Finally, in 1846 a series of droughts, floods, and canal cave-ins, coupled with railroad line extensions, did in the Farmington Canal.

▶ Ground was broken for the Farmington Canal on July 4, 1825.

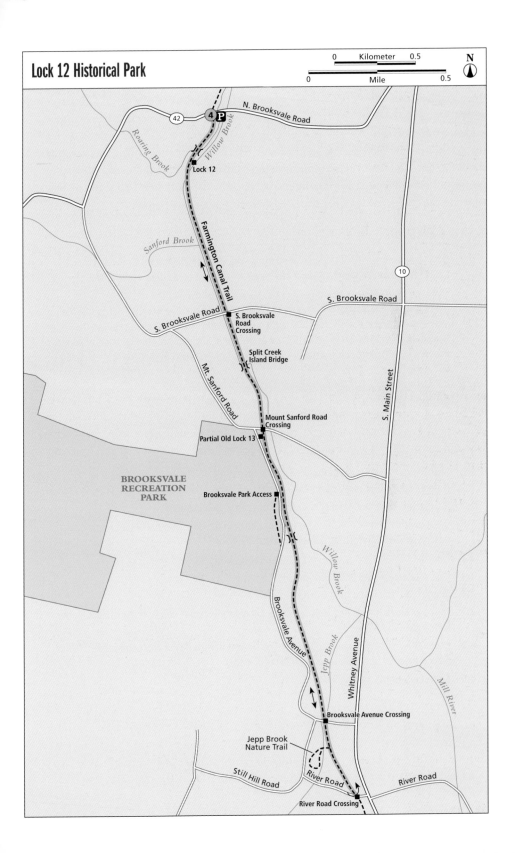

Lock 12 Historical Park

0 Kilometer 0.5

0 Mile 0.5

N

42

N. Brooksvale Road

4 P

Willow Brook

Roaring Brook

Lock 12

Sanford Brook

Farmington Canal Trail

S. Brooksvale Road

S. Brooksvale Road

S. Brooksvale Road Crossing

Split Creek Island Bridge

10

Mt. Sanford Road

Mount Sanford Road Crossing

Partial Old Lock 13

S. Main Street

BROOKSVALE RECREATION PARK

Brooksvale Park Access

Willow Brook

Brooksvale Avenue

Jepp Brook

Whitney Avenue

Mill River

Brooksvale Avenue Crossing

Jepp Brook Nature Trail

Still Hill Road

River Road

River Road

River Road Crossing

Over its life, investors lost over $1 million.

Only twelve years after the canal's demise, a railroad line was laid over the old towpath. The steel wheels were in operation until the early 1980s, when floods irreparably damaged the line. The right-of-way lay dormant until America's penchant for building transportation corridors was reborn in the form of rail trails, greenways for the public to travel for exercise and fun, or take a historic hike. Today we have the Farmington Canal Trail, once again spreading its wings from the Connecticut coast to Massachusetts. Individual communities and counties maintain their trail segment. Stay tuned as the trail—part of the greater East Coast Greenway—grows.

Miles and Directions

0.0 Start from the Lock 12 Historical Park parking area. Walk briefly toward CT 42 and then turn south on the Farmington Canal Trail, entering woods. Shortly pass over the first of many canal bridges.

0.2 Come to Lock 12, on your left. Check out the stone basin and the wooden lock gates. The lock tender's house stands adjacent to the lock. A nearby wooden building houses the irregularly open Lock 12 Museum. Return to the canal trail, quickly passing another bridge, this one an elaborate stone structure. The asphalt trail bordered in pea gravel is canopied by hardwoods.

0.6 Sanford Brook comes into the canal on your right. Natural streams were important to ensure the canal had adequate water for floating barges.

0.9 Reach and cross South Brooksvale Road. Continue south along the popular pathway. Brooksvale Stream comes in on your right.

1.1 Cross the Split Creek Island Bridge. Keep south.

1.3 Bisect Mount Sanford Road. On your right is the unrestored Lock 13. Compare it to restored Lock 12 at trail's beginning.

1.7 A bridge and spur trail lead right to Brooksvale Park. Keep straight.

1.8 Cross another bridge. The canal here is still, almost pond-like. In other places it is a fast-moving stream, dammed by beavers, or even silted in.

2.2 Walk through an open grassy area under a power line.

2.4 Pass a closed private bridge on your right. Keep south under woods.

2.6 Bridge Jepp Brook and then cross Brooksvale Avenue.

2.7 The Jepp Brook Nature Trail leaves right as a footpath entering woods. Keep straight on the Farmington Canal Trail.

3.0 Reach River Road. The canal trail continues straight to New Haven and points south. This is a good place to turn around and retrace your steps.

6.0 Arrive back at the parking area.

5 The Tower of the Sleeping Giant

This hike takes place at one of Connecticut's most treasured state parks. You will follow a wide trail up to a 1930s-built castle-like observation tower, where views range in all four cardinal directions. The hike then continues along a rocky ridge before turning back. Here you will pass a huge stone quarry, the ultimate reason for the park being saved, along with remaining infrastructure of the quarry as well as an old streamside milldam.

Start: Sleeping Giant State Park entrance
Distance: 3.9-mile loop
Hiking time: 2.5–3 hours
Difficulty: Moderate due to one very rocky segment
Trail surface: Gravel, natural
Best season: Year-round; clear days for best views
Other trail users: None

Canine compatibility: Dogs allowed
Land status: State park
Fees and permits: No fees or permits required
Schedule: Open sunrise to sunset year-round
Maps: Sleeping Giant State Park
Trail contact: Sleeping Giant State Park, 200 Mount Carmel Ave., Hamden, CT 06518; (203) 287-5658; ct.gov

Finding the trailhead: From exit 10 (Hamden/Cheshire/Hwy 40) on I-91 northwest of New Haven, Connecticut, take the Mount Carmel Connector west to reach CT 10 in 2.5 miles. Turn right onto CT 10 north and follow it 1.3 miles. Turn right onto Mount Carmel Avenue and follow it for 0.2 mile to Sleeping Giant State Park on your left. Park on the right immediately after entering the park. **Trailhead GPS:** N41 25.298'/W72 53.962'

The Hike

The state of Connecticut is blessed with many beautiful places. In the state's earlier history, gems such as the Sleeping Giant—a linear ridge of hills resembling a man lying on his back—stood undisturbed. However, times change. This fascinating rocky ridge, once known as Mount Carmel, peppered with vistas of the surrounding hills and waters, suddenly was being quarried for its fine granite. Regrettably, the granite-mined area was the head of the sleeping giant. His head was being hacked away day by day! This did not sit right with Yale Forestry School professor James W. Toumey, though truth be known, it was the noise of the quarry as much as the Sleeping Giant's permanent alteration that bothered him. Along came Arnold Dana, who ultimately spearheaded the effort to save the Sleeping Giant, which led to its protection and establishment of what became Sleeping Giant State Park.

Arnold Dana had visited the park as a kid. On June 18, 1875, 12-year-old Arnold and a pair of companions decided to climb the Sleeping Giant. On the way back down Arnold fell down the mountain. Luckily for him—and for us—Arnold survived, but

The tower of the Sleeping Giant State Park has many levels.

his experience stayed with him for the rest of his days. Later he found himself at the forefront of the Sleeping Giant Park Association, saving the place he loved—and the one that almost killed him.

The publicity of the park being preserved caught the eye of the federal government. About this time, the Great Depression hit and Franklin Delano Roosevelt created his Civilian Conservation Corps (CCC) works program, putting unemployed folk to work developing parks such as Sleeping Giant, as well as other preserves throughout New England and the country at large. Today we can walk the Carriage Road up to an observation tower built on Mount Carmel by the CCC. Interestingly, the Feds chose a medieval castle design for the tower, which surprises and certainly catches the eye of hikers who reach the top.

After climbing the tower steps, you emerge at a perch where the views stretch as far as the sky allows. Clearly visible are Long Island Sound and the buildings of New Haven, as well as wooded hills both east and west. Pick a clear day for your hike and you will not be disappointed.

Nevertheless, that is not the end of your historic adventure. Leave the tower and the crowds behind, continuing along the ridge. Natural rocky vistas open as you pick your way through stone-pocked woods before turning back toward the trailhead on a more foot-friendly track. This takes you along the north slope of the ridge. Descend to the aforementioned quarry site, where you can see not only the exposed granite cliff of the quarry but also relic infrastructure used to move and ship the valuable stone to market. This includes a spur railroad loading area and concrete steps integrated into the trail.

▶ The Sleeping Giant Park Association purchased the quarrying lease of the Sleeping Giant's head in 1933, thus saving his scalp, and eventually purchased the rest of the series of hills that form the full-bodied Sleeping Giant.

From there, dip to the Mill River, where you can view an old milldam squeezed into a rock-lined gorge through which the river passes. Finally, emerge at the state park picnic area with one Sleeping Giant experience under your belt, yet realizing you hiked only one-tenth of the trails available at this natural gem of Connecticut.

Note: The elaborate and extensive trail system here is marked with color-coded blazes and has seemingly innumerable trail intersections, as well as user-created shortcuts that the park tries to keep closed. Occasional numbers are painted onto trailside rocks and trees to help you keep apprised of your position—and allow park personnel to know where you are in case you call and say you are lost. Bring a trail map with you to ensure your position. They are available on the state park website and at the trailhead. One glance at the park map and you will see that this is but one of dozens of loop hike possibilities.

Miles and Directions

0.0   Start from the main parking area at the park entrance. Walk toward the park picnic area and pick up the wide Carriage Trail. Climb the northwest slope of Mount Carmel. Frequent trail intersections lie ahead, but stay with the gravel Carriage Trail under hardwoods mixed with mountain laurel.

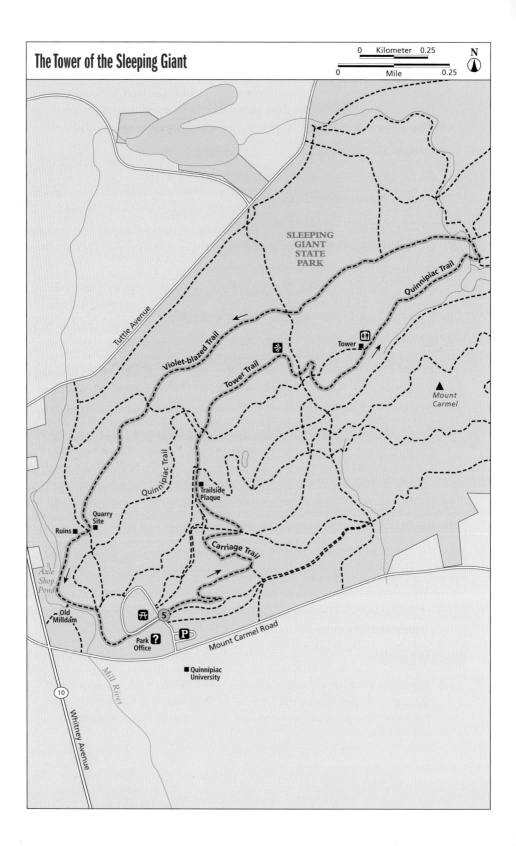

The Tower of the Sleeping Giant

| 0 | Kilometer | 0.25 |
| 0 | Mile | 0.25 |

N

SLEEPING
GIANT
STATE
PARK

Tuttle Avenue

Quinnipiac Trail

Violet-blazed Trail

Tower Trail

Tower

Mount
Carmel

Quinnipiac Trail

Trailside
Plaque

Quarry
Site

Ruins

Carriage Trail

Axle
Shop
Pond

Old
Milldam

5

Park
Office

P

Mount Carmel Road

10

Mill River

Whitney Avenue

Quinnipiac
University

0.7 Enter a rocky, bouldery draw. The granite bluff where Arnold Dana fell as a boy is partly visible through the trees to your left. Don't miss the bronze plaque on the right honoring Dana. Singletrack side trails continue to spur from the wide Carriage Trail.

0.9 Pass through a gap in the ridge. Keep gently ascending, curving northeasterly.

1.2 Pass an overlook on your left. Views open northwesterly. Make the final push around the southeast slope of Mount Carmel.

1.6 Reach the stone observation tower. Enter the castle-like structure and wind your way to the top. Note "1937," the year the tower was completed, inscribed into the concrete as you walk up. Incredible views open, especially southward toward Long Island Sound and New Haven. A restroom is nearby. After soaking in the views, take the light blue–blazed singletrack Quinnipiac Trail, heading northeasterly.

1.7 Reach a natural rock outcrop overlook extending northeast. Keep northeasterly, descending through rocky, stunted woods of hickory and oak.

1.9 After dropping through a rock garden that is hard on the feet, cross a creeklet and come to a red-blazed trail with circular blazes. Head left on the red-blazed trail. Go 200 feet to another trail intersection. Turn left here, re-crossing the creeklet after joining a violet-blazed path. You are now westbound. The walking is much easier, on level land deep under hardwoods.

2.5 Cross a normally dry creekbed and immediately reach a red circular blazed trail. Keep straight on the violet-blazed trail, rolling along the north slope of the mountain.

3.0 Cross a trail blazed with red hexagons. Keep straight on the violet-blazed trail, going down more than not. The quarry site comes into view through the trees.

3.3 Reach the huge quarry on your left. A concrete-block building stands to your right, with the granite loading structure below. After viewing the quarry, follow the violet-blazed trail steeply down toward the railroad granite-loading area. Interestingly, the path integrates old concrete steps into its descent. Come to a field where the concrete remains of the granite-loading area are located. Follow the violet-blazed path back into woods left, now on a wide jeep road.

3.4 Come along the Mill River, once backed up here as Axle Shop Pond. Ahead, the trail seems to dead-end at the water; stay left on a singletrack path on a rocky slope, running parallel to the water. Work over big emergent rocks and boulders, squeezing between boulders at one point.

3.5 Come alongside an old milldam, constructed here since the river was already constricted by a stone gorge. Keep downstream as the rocks give way to a more foot-friendly trail.

3.6 Intersect a blue-blazed trail. Stay right here (downstream) to quickly reach another intersection. Veer left, still with the violet-blazed trail. Climb a bit away from the Mill River.

3.8 Emerge at the park picnic area. Keep straight, passing restrooms on your left.

3.9 Arrive back at the main parking area.

6 Talcott Mountain

This hike climbs a mountain overlooking the Farmington River valley and the site of a fascinating home with a 165-foot observation tower. The walk to the tower is short but steep in places. However, the views from atop Talcott Mountain and the mountaintop castle make the hike worth it. Picnicking is also available at Talcott Mountain State Park.

Start: Yellow Trail parking area
Distance: 2.6 miles out and back
Hiking time: 2–2.5 hours
Difficulty: Moderate
Trail surface: Mostly gravel
Best season: When tower is open (see right)
Other trail users: None
Canine compatibility: Dogs allowed
Land status: Connecticut state park

Fees and permits: No fees or permits required
Schedule: Park open 8 a.m. to sunset; tower open 10 a.m. to 5 p.m. Thurs through Sun from May 24 through the end of Aug, daily from Labor Day weekend through Oct 31
Maps: Talcott Mountain State Park
Trail contact: Talcott Mountain State Park, 57 Gun Mill Rd., Bloomfield, CT 06002; (860) 242-1158; ct.gov

Finding the trailhead: From exit 35B on I-91 north of Hartford, take CT 218/Cottage Grove Road. Follow Cottage Grove Road, heading west to CT 185. Turn right onto CT 185 toward Simsbury. At the top of the hill, the entrance to Talcott Mountain State Park/Heublein Tower will be on your left. Turn left into the state park and continue 0.3 mile to the trailhead. **Trailhead GPS:** N41 50.379'/W72 47.550'

The Hike

Gilbert Heublein was a romantic fellow. And he backed up what he said. Back in 1875, while hiking atop what later became Talcott Mountain State Park, Heublein told his then fiancée, Louise Gundlach, that he would build her a castle on one of the mountain's many overlooks. And he did. The building you see, of castle proportions, was constructed to withstand rigorous weather atop the mountain. The elaborate structure, capped with a 165-foot high tower, was completed in 1914. The Heubleins planned to use the place as a summer home and to entertain friends and clients of the food and beverage magnate.

However, external forces were at work. World War I was brewing, and folks began to wonder if Heublein—of German descent—wasn't using his tower to spy down on the Americans. After all, the tower presents clear-day vistas stretching from Long Island Sound in the Atlantic to Mount Monadnock over New Hampshire way. In the near, the Farmington River valley stretches out below, with the Berkshires rising in the distance.

Heublein did not like being under suspicion. He was an American. To quell any doubt about whose side he was on, Heublein offered the tower to American forces

The view from the front door of the Heublein Castle is gorgeous.

from which to reconnoiter the Germans! The uproar died, and the man behind A1 Steak Sauce—his number-one product—enjoyed the retreat atop Talcott Mountain until he died in 1937, at age 88.

In 1943 the tower and building were acquired by the *Hartford Times*. They planned to use the spot for a radio tower and also for entertainment. It was at this retreat, in 1950, that Dwight D. Eisenhower decided to make his bid for the presidency, which he won in 1952. The former general was visiting Connecticut senator Prescott Bush, who talked Eisenhower into making a run. Prescott Bush was the father of future President George H. W. Bush and grandfather to President George W. Bush.

In 1962 the *Hartford Times* sold the tower and the land around it. An investment group had formed to develop homesites atop Talcott Mountain using the Heublein property. Citizens of the surrounding Farmington River valley rallied and pressed the State of Connecticut to purchase the property, which it did. The state, along with a philanthropic outfit called Friends of the Heublein Tower, has worked to restore and maintain the facility. Through the years the tower has been reworked several times. It was originally constructed to withstand 100-mile-per-hour winds. When it's open, hikers can walk to the top of the tower to enjoy unparalleled vistas. Even if the home

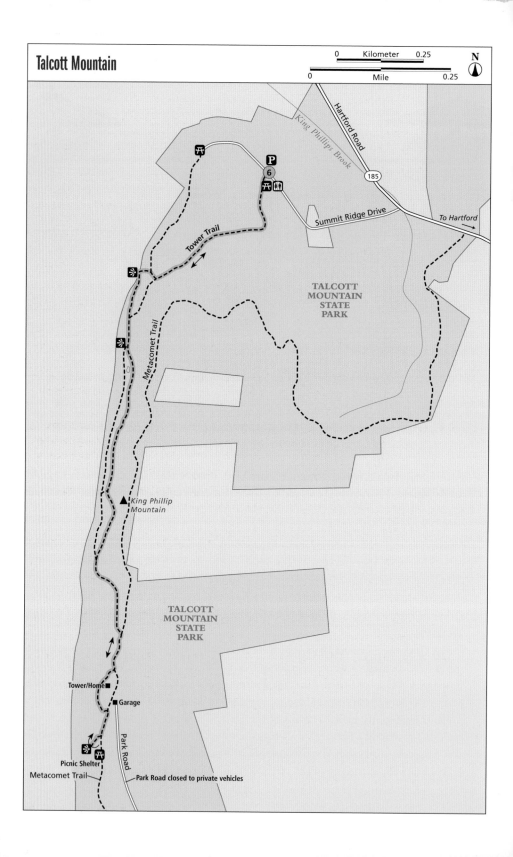

Talcott Mountain

0   Kilometer   0.25

0   Mile   0.25

N

Hartford Road

King Phillips Brook

185

P

6

Summit Ridge Drive

To Hartford

Tower Trail

TALCOTT
MOUNTAIN
STATE
PARK

Metacomet Trail

King Phillip
Mountain

TALCOTT
MOUNTAIN
STATE
PARK

Tower/Home

Garage

Park Road

Picnic Shelter

Metacomet Trail

Park Road closed to private vehicles

and tower are not open, hikers will gain extensive views from the natural rock over-looks along the mountain.

You can only reach the home by foot. That is what makes this historic hike special. You *earn* the vistas; you *earn* the examination of the house and grounds.

Hike a wide gravel trail rising quickly from the parking area. Wind your way up the northeast side of Talcott Mountain until leveling out on a ridge, reaching the first of several eye-popping overlooks. The hike turns southbound, running directly alongside the edge of the ridgeline overlooking the Farmington River val-ley, passing more vistas. Spur trails lead to other over-looks and other paths that run parallel to the main wide path that ultimately takes you to the Heublein Tower and home. Hopefully the tower will be open during your visit. Check ahead for open dates and times. If it is open, you can see other parts of the house in addition to the tower. Take the time to explore the gardens and grounds. Consider bringing a meal up here to enjoying the picnic area and shelter near the house.

▶ The Heublein Tower atop Talcott Mountain was the home of Connecticut's first elevator.

Miles and Directions

0.0 Start from the trailhead on the wide blazed Tower Trail. Pass around a pole gate. Travel by a picnic area and restrooms. Ascend through hardwoods of maple, birch, and witch hazel. The gradient is fairly steep, but trailside resting benches are widespread.

0.4 Top out on the northern end of Talcott Mountain. A spur trail heads right to a picnic area. Ahead, a vista opens. Begin a series of off-and-on unblazed paths running along the ridge-line, especially directly along the bluff dropping west from Talcott Mountain. Craggy cedars hang onto the edge of the frequent outcrops. Turn south along Talcott Mountain.

0.6 Pass a small pond on your right. Continue through woods, with the cliffs of Talcott Moun-tain beyond. More parallel trails spur off and on the wide Tower Trail.

1.0 Walk beside an exposed cliff to your left.

1.1 The Metacomet Trail leaves left for the east side of the mountain and CT 185. Stay straight on the Tower Trail.

1.2 The trail splits. The trail going left heads around the east side of the tower/house and to public restrooms. Stay right toward the cliffs of Talcott Mountain to emerge on a rock out-crop and the front of the Heublein Tower. An amazing view is available from the front porch of the home/tower. The front door here is where you enter to climb the tower. After enjoying the tower, keep south on the grounds, passing the garage.

1.3 Reach a rock outcrop with extensive views of the Farmington River valley and wooded hills and mountains beyond. The picnic shelter is just ahead. From here the Metacomet Trail continues south, but this hike backtracks. Explore more of the grounds before retracing your steps to the trailhead.

2.6 Arrive back at the trailhead.

7 Gillette Castle

This hike explores the intriguing home and grounds of Gillette Castle, overlooking the Connecticut River. Here actor William Gillette, known for his characterization of Sherlock Holmes, built an imposing yet whimsical stone dwelling. Beyond the home, you can explore a trail network that includes the grade of a narrow-gauge train that once coursed through the woodsy property.

Start: Visitor center and Gillette Castle parking area

Distance: 3.0-mile trail network

Hiking time: 1–2 hours

Difficulty: Easy

Trail surface: Natural

Best season: When castle is open for tours

Other trail users: None

Canine compatibility: Dogs allowed

Land status: Connecticut state park

Fees and permits: No entrance fee but fee to tour castle

Schedule: Park open 8 a.m. to sunset; last castle tour at 5 p.m.

Maps: Gillette Castle State Park

Trail contact: Gillette Castle State Park, 67 River Rd., East Haddam, CT 06423; (860) 526-2336; ct.gov

Finding the trailhead: From the traffic circle intersection of CT 82 and CT 85 just south of Salem, Connecticut, take CT 82 west for 8.2 miles. Turn right at a stop sign and stay with CT 82 west. Continue for 1.4 miles and turn left onto Hemlock Valley Road. Continue 7 miles and turn right onto Bone Mill Road. Follow Bone Mill Road for 0.1 mile. Turn right onto River Road/CT 431 and then make a quick left into Gillette Castle State Park, driving until you reach the large parking area near the castle. **Trailhead GPS:** N41 25.4264' / W72 25.6554'

The Hike

William Gillette was a genius whose passion for theater shaped not only his career but also his outlook on life. And nowhere is it more visible than at the mansion he dubbed "The Seventh Sister" for being located on the most southerly of seven hills overlooking the Connecticut River. Taken over and then restored by the State of Connecticut, the estate was renamed Gillette Castle. Not only is the stone structure striking but the grounds are conspicuous as well, laced with trails designed by William Gillette himself. Some of these trails follow the miniature railroad line the actor had on his property. Over 3 miles of track once coursed through the 184-acre property, using trestles and even a tunnel. The train was large enough to carry twenty-eight passengers, and the world-renowned actor often entertained guests by conducting trips. Today you can walk these railroad grades as well as other hiking trails in combination with a visit to the Gillette Castle.

William Gillette was born of upper-crust Connecticut lineage in 1853. His former-senator father was not enamored of his son's aspiration for the stage. However, sometimes our passions are too strong to ignore, despite the odds of failure and the admonitions of a stern parent. Gillette had the acting bug from an early age. Like many erstwhile famous actors, he started in local productions but got his break when the lead actor in a play fell ill and Gillette stepped in—to the approval of audience and critics alike. His career grew wings. Fellow Connecticut resident Mark Twain recommended William Gillette for his play *The Gilded Age* in 1875. This run further cemented Gillette's reputation and kept him in work.

Somewhere along the way, Gillette realized that if he could act, direct, and even write plays, his income would rise. And that he did, continually honing his craft, even inventing sound and visual props for plays in addition to wearing the three hats of writing, directing, and acting. However, it was his portrayal of Sir Arthur Conan Doyle's Sherlock Holmes that would make Gillette a world-recognized actor. Sir Arthur, in need of money to build his own English estate, decided to generate revenue by putting his best-known character in a play, since he had killed Holmes off in the final book of his Sherlock Holmes series. Through a few twists of fate, the role of

The imposing Gillette Castle has a bit of whimsy too.

the famous detective came to William Gillette, who had wide latitude in interpreting the role. Gillette and the play were raging successes throughout the world. Over the course of 1,300 performances and a 1916 silent movie, Gillette fashioned the Sherlock Holmes we know today: the man of the plaid deerstalker cap, the curved pipe, the magnifying glass, and the studied way of speaking.

Thus we find William Gillette as a world-famous actor beginning to build his architectural masterpiece on a hill atop the Connecticut River in 1914. It took twenty full-time men five years to complete the stone structure, built on a steel framework. Not only is the outside eye-catching, intricate detail was also used on the inside, all directed by Gillette. His use of interior windows and forty-seven unique doors captures the theatrical outlook developed by a lifetime on stage.

▶ William Gillette was son of former US Senator Francis Gillette and Elizabeth Daggett Hooker Gillette, descendent of Thomas Hooker, founder of Hartford, Connecticut.

His fascination with trains was borne out by the narrow-gauge track he built on the grounds. You can follow the old grades, as well as the hiking trails he constructed. The spiderweb of pathways and old railroad grades afford many opportunities to create your own exploration of the grounds. After Gillette passed away in 1937, at the age of 83, his train was moved to an amusement park in Bristol, Connecticut, where it operated for nearly fifty years. The locomotive has since been returned to the park grounds and is on display at the castle visitor center. As you will see, the locomotive is no toy train; it is bigger than you might imagine.

Gillette would be pleased at the return of his locomotive. Later in life, he became extremely concerned about the disposition of his estate after his death. In his own words, he didn't want it to end up in the hands of "some blithering sap who had no conception of where he is or with what surrounded." Luckily, the State of Connecticut bought the property in 1943. Through the years, Gillette Castle has grown as a tourist attraction, and today the house—on the National Register of Historic Places—receives around 150,000 visitors annually. The castle is open for self-guided tours, with on-site personnel to answer your questions. In addition, plays are held on the grounds of Gillette Castle; check ahead for dates.

You will have to come up with your own tours of the trails at Gillette Castle. "Why it's elementary, my dear Watson," as Sherlock Holmes used to say. Grab a trail map at the visitor center or print one out from ct.gov before you arrive. Do not try to resist touring the Gillette Castle first. The unique dwelling is fascinating inside and out. During summer, the gardens around the house are attractive and colorful. The view from the back deck overlooking the Connecticut River and the surrounding countryside will leave no doubt that Gillette picked a prime location for his home. Stop by "Grand Central Station," a stone station house for his train.

If you want to follow the railroad grade for your hike, pick it up at the top of the castle driveway, near where it meets the park road, just before the park road enters

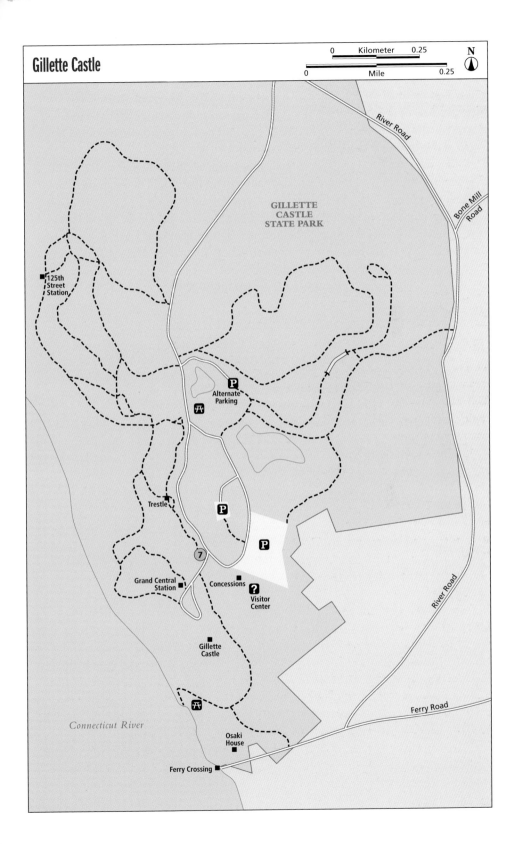

Gillette Castle

0   Kilometer   0.25
0   Mile   0.25

N

River Road

Bone Mill Road

GILLETTE CASTLE STATE PARK

125th Street Station

P Alternate Parking

Trestle

P

P

7

Grand Central Station

Concessions

? Visitor Center

Gillette Castle

River Road

Ferry Road

Connecticut River

Osaki House

Ferry Crossing

the large visitor parking lot. The proper path will be the trail that keeps a level grade. The grade quickly cuts through a hill and bridges a walking trail. If you keep going, you will pass a small shelter disguised as another train stop. The entire train line is not intact, as parts of the grade were destroyed when the park entrance road was redone. However, you can follow a lot of it. Make sure and go through the train tunnel too. Ponds and picnic areas complement the woodsy terrain.

Other trails are less level. They wind through hills and intermingle with the railroad grades. You can explore the wooded hilly terrain that slopes down to the Connecticut River. Walk down to the river to where the *Aunt Polly* docked, the houseboat Gillette lived on during construction of the castle. You can also see the Osaki House, where Gillette's caretaker resided. The historic Chester-Hadlyme Ferry first crossed the river in 1769 and continues to ply the waters here at the edge of the park grounds.

By combining a visit to the castle, the trails, and the river—and perhaps taking in a play—you will gain an appreciation for the genius of William Gillette.

Miles and Directions

0.0 Start by touring Gillette Castle. Foot trails begin behind the castle, through a stone archway near Grand Central Station. The railroad grade starts near the upper end of the castle driveway (closed to the public) and the one-way park road just before it enters the large public parking area. Create your own loops, stopping by the ponds and following the gated park road down to the Connecticut River.

3.0 After exploring to your heart's content, arrive back at the castle parking area.

Rhode Island

Mansions of the Gilded Age grace the Newport Cliff Walk (hike 8).

8 Newport Cliff Walk

This world-recognized footpath travels cliffs straddling the Atlantic Ocean on one side and the impressive mansions of Newport on the other. Recognized as New England's first national recreation trail, this high-wire act combines natural and architectural splendor while overlooking the shores of Rhode Island Sound. Most of the trail is level asphalt hiking, but the last part works over rocks and irregular natural terrain as it circles around Rough Point to end on Bellevue Avenue, home of Newport's swankiest estates.

Start: Memorial Avenue west of Easton Beach
Distance: 6.8 miles out and back
Hiking time: 3.5–4 hours
Difficulty: Moderate
Trail surface: Mostly asphalt, some natural
Best season: Summer for beach and flowers
Other trail users: None
Canine compatibility: Dogs allowed

Land status: Public right-of-way over private property
Fees and permits: Parking fee almost certain
Schedule: Open sunrise to sunset
Maps: Newport Cliff Walk
Trail contact: City of Newport, 43 Broadway, Newport, RI 02840; (401) 845-5300; new .cityofnewport.com; cliffwalk.com

Finding the trailhead: From the intersection of US 1 and RI 138 near Allenton, Rhode Island, take RI 138 east for 8.3 miles, crossing a toll bridge along the way. Veer right onto RI 238 south for Scenic Newport. Pass through touristy Newport as the road becomes RI 138A. Look for signs for Bellevue Mansions. However, at 1.5 miles keep straight on RI 138A past Bellevue Avenue and continue for 1 mile to reach public parking at Easton Beach, on your right. To begin the Cliff Walk, walk back west along the road about 100 yards, then start the walk at a break in a rock wall. **Trailhead GPS:** N41 29.110'/W71 17.847'

The Hike

This is one spectacular hike—very unusual and very historic. The trail was initially developed over a forty-year period, 1880 to 1920, by the Newport estate owners themselves, making it one of the oldest walking paths in New England. The trail still passes through sixty-four individual parcels of private property on a public right-of-way. It is now a federally designated National Recreation Trail in a federally designated National Historic District. Hurricanes and storms have battered the path through the years, and disputes have broken out concerning continued access of the Cliff Walk as it passes through seaside estates. However, the path remains a public right-of-way and continues to host thousands of visitors annually. The Cliff Walk is a huge draw for visitors to the Ocean State.

Of course the magnates of the Gilded Age came first—the Vanderbilts, the Astors, and the Dukes—drawn to Newport's idyllic summer climate. And where better to put a home than on the cliffs overlooking Rhode Island Sound? And come they

Views like this make the Cliff Walk a perennial attraction.

did, from the prominent Morris family of New York to wealthy trade merchants like William Wetmore and coal barons like E. J. Berwind. The elites are gone, but their magnificent mansions remain. Today you can tour these fantastic castles, learning about a lifestyle lived by very few. Some of the historic mansions are now part of Salve Regina University, situated in the heart of Newport's mansion district.

The Cliff Walk leaves Easton Beach and Easton Bay to your left. The first part of the trail travels a fine asphalt path with a couple sets of stairs. Eventually you will get used to gawking at the stellar ocean and shoreline panoramas on one side of the trail and the impressive estates on the other side. In some places the path is hemmed in by vegetation, but even then you will hear the crash of the ocean against the rocks below and smell trailside flowers and estate gardens along with salty wafts from the sea.

If you don't feel like backtracking on the Cliff Walk, you can walk back via Bellevue Avenue, promenading past the fronts of impressive mansions that

▶ The Rhode Island State Constitution guarantees the public "rights of fishery and the privileges of the shore to which they have heretofore been entitled." In other words, citizens can access the shore to fish—or walk—even on private lands that abut the shore.

Touring the Mansions

After your trek along the Cliff Walk, you may want to tour some of the mansions you passed. The Preservation Society of Newport County website details each of the major mansions available to tour. Some are self-guided, some are guided only, and some offer both. These tours operate most of the year, but each mansion has its own schedule. Most mansions have free off-street parking. The estates are located close enough to one another that you can walk from one to the next. There are even tours that focus on the life of the servants who worked on these estates. For more information visit newportmansions.org.

once housed the potentates of the Gilded Age. Many of these big homes are part of the Preservation Society of Newport County and are open for tours. In addition, public transportation is available and can get you back to RI 138A, not far from Easton Beach. Check the City of Newport website for schedules. Consider incorporating a few hours at Easton Beach, with its convenient Cliff Walk parking, into your schedule.

Miles and Directions

0.0 Start south on the Cliff Walk after heading west from the Easton Beach parking area. Join an asphalt trail passing between large houses to the right and the Atlantic Ocean to the left. The trail is built on a cliff, with the water well below. Hedges and/or fences hem the trail in on one side or the other. It is a sharp drop to the water below. Excellent views open to the south and west to the Atlantic Ocean, Sachuest Point, and Sakonnet Point, as well as southward along the cliffs of the Cliff Walk.

0.2 Pass the Seaview Avenue access. Very rough user-created trails drop toward the ocean. Use these at your own risk. The trail continues past wind-stunted vegetation on the seaward side. Pass occasional repose benches.

0.7 Come to the Narragansett Avenue access and the famed 40 Steps leading to a balcony above the ocean. Here employees of the area manses once gathered for their own socializing.

0.8 Reach the Webster Street access. Ahead you will pass the four former estates and properties that now compose Salve Regina University, the most famous of which is the Astor estate known as The Breakers.

1.1 Reach Shepard Avenue and the heart of Salve Regina University.

1.3 Come to Ochre Point and a stellar view. Here look back toward Easton Beach as well as eastward across Rhode Island Sound. An enthralling vista stretches south of the Cliff Walk along the coast, backed by regal dwellings. The Ruggles Avenue access is just ahead. Turn into Sheep Point Cove.

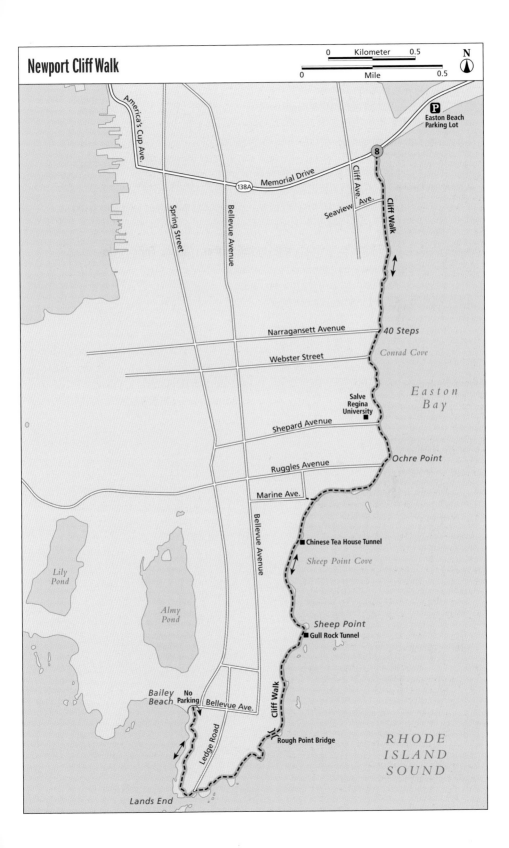

Newport Cliff Walk

Kilometer 0 0.5
Mile 0 0.5

N

Easton Beach Parking Lot

America's Cup Ave.

Spring Street

Bellevue Avenue

Memorial Drive 138A

Cliff Ave.

Seaview Ave.

8

Cliff Walk

Narragansett Avenue

40 Steps

Conrad Cove

Webster Street

Salve Regina University

Easton Bay

Shepard Avenue

Ochre Point

Ruggles Avenue

Marine Ave.

Bellevue Avenue

Chinese Tea House Tunnel

Sheep Point Cove

Lily Pond

Almy Pond

Sheep Point
Gull Rock Tunnel

Bailey Beach

No Parking

Bellevue Ave.

Ledge Road

Cliff Walk

Rough Point Bridge

RHODE ISLAND SOUND

Lands End

1.6 Pass the Marine Avenue access. This is the last public access point for 1.5 miles, until Ledge Road. Pass Rosecliff Mansion, used in the 1974 movie *The Great Gatsby*. Ahead you will walk near the Chinese Tea House and go through the Tea House Tunnel.

2.1 Reach Sheep Point and pass through the shorter Gull Rock Tunnel. The trail becomes rougher here.

2.5 Work your way around Rough Point and its bridge. Watch the waves crash below. Keep southwesterly on a path marked with round metal circles attached to the rocky shore. Continue on a mix of rocks, soil, and man-made pathway.

3.0 Come to the Ledge Avenue access. The Cliff Walk continues on a combination of rock and natural surface. Stay with the circular markers embedded into rock as the path curves north past Lands End. Pass rock outcrops, small sand and rock beaches, tidal pools, and scenic coastline.

3.4 Emerge on Bellevue Avenue just east of Bailey Beach. You can backtrack on the Cliff Walk, stroll Bellevue Avenue past the mansions, or walk to a bus stop. Buses and trolleys regularly travel Bellevue Avenue in the mansion area.

6.8 Arrive back at RI 138A near Easton Beach.

9 Blackstone River Valley

Explore the birthplace of American industry in Blackstone River Valley. The trek follows a paved trail meeting the towpath of the old Blackstone Canal, built to transport products, primarily textiles, from America's first water-powered factories. Walk the towpath and the Blackstone River. Visit old power-generating dams, an intact segment of the Blackstone Canal, an early mill site, and a mill manager's house.

Start: Blackstone River State Park Visitor Center
Distance: 7.2 miles out and back
Hiking time: 3.5–4.5 hours
Difficulty: Moderate, mostly level
Trail surface: Asphalt, a little natural surface
Best season: Warm season to see the Kelly Museum
Other trail users: Bicyclers, inline skaters, joggers

Canine compatibility: Dogs allowed
Land status: Rhode Island state park
Fees and permits: No fees or permits required
Schedule: Open sunrise to sunset
Maps: Blackstone River Valley Bikeway
Trail contact: Lincoln Woods State Park, 2 Manchester Print Works Rd., Lincoln, RI 02865; (401) 723-7892; http://riparks.com

Finding the trailhead: The Blackstone River State Park Visitor Center is located between exits 9 and 10 on I-295 in Lincoln, Rhode Island. the visitor center doubles as an interstate rest area, and thus may not seem like the right place when you arrive. *Note:* The visitor center is only accessible while heading north on I-295, after passing exit 9 and before reaching exit 10. **Trailhead GPS:** N41 56.385'/W71 26.661'

The Hike

New England in the 1780s was an agrarian society. Small farms dotted the vast woodlands where persistent men coaxed crops from the stony soil. Then an English immigrant named Samuel Slater made his way from old England to Patuxent, Rhode Island, set in the lower Blackstone River valley. By 1793 Slater had established the first American mill powered by water. With a consistent drop on its 46-mile run from Worchester, Massachusetts, to Narragansett Bay in Rhode Island, the Blackstone River was perfect for this. Its gravity-forced water turned the wheels that powered the textile mills that soon popped up along the Blackstone River.

The valley became a hotbed of technological innovation. New ways of using waterpower to operate the mills and new ways of milling made the valley an exciting place to work. Area farmers began moving to the city, taking advantage of this new way to earn a living—working 12-hour days for "wages." The mills expanded beyond spinning cotton and wool and moved on to making other products such as shoes, tools, and machinery. The problem of efficient mass production had been solved, lowering the cost of goods; but shipping these products became the new challenge,

Crossing the Blackstone River at an old mill site.

for the roads of New England were miserable. At the time it cost the same to ship a product 30 miles by land across local roads as it cost to ship something from Boston to England by water!

Local merchants decided to try another English innovation that was spreading across America—canals. Channels were dug alongside the Blackstone River (in places the channel was integrated with the river); locks were installed. By 1830 most of the mill products of the Blackstone River valley were being shipped south through Rhode Island rather than east through Boston.

▶ The Blackstone Canal merged with navigable portions of the Blackstone River for about 10 percent of its 45-mile length. The rest was hand-dug canal like you see along this hike.

Irate Boston shippers decided to build a railroad line linking Worcester, Massachusetts, with Boston. Railroads at this time were an iffy experiment, an unproven technology in much the same way as large-scale factory-driving water power had been decades earlier. By 1835 the Boston & Worcester Railroad was moving products easterly to the Atlantic at the "lightning" speed of 10 to 15 miles an hour. Railroads had the additional advantage of year-round operation, as opposed to the drought-, flood-, and ice-plagued canals. This was the beginning of the end for the canal, especially after the opening of the Providence and Worcester Railroad in 1847, which ran the length of the Blackstone Valley.

Meanwhile, dams were erected at every major drop in the river and a factory was built nearby to use the waterpower. The scale of factories in the valley grew. Two hundred workers were employed in a factory where twenty had been the decade before. The local labor force was used up. Factory managers began advertising both locally and internationally for textile workers to labor in the Blackstone River Valley. Workers came from throughout Europe to toil in the increasingly productive plants lining the river. By 1880 it was said that the Blackstone was the "hardest working river in America."

This combination of factory mass production via waterpower and efficient national shipping using railroads literally changed the face of America—the first morphings from Thomas Jefferson's agrarian ideal to the modern urban melting pot we live in today. And it started here in the Blackstone Valley.

This hike begins along the modern transportation corridor of I-295 in Rhode Island. From there you join a trail winding east to the Blackstone River. Immediately reach one of the best-preserved sections of the Blackstone Canal, where hand-placed bank stones form parallel lines along the waterway. Check out the Ashton Dam, once used to power the huge brick Ashton Mills factory across the river, now condos.

Visit the site of the Kelly Mill, an early factory, seemingly quaint in size. The trailside Kelly Museum is a real highlight. Visit the preserved house of Wilbur Kelly, factory superintendent, and soak in the interpretive information of that era. The walk then passes a housing site for Kelly's workers and then along a preserved section of

Creative Destruction

Economist Joseph Schumpeter developed the economics theory known as creative destruction. And it fits the Blackstone River valley to a T. The theory states that when a new process is created, an old one is destroyed. And so it went, with the canals being replaced by trains. As economics goes, someone is always coming along to do something faster, using more efficient technology and cheaper labor. The same thing happened here along the Blackstone. The factories built along the river were outmoded; so was the equipment. Cheaper, non-union labor could be found working modernized mills down South. By the 1920s more than half the textiles manufactured in the United States were made below the Mason-Dixon Line. Today there is very little mill operation in the Blackstone River Valley. However, you can still see this history via the Blackstone Canal towpath, now re-created as a history trail.

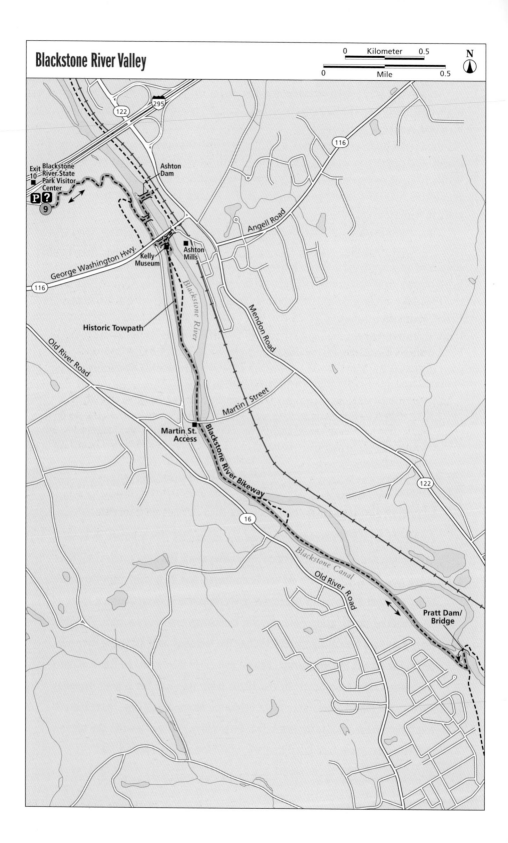

Blackstone River Valley

0   Kilometer   0.5

0   Mile   0.5

N

122

295

116

Exit 10

Blackstone River State Park Visitor Center

P

9

Ashton Dam

Angell Road

George Washington Hwy.

116

Kelly Museum

Ashton Mills

Mendon Road

Blackstone River

Historic Towpath

Old River Road

Martin Street

Martin St. Access

Blackstone River Bikeway

122

16

Blackstone Canal

Old River Road

Pratt Dam/ Bridge

the old towpath, where mules pulled 30 tons of boat-laden goods 3 miles an hour for twenty years, from 1828 to 1848. Enjoy walking down the valley with the canal on one side and the Blackstone River on the other. The trail is mostly level except the beginning part, where you descend from the visitor center to the river. Check out the wetlands upstream of the Pratt Dam. Eventually cross the Pratt Dam, another factory impoundment, on an innovative trail bridge that runs atop the dam. View the old dam from different angles before backtracking along the Blackstone River, looking for more signs of the history that changed the land.

Miles and Directions

0.0 Start from the Blackstone River State Park Visitor Center on an asphalt path (to the right as you face the visitor center). Descend past picnic tables and enter woods. Noisy I-295 rumbles to your left.

0.5 Reach a trail intersection on a bluff above the Blackstone River. The trail leading right heads to alternate parking. Stay left toward the Kelly Museum, southbound and down-stream along the Blackstone River.

0.7 Leave left from the path, crossing a bridge over the Blackstone Canal. Check out the straight lines of the waterway. After crossing the bridge, head left to see the Ashton Dam, once used to power a factory. Note where the canal was integrated with the river, working around rock bluffs. Return to the trail, continuing downstream.

1.0 Reach the Kelly Museum site after passing under the RI 116 Bridge. To your left, the site of the Kelly Mill lies under the bridge. A leg of the Blackstone River Trail crosses the Blackstone River. Head toward the Kelly Museum, open during the warm season. Tour the house, viewing the displays and also the foundations of adjacent buildings. From there keep south along the old towpath beside the canal.

1.8 Pass under the Martin Street Bridge. A trail access comes in here.

2.3 Cross a small bridge. Note the wider canal here. A spur dirt path leads through woods 0.25 mile then returns to the main track. New Pond wetlands are to your left.

3.5 Reach a trail intersection. Go acutely left, crossing the old Pratt Dam on an innovative trail bridge. View the milldam from different angles.

3.6 Begin backtracking toward the visitor center.

7.2 Arrive back at the visitor center.

Massachusetts

The silent Stanley Woolen Mill reflects in the stillness of the Blackstone Canal (hike 18).

10 Fort Hill Trail at Cape Cod

This circuit explores an early Pilgrim settlement on Cape Cod. View the boundary marker of a 1700s preacher, then soak in natural beauty on a swamp boardwalk. From there reach an overlook of Nauset Marsh and Nauset Lighthouse on the Atlantic Ocean. Stop by Indian Rock, where the Wampanoag sharpened their stone tools. Walk by old rock walls and then climb Fort Hill, possible site of English defense works. Finally, visit the ornate Penniman House, home of a Cape Cod whaler.

Start: Penniman House trailhead
Distance: 1.6-mile loop
Hiking time: 1–1.5 hours
Difficulty: Easy
Trail surface: Natural, gravel, plus boardwalk
Best season: Fall for color in red maple swamp
Other trail users: None
Canine compatibility: Dogs not allowed

Land status: National seashore
Fees and permits: Entry permits required from late June through Labor Day
Schedule: Open sunrise to sunset
Maps: Fort Hill Trail
Trail contact: Cape Cod National Seashore, 99 Marconi Site Rd., Wellfleet, MA 02667; (508) 255-3421; nps.gov/caco

Finding the trailhead: From exit 13 on US 6 in the town of Orleans, Massachusetts, stay with US 6 east toward Wellfleet. At 1 mile veer right onto Governor Prence Road. Follow it 0.1 mile and then veer right onto Fort Hill Road. Trailhead parking is on the left, just after you pass the Penniman House. **Trailhead GPS:** N41 49.135' / W69 57.881'

The Hike

This is but one of many short historic interpretive trails at Cape Cod. If this one is too brief, simply combine it with other trails at the seashore detailed below. Back in 1644, Plymouth colonists founded Eastham, overlooking Nauset Marsh, adjacent to the Atlantic Ocean. The Nauset area contained some of the most fertile land on Cape Cod. The colonists cleared the forest and planted rye and corn for themselves and hay for their livestock, including sheep to make wool clothing for the long, windy winters. They worked the Nauset Marsh below for shellfish.

The land had already gone through other claimants, starting with the French. Intrepid explorer Samuel de Champlain had stopped here, searching for a better place to colonize after a wicked winter in what became New Brunswick. He called the place Port Malabar, for the dangerous shoals just off Cape Cod. However, the French were destined to stay north. To the south, the Dutch had already settled Manhattan and were vying for more land. The Plymouth colonists were ordered to build a fort at the local high point in the early 1650s to fend off a potential Dutch invasion. The war was not to be. The only thing left is the name Fort Hill. No one is sure if the English ever did build "breast works with flankers" as ordered. The Plymouth settlers continued clearing Eastham for farming and fuel. The trees were quickly depleted, and cultivated soils blew with the relentless winds, leaving the land nearly barren.

Meanwhile, the Eastham settlers were staying true to their mission of practicing Christianity the way they saw fit, a way not allowed back in Europe, where they had run afoul of the Church of England. They invited the Reverend Samuel Treat to sermonize their flock. He settled on 20 acres, the northwest boundary marker of which you can still see today. The reverend preached for forty-five years in Eastham, not only tending his congregation of worshipers but also doing mission work with the local Nauset Indians, part of the greater Wampanoag federation of tribes occupying Cape Cod.

The Nauset had been on the cape as far back as their history went, even to the time when the first cranberry was created. Wampanoag legend has it that Granny Squannit, who lived by one of the bogs nestled between the hills of the cape, cut her finger. Out came water, not blood. In distress, she hollered to her brother Mausep, a giant of a man, "The water is pouring out of me! Soon I will be no more!" Mausep

Whalebone entry greets visitors to the Edward Penniman House.

More Historic Hike Options

In addition to this historic hike, Cape Cod National Seashore offers other short trails interpreting New England's coastal past. The Atlantic White Cedar Swamp Trail, a 1.2-mile loop, visits a wetland and then returns via the "Wireless Road," where Guglielmo Marconi first telegraphed a message across the Atlantic Ocean in 1903. The Pamet Area Trail System presents 1.2 miles of hiking trails plus more walking on fire roads. Start at a former Coast Guard station, climb past views, and then visit a cranberry bog house. Next, take off on the Kings Highway, a road used by settlers that traces an even older Wampanoag path. The Pilgrim Spring Trail makes a 0.7-mile loop to a spring believed to be where the Pilgrims drank their first freshwater upon landing in New England. The Smalls Swamp Trail makes a 0.6-mile loop through a site occupied by the Wampanoag for thousands of years and then later by European settlers. Stop at the park's Salt Pond Visitor Center for maps and directions to these additional historic hikes, or visit their website for details.

then pricked his own finger, to drop blood on Granny Squannit's cut and staunch the bleeding. He stretched his giant arm across the marsh toward Granny Squannit, but the wind blew his red blood into the bog, where it became the first cranberry. The rosy delicacy soon spread to every freshwater bog on the cape. By the way, Mausep did save his sister with a second drop of blood that sealed her wound.

On this hike you will see tangible evidence of the Nauset at Indian Rock, where they sharpened their stone axes and fishhooks for ages. The grooved lines in the granite provide a link to their day. Imagine the amount of time spent at this rock by generations of Nauset in order to leave the parallel grooves you will see. In 1965 the National Park Service moved the rock from the edge of Nauset Marsh up to the hill overlooking the marsh.

The Penniman House is another visible connection to the past you will see on this walk. Edward Penniman was a whaler on Cape Cod. Despite whales being long gone from the Massachusetts coast, the area was still the epicenter of American whaling, with generations of world-traveling whalers calling this area home. Penniman was one of the last such men, born

▶ The Nauset Lighthouse, visible during this hike, was moved in the vicinity in 1996 and is still used as a navigational aid.

in 1831. He grew up in Eastham, and prospects did not look good. What little land there was on the cape was mostly depleted. Nevertheless, water was plentiful—an

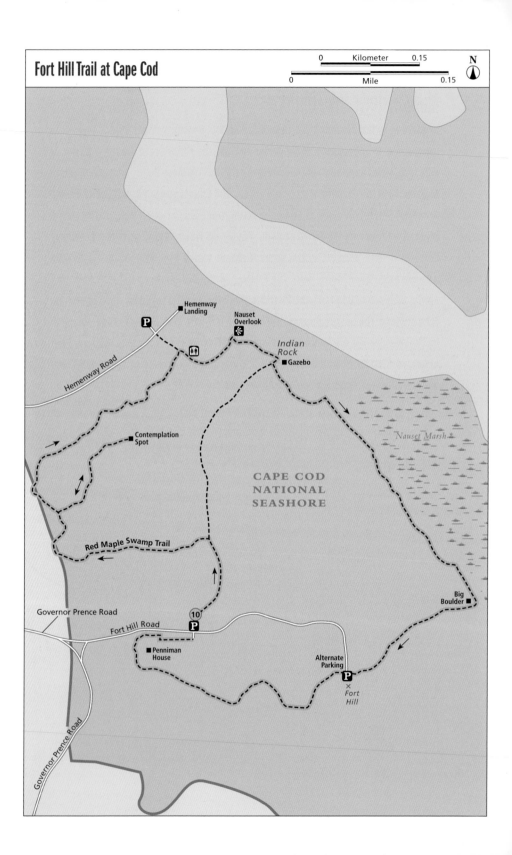

Fort Hill Trail at Cape Cod

N

0   Kilometer   0.15
0   Mile   0.15

Hemenway Landing

Nauset Overlook

Indian Rock

■ Gazebo

Nauset Marsh

Hemenway Road

P

■ Contemplation Spot

CAPE COD NATIONAL SEASHORE

Red Maple Swamp Trail

Big Boulder ■

Governor Prence Road

Fort Hill Road

10
P

■ Penniman House

Alternate Parking
P

✕ *Fort Hill*

Governor Prence Road

ocean full. Penniman turned his eye seaward and was working on a whaling ship at age 11. By age 21, he had graduated to harpooner on the *Isabella*, a schooner out of New Bedford. Penniman proved his mettle and was captaining his own whaling vessel by age 29. For the next two-plus decades, the captain made seven major whaling missions. And they *were* missions—whalers were often gone for years at a time, sailing from the South Seas to the Arctic Ocean, questing for the aquatic monsters.

In between adventures, about 1868, Penniman built the house you see on this hike and finally retired there in 1884. The cupola atop the ornate two-story structure allowed the old salt to look upon the beloved ocean beyond Nauset Marsh, and down on his grandchildren too.

The hike also takes you by natural features. After passing Reverend Treat's boundary marker, inscribed with a "T," you will visit a red maple swamp on a pair of boardwalks. Back in Reverend Treat's day, this swamp had been denuded of trees for firewood and lumber. Nauset Marsh is also visible along the hike. The park service has cleared trees in places, re-creating a historical landscape recalling the Eastham settlers' era.

Miles and Directions

0.0 Start north from Fort Hill Road, away from the Penniman House. Walk a gravel track through open terrain, with Nauset Marsh visible to your right. Ahead, pass the Treat boundary marker, inscribed with a "T."

0.1 Reach a trail intersection. Turn left here, joining the Red Maple Swamp Trail. Enter woods and descend. Shortly join a boardwalk, meeting swamp woods.

0.3 The boardwalk splits. Stay right and enter the heart of the swamp to reach a contemplation spot. Backtrack and resume the main boardwalk.

0.7 Leave the boardwalk and reach a trail intersection. Here an asphalt path heads left toward the parking area at Hemenway Landing. This hike heads right on the asphalt trail, shortly passing seasonally open restrooms.

0.8 Open onto a high point and cleared view of Nauset Marsh in the foreground and Nauset Light in the distance.

0.9 The path reaches a gazebo and Indian Rock, also known as Sharpening Rock. Stay left here (the path going right heads to the trailhead). Walk along the bluff above Nauset Marsh.

1.2 Turn right at a big boulder, toward Fort Hill. A user-created trail keeps straight.

1.3 Top out at the parking lot on Fort Hill, perhaps the site of defense works in the mid-1600s. Keep straight through the parking lot; descend a draw and then climb.

1.5 Circle behind the Penniman House. Note the elaborate structure of the home, which included a lead-lined cistern in the attic and a kerosene-burning chandelier.

1.6 Arrive back at the trailhead.

11 Great Island Trail at Cape Cod

This Cape Cod National Seashore hike first stops by an Indian grave then explores a series of now-connected islands inhabited by early settlers. Walk the shore and bluffs of Wellfleet Harbor, visiting the site of an old whaler's tavern from the early 1700s. Continue south on Great Island in once-settled woods. Drop to a marsh and then climb Great Beach Hill. Ahead, gaze out on Jeremy Point and the shoals of once-inhabited Billingsgate Island before turning north and beach walking along Cape Cod Bay.

Start: Great Island Trail parking area
Distance: 6.6-mile loop
Hiking time: 4–5.5 hours
Difficulty: Strenuous due to sand walking
Trail surface: Natural
Best season: Summer
Other trail users: None
Canine compatibility: Dogs not allowed Apr 1 through Sept 30 due to bird nesting

Land status: National seashore
Fees and permits: Entry permits required from late June through Labor Day
Schedule: Open sunrise to sunset
Maps: Great Island Trail
Trail contact: Cape Cod National Seashore, 99 Marconi Site Rd., Wellfleet, MA 02667; (508) 255-3421; nps.gov/caco

Finding the trailhead: From exit 13 on US 6 in the town of Orleans, Massachusetts, stay with US 6 east toward Wellfleet. At 11 miles turn left at a traffic light onto Main Street toward Wellfleet Harbor. Follow Main Street 0.2 mile and veer left onto East Commercial Street. Stay with East Commercial Street as it becomes Kendrick Avenue after 0.7 mile. After 1.5 miles veer left on Chequessett Neck Road. At 1.6 miles turn left into the Great Island Trail parking area, marked with a brown national park sign. **Trailhead GPS:** N41 55.971' / W70 4.145'

The Hike

Times change, people change, even the land changes. Such is the case here in the Great Island area of Massachusetts's Cape Cod National Seashore. Go back in time 400 years. Cape Cod is a glacially sculpted spit inhabited by the Wampanoag—a loose association of Indian tribes occupying this land of salty waters, high dunes, freshwater ponds and streams, and pockets of forest roamed by bears, deer, even wolves.

Meanwhile, a persecuted group of Christians leaves England for the opportunity to worship as they please in a new land. They aim for a place called Virginia but end up north of their intended destination. It is late in the year, and they decide to stay where they are and make a life for themselves in what became known as Massachusetts. The Wampanoag have mastered living on Cape Cod and share their knowledge with the settlers. By the late 1600s some settlers are dwelling on a series of islands dividing Wellfleet Harbor from Cape Cod Bay. As the Wampanoag did, the settlers hunt whales, gather oysters, and grow crops in the summer.

Looking south into Cape Cod Bay

Times were good for the settlers. Whaling became serious business, as whales were prized for their oil to light lanterns on the seemingly endless winter nights. These whalers gathered at Smith Tavern, situated on a high bluff of Great Island. From around 1690 to 1740, between times spent on the lookout towers spying for whales and alerting men in boats as to the mammals' whereabouts, then whaling, the men gathered in the tavern to tell their tales to sympathetic dames. Eventually the whales were overharvested. The local whaling industry died, and Smith Tavern went with it.

The settlers of Great Island and other adjacent islands adjusted, raising livestock and growing cranberries on the now-deforested islands. Concurrently, the ceaseless tide moving in and out of Cape Cod Bay built sand dunes, followed by marshes, linking Great Island and its neighboring lands. Yet within sight to the south, Billingsgate Island, with over thirty families in residence and a lighthouse to boot, was slowly being eroded.

By 1800 Great Island was deserted, though it now stands tall and proud along with Great Beach Hill, both cloaked in trees again. Billingsgate Island would last another century before its residents were forced to move, losing their land through tidal erosion. By 1915 even the Billingsgate Lighthouse and its adjacent residence had succumbed to the tides.

A Little Publicity Never Hurt

Legend has it that the Smith Tavern sign, visible from the shore, went like this:

Samuel Smith, he has good flip

Good toddy if you please

The way is near and very clear

Tis just beyond the trees.

Today Griffin Island, Great Island, and Great Beach Hill are all linked by land, changed from the early settler days four centuries back by the currents and tides of the Atlantic. This connection enables us to explore this formerly inhabited locale, now under the auspices of the National Park Service. Your hike leaves the trailhead at Griffin Island, passing the grave of an unknown Wampanoag woman before descending to the mouth of the Herring River, which once flowed into Cape Cod Bay but now enters Wellfleet Harbor. Curve around "The Gut," a stomach-shaped bay.

Slow sand slogging leads to Great Island and a hike in hilly pitch pine–scrub oak woods. Grab a boundless view of Wellfleet Harbor before turning inland again to reach the site of Smith Tavern. Though no remains are visible, archaeologists excavated the site in 1970. More than 24,000 artifacts were found and cataloged. Persistent legends of a tavern on Great Island were proven true.

From the tavern site, wander through more woods before passing a monument quoting Captain William Bradford, arguably the glue that held the settlers of the ship *Mayflower* together. The inscription declares the role of God in changing the small colony of Plimoth Plantation to what would become the United States. It ends like this: . . . "as one small candle may light a thousand, so the light here kindled hath shone unto many, yea in some sort to our whole nation."

From there, drop off Great Island and circle Middle Meadow Marsh. Here the hike ascends Great Beach Hill then drops to its south side. Scan toward Jeremy Point and the shoals where the lighthouse of Billingsgate Island once stood. If you try to head toward Jeremy Point, realize that the access will be cut off when the tide rises. In addition, parts of the hike, especially when you are walking along marshes, will use different routes depending on the tides.

Beyond the Jeremy Point Overlook, the hike turns north. Walk along the sandy shore below dunes of Cape Cod Bay. Cross the dunes only where signed, and please allow the dunes to remain in their natural state. *Note:* Portions of the beach may be closed due to nesting birds. Closures will be noted and alternate routes given.

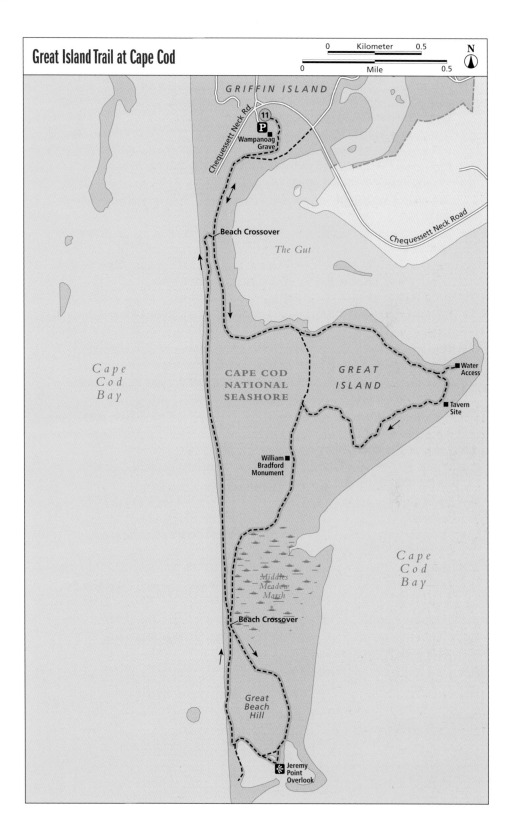

Great Island Trail at Cape Cod

GRIFFIN ISLAND

11

P

Wampanoag Grave

Chequessett Neck Rd.

Beach Crossover

The Gut

Chequessett Neck Road

Cape Cod Bay

CAPE COD NATIONAL SEASHORE

GREAT ISLAND

Water Access

Tavern Site

William Bradford Monument

Middles Meadow Marsh

Cape Cod Bay

Beach Crossover

Great Beach Hill

Jeremy Point Overlook

0   Kilometer   0.5

0   Mile   0.5

N

Miles and Directions

0.0 Start at the Great Island trailhead on a signed path entering woods. Immediately pass the grave of a Wampanoag Indian woman, who was reinterred here in 1976. Continue through stunted pines.

0.2 Reach the shore of The Gut, the outflow of the Herring River. Turn right here, walking along the marsh. Depending on the tide, you may be walking a sandy track or along the grasses. Pass a private hilltop house on your right. Look for critter tracks in the sand.

0.5 Reach an intersection. Here a marked cross-dune path leads right to the beaches of Cape Cod Bay. Stay straight here on a slow, sandy track, keeping The Gut to your left and dunes to your right.

0.9 Curve left around The Gut. Work easterly along a grassy, sandy shore, perhaps walking atop ocean detritus.

1.2 Come to a trail intersection. Here the main trail leads right into the heart of Great Island. Stay left toward the Smith Tavern site, still running alongside The Gut.

1.4 The path leaves the shore and ascends right, entering a pine forest. Be vigilant—this right turn is easy to miss. Work uphill among stunted pines, small oaks, bronze needles, and mosses.

1.8 Open onto an elevated view of Wellfleet Harbor and a trail intersection. Here a marked spur goes straight to the bay below. This loop heads right, reentering forest.

2.0 Reach the marked site of the Smith Tavern. A spur heads left to a view. The loop heads right, still in woods.

2.7 Come to a trail intersection. Turn left on the main pathway (southbound) in the heart of wooded Great Island.

2.9 Reach the memorial to William Bradford. Keep straight in rolling pine woods.

3.1 Open onto Middle Meadow Marsh, once the site of a cranberry operation. Circle right, coming alongside dunes.

3.6 Reach a beach crossover, but stay straight on sand to work your way up wooded Great Beach Hill.

4.1 Emerge on the south side of Great Beach Hill. Keep right along a marsh. Views open of Jeremy Point.

4.2 Reach Jeremy Point Overlook and your farthest south position. Turn north.

4.3 Come to the shoreline of Cape Cod Bay. Head north. (**Note:** Southbound hiking toward Jeremy Point is subject to tidal inundation.)

4.7 Return to the south beach crossover. Stay straight, mimicking the curves of the bay shore.

6.1 Arrive at the north beach crossover. Leave Cape Cod Bay and begin backtracking north along the north part of The Gut.

6.6 Arrive back at the Great Island trailhead.

12 World's End

This entire hike is historic, since you travel trails designed by world-famous landscape architect Frederick Law Olmsted. The scenery is spectacular too as you walk carriage paths and foot trails over a peninsula jutting into Boston Harbor. Grab sweeping views from open hills and oceanside rocks. Visit an old sheepfold and an ice pond at this place of many past incarnations.

Start: World's End entrance station
Distance: 4.2-mile loop
Hiking time: 2–2.5 hours
Difficulty: Moderate
Trail surface: Gravel, natural
Best season: Year-round
Other trail users: Equestrians with special permit, cross-country skiers in winter
Canine compatibility: Leashed dogs allowed

Land status: Trustees of Reservations
Fees and permits: Entrance fee required if not member of Trustees of Reservations
Schedule: Open 8 a.m. to sunset on weekdays; 7 a.m. to sunset on weekends
Maps: World's End Trail Map & Guide
Trail contact: The Trustees of Reservations, 396 Moose Hill St., Sharon, MA 02067; (781) 784-0567; http://thetrustees.org

Finding the trailhead: From exit 14 on US 3 near Hingham, Massachusetts, southeast of Boston, take MA 228 north for 6.5 miles, passing through the town of Hingham. Turn left onto MA 3A and continue 0.4 mile to turn right on Summer Street at a traffic light. Follow Summer Street and keep straight at another traffic light, where Summer Street becomes Martins Lane. Follow Martins Lane to dead-end at World's End after 0.7 mile. You must park inside the World's End Reservation; no street parking is allowed. **Trailhead GPS:** N42 15.504'/W70 52.420'

The Hike

The spot known as World's End, in the southeastern section of greater Boston Harbor near Hingham, has undergone many incarnations. During pre-colonial days, World's End was its own separate island, linked only to the mainland by a bar at low tide. Early settlers wanted to use World's End for agriculture and built an above-water land bridge, making World's End no longer an island. After generations as an agricultural site where hay and other crops were raised as well as sheep, the land overlooking the isles, peninsulas, and shoreline of Hingham Harbor became the home of wealthy businessman John Brewer. Brewer decided to subdivide his farming estate into 160 lots and hired Frederick Law Olmsted to plot the subdivision. It was then that the renowned landscape architect laid out the carriage paths we walk today. He also planned the strategic tree plantings that shade the way, providing depth and texture to the

▶ In 1895 Frederick Law Olmsted suffered a mental breakdown; he spent the last eight years of his life in an asylum.

Overlooking Weir River and Hampton Hill from Planters Hill

often-open landscape, with its dramatic views of the surrounding waters and lands of the harbor.

In the 1940s World's End was thought to be ideal to house the United Nations, ultimately losing out to New York City. World's End's proximity to water and a burgeoning power-hungry Boston metropolis then made it a likely site for a nuclear reactor. That is when local residents decided to have a say in the matter. By 1967 people and politicians had banded together to stop the reactor and bring the property under the umbrella of The Trustees, a member-driven philanthropic outfit managing over one hundred properties in Massachusetts.

Today we can visit World's End, appreciating the nearly continuous views of the south end of Boston Harbor and the natural components of the reserve, where deer and birds thrive on the land and sea life inhabits the tidal wetlands.

Miles and Directions

0.0 Start from the parking area and walk back toward the entrance station. Join the wide, gravel Brewer Road carriage path heading north. Cross the outflow of Damde Meadows tidal marsh, once dammed, drained, and used for pasturage. Views open left into Martins Cove and right into the tidal marsh. Just after the bridge, a narrow grassy track heads left. Stay straight on Brewer Road.

The Man Who Invented Landscape Architecture

Frederick Law Olmsted was born in Hartford, Connecticut, but soon left the nest, exploring different places and methods of employment, from farmer to sailor. He attended multiple schools and later worked as a newspaper correspondent and publisher. In 1857, at age 35, Olmsted found himself superintendent of New York's Central Park. He and another fellow had implemented their winning park development plan, which included winding paths, scenic views, and large green spaces—many of the features we see in today's parks throughout the country.

Central Park established Olmsted as a man who could enhance outdoor space to be both attractive and functional. He lent his skills throughout the country, from preserving Yosemite Valley in California to landscaping Chicago's World's Fair to designing the grounds of the US Capitol. He eventually moved to Boston, where his notable accomplishment was creating the Emerald Necklace—the chain of nine parks ringing Boston. It was not until decades after his death that Olmsted was recognized for his genius and for establishing what came to be known as landscape architecture.

0.1 Keep straight as Barnes Road carriage path leaves right. Begin climbing Pine Hill. Redwing blackbirds and other avian life cheer you on.

0.2 Top out on Pine Hill. Note the planted trailside trees, adding variety, color, and texture to the rolling landscape. Keep straight as a grassy track comes in on the left. The mix of field and forest is favorable for deer; you may see one on your hike.

0.3 Stay straight, joining the Planters Hill Loop as Brewer Road leaves left. Views open of greater Boston Harbor in the far and the peninsula of Nantasket and Hull in the near. A footpath enters on the right. Note the rock walls from agricultural days centuries back.

0.5 Take the spur leading left to the Edwards Monument atop Planters Hill. Backtrack and continue the Planters Hill Loop. More panoramas open as you turn north.

0.6 Reach Brewer Grove, a bench, and a view of the Boston skyline. Behind you, picnic tables provide a dining option. Ahead, a slender trail drops north toward World's End. Grab a seat at the bench and soak in the vista of Boston Harbor and the skyline. Continue on the Planters Hill Loop.

0.7 Take an acute right, rejoining Brewer Road. Descend.

1.0 Come to The Bar, the link between World's End and the mainland on the land bridge. Views open of Hingham Harbor on your left and Rocky Neck on your right. The stone sheepfold foundation is in the woods to your left after you cross onto World's End. It is better seen and accessed when the foliage is off the trees.

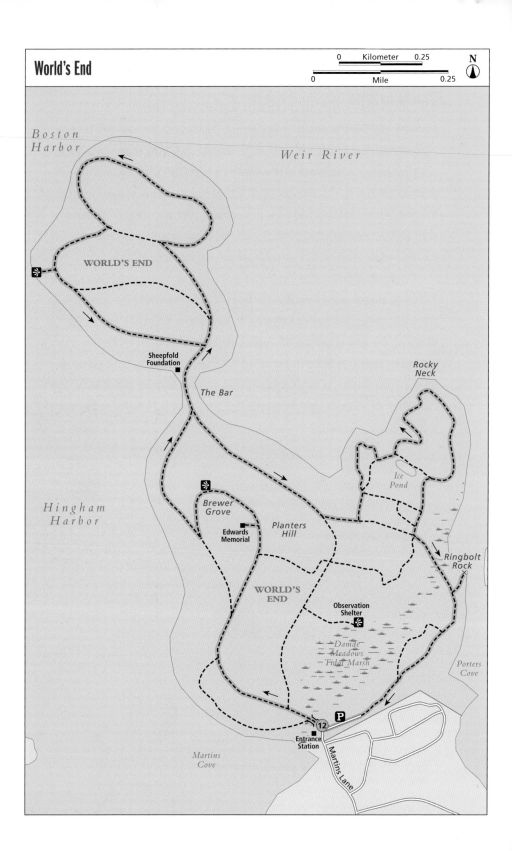

World's End

| 0 | Kilometer | 0.25 |
| 0 | Mile | 0.25 |

N

Boston Harbor

Weir River

WORLD'S END

Sheepfold Foundation

The Bar

Rocky Neck

Ice Pond

Hingham Harbor

Brewer Grove

Edwards Memorial

Planters Hill

Ringbolt Rock

WORLD'S END

Observation Shelter

Damde Meadows Tidal Marsh

Porters Cove

12

P

Entrance Station

Martins Cove

Martins Lane

1.1 Stay right as the carriage road splits. Begin a counterclockwise loop of World's End.

1.2 Stay straight as a carriage road bisects World's End.

1.4 Turn sharply right as a carriage road bisects "The Valley." Continue the widest loop on World's End. The woods thicken on the north side of World's End as parts of Olmstead's landscape plantings have been allowed to naturally reforest.

1.9 Reach the other end of the carriage road passing through The Valley. Turn right here, cruising the slope of a hillside.

2.0 A grassy trail leaves right to a fine view of Hingham Bay, Bumpkin Island, and the Boston skyline. Resume the loop on World's End.

2.2 Stay right as a carriage road heads left to bisect World's End.

2.4 Descend toward the land bridge. This is a chance to access the sheepfold foundation. Look for a break in the woods and a slender path to your right. Find a three-sided rock wall built into the hillside, formerly roofed, to protect the animals from weather and predators. Note that the sheepfold is on the south side of World's End, shielded from northerly winds and facing the sun.

2.5 Stay left on Barnes Road after crossing the land bridge back to the mainland. Big trees border the carriage road.

2.8 Split left on Weir River Road. Barnes Road keeps straight. Descend just a bit and then split left on a singletrack path circling the peninsula of Rocky Neck. Spur trails split to open outcrops that make for rewarding viewing and relaxing locales. Just keep the water to your left and you won't get lost.

3.2 Come near the ice pond at a trail intersection. Stay left, still looping around Rocky Neck on a narrow, stony trail. Access gravelly beaches here at low tide.

3.4 Reach the most northerly part of Rocky Neck. Curve back south. The path widens.

3.6 Stay left at the intersection on the east side of the ice pond, much of which is marsh these days. Pass short spur trails leaving right.

3.7 Turn left onto Weir River Road, a full-blown carriage path. Pass a spur leading right to an outcrop near Damde Meadows.

3.8 Cross the old easterly dam of Damde Meadows. Look southwest across the tidal marsh and you can see the bridge at hike's beginning. Ahead, to your left, a slender trail leads left to Ringbolt Rock, a popular fishing spot on the Weir River. Keep southwest on Weir River Road. Pass spurs leading right that come along the tidal marsh.

4.1 Pass around a gate and reach parking areas that are opened as needed.

4.2 Arrive back at the main parking area.

13 Deer Island

Overlooking Boston Harbor, Deer Island has been home to an Indian incarceration center, a defensive fort, an immigration quarantine area, a county prison, a hospital, a lighthouse, and a pump house now on the National Register of Historic Places and today home to a contemporary sewage treatment plant that was a major force behind the amazing cleanup of Boston Harbor. Add trails with nearly continual panoramas of the dramatic coastline and you have a scenic and historic hike.

Start: Deer Island parking area

Distance: 3.0-mile loop

Hiking time: 1.5–2 hours

Difficulty: Easy to moderate

Trail surface: Natural

Best season: Year-round

Other trail users: Bicyclists

Canine compatibility: Leashed dogs only

Land status: National park

Fees and permits: No fees or permits required

Schedule: Parking area open sunrise to sunset

Maps: Deer Island

Trail contact: Boston Harbor Islands Partnership, 15 State St., Ste. 1100, Boston, MA 02109; (617) 223-8666; bostonharbor islands.org

Finding the trailhead: From the intersection of MA 16 and MA 145 in Revere, Massachusetts, take MA 145, Revere Beach Parkway 0.6 mile toward Winthrop, then stay straight on Winthrop Avenue for 1.2 miles, where it becomes Revere Street. Keep straight on Revere Street, with the ocean to your left. The road then becomes Winthrop Shores Drive. After 0.8 mile turn right onto Underhill Street. Go for 0.1 mile, then turn left onto Shirley Street and continue 1 mile. Make a left onto Eliot Street and then a quick right onto Tafts Avenue, which you follow 1 mile to end at Deer Island. Parking is on the left. Deer Island Address: 290 Tafts Ave., Winthrop, MA. **Trailhead GPS:** N42 21.318'/W70 58.048'

The Hike

You could call Deer Island of the twenty-first century an industrial site, but do so with pride. The sewage treatment plant occupying the island's center played a major role in bringing the waters of Boston Harbor—once known as the dirtiest harbor in New England—up to standard. Deer Island has seen its share of changes over the past 400 or so years. Once a shelling and fishing ground of the Wampanoag Indians, as were other isles of the harbor, Deer Island became an internment center for natives during King Philip's War (1675–76).

During this conflict, the English tried and executed three Wampanoag for killing a Christian convert from their tribe. Metacom, chief of the Wampanoag, struck back at the English, touching off retaliatory raids and battles. Fearful that the "Praying Indians," the ones converted to Christianity, would side with Metacom, the English settlers herded the converts onto Deer Island for the winter of 1675–76. Lacking provisions and firewood, hundreds died from starvation and exposure. A spot on the hike passes a memorial to the fallen Wampanoag.

Later, Deer Island became an agricultural site, primarily for livestock. Then events half a world away came into play. In the 1840s the potato blight hit Ireland; thousands were starving. America—Boston in particular—became the place to escape to. Deer Island became an immigrant processing center. However, so many arrivals were ill that a hospital was set up to handle them.

In the 1850s a poorhouse was located on Deer Island. Here the city of Boston shipped the destitute, children and adults alike. Over the decades it morphed into a low-level jail for petty criminals. Finally, in 1880, Suffolk County established its primary House of Correction here on the island. For a century, Deer Island housed more than 1,000 inmates at a time.

You may be getting the feeling Deer Island was not considered for its beauty. Then the place really did become a dumping ground. In the 1880s a sewage treatment plant was first located on Deer Island. The attractive brick structure you see

The Mazzone Memorial overlooks the Boston Skyline.

today, the one with lots of windows, is on the National Register of Historic Places. As Boston grew and technology advanced, the old pump house was replaced. Yet the population was growing faster than the plant could accommodate. Boston's harbor became a foul place, and swimming bans became routine.

In the early 1980s the city of Quincy sued the Greater Boston Metropolitan Planning Commission, stating that the Deer Island facility was the heart of the problem, dumping sludge directly into the harbor. Eventually Judge David Mazzone ruled, "The law secures to the people the right to a clean harbor." The handwriting was already on the wall, and by the early 1990s, the Suffolk County Jail was razed to make way for the state-of-the-art plant we see today. The harbor is no longer dirty, and part of Deer Island, where you can grab a stellar view of downtown Boston, is known as Mazzone Park.

▶ One newspaper account recalls a man caught trying to escape Deer Island's jail by swimming across Boston Harbor aided by a pair of tire tubes!

Circling around the island, pass the monument to the Wampanoag, then work beyond the sewage plant gatehouse. In places the trail will be fenced from the facility. Rest assured that the trail is open completely around the island, with intersections clearly marked and labeled.

While circling Deer Island, it is truly hard to comprehend the island's many faces. The asphalt trail travels along the shore's edge for much of its way, presenting nearly continuous sweeping views of Boston Harbor and its islands and coastline. Most of the nearer isles are part of the Boston Harbor Islands National Recreation Area, as is Deer Island. Unlike Deer Island, they are accessible by ferry only. Historic sites abound. Georges Island has old Fort Warren, where Confederate soldiers and officials—including the vice president of the Confederate States of America, Alexander H. Stephens—were housed. Peddocks Island also has military ruins.

Just off the south point of Deer Island once stood the Deer Island Lighthouse, originally built in 1890. The cast-iron structure was built in shallows and included a light keeper's house. The storm-battered foundation lasted into the 1970s, when the light was dismantled and the new slender fiberglass light you see today erected. Circling around, the trail opens toward the Atlantic, high atop a seawall. Fort Dawes, a coastal defense first established in the early 1900s, stood here. It was razed for the new treatment plant. Toward the end, the walk climbs a glacially carved hill and passes a cemetery, Rest Haven, where many Irish immigrants are interred, never having reached the US mainland. The sweeping views are breathtaking. One vista affords a view to nearby Shirley Beach. Here a channel known as Shirley Gut once separated Deer Island from the mainland. But the great 1938 hurricane that swept across New England closed the channel, making Deer Island an island no more.

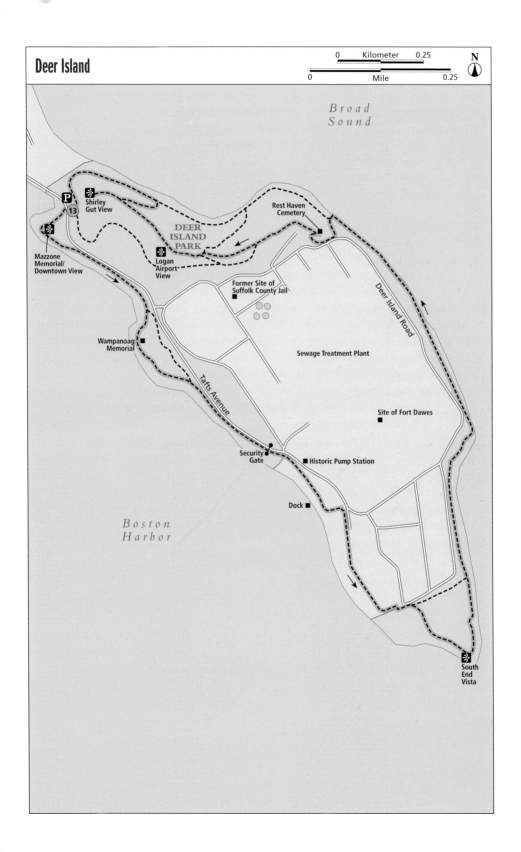

Deer Island

0   Kilometer   0.25

0   Mile   0.25

N

Broad Sound

P
13
Shirley Gut View

Rest Haven Cemetery

DEER ISLAND PARK

Mazzone Memorial/ Downtown View

Logan Airport View

Former Site of Suffolk County Jail

Deer Island Road

Wampanoag Memorial

Tafts Avenue

Sewage Treatment Plant

Site of Fort Dawes

Security Gate

Historic Pump Station

Dock

Boston Harbor

South End Vista

Miles and Directions

0.0 Start from the Deer Island parking area and cross the road entering the Deer Island Plant, beginning a counterclockwise loop of Deer Island on an asphalt trail.

0.1 Reach the memorial to David Mazzone, the judge who sparked the cleanup of Boston Harbor. Soak in the stellar view of the Boston skyline. Nearer aquatic views abound. Turn south on the asphalt trail.

0.3 The trail splits. The path going left climbs a small glacial hill. Stay right along the shore and pass a memorial to the incarcerated Wampanoag. A gravel beach is exposed below at low tide.

0.5 Come to another trail intersection. The hilltop path rejoins the main loop, where westerly harbor views are unmatched.

0.7 Pass the plant's security gate. Continue along the path and look left for the old brick pump station. Pass the large island boat dock on your right, much of the plant on your left, as well as huge wind turbines and solar panels.

1.1 Reach a trail intersection on the south side of the island. An asphalt path shortcuts left. Stay right on the asphalt path heading to the tip of Deer Island. A hill rises to your left.

1.2 Reach the south end of Deer Island. The Deer Island Lighthouse is in the near. A plethora of isles dot Boston Harbor; a display helps you identify adjacent islands. Curve north, now along a seawall. Views of the Atlantic extend as far as the eye allows.

1.3 Pass the other end of the south-end shortcut. The plant is still to your left.

2.1 Leave the main trail and climb left, up a glacial drumlin. Soon pass Rest Haven Cemetery, on a knoll. Keep climbing.

2.3 Reach a high point of the island; soak in more views, including down into the water treatment plant. Pass a trail dropping left. Keep straight and quickly come to a three-way intersection. Stay straight atop the linear ridge.

2.5 Pass an overlook of Logan Airport. Keep straight.

2.6 Take the asphalt spur to Shirley Gut Overlook and then backtrack. Stay on asphalt and dip to the northeast end of the island, rejoining the main trail. Circle past Shirley Beach.

3.0 Arrive back at the trailhead parking area.

14 Walden Pond

Circle the very pond beside which Henry David Thoreau resided for two years in the 1840s, writing his timeless treatises on nature's value to mankind. The busy, popular destination offers trails aplenty. Our hike circles Walden Pond, stopping by the site of Thoreau's Cabin. Leave Walden Pond for Heywood Meadow, a marsh, and then climb to Emersons Cliff, named for Thoreau's friend Ralph Waldo Emerson. From there you complete the circuit around Walden Pond, passing the main beach area.

Start: MA 126 crosswalk on east side of Walden Pond
Distance: 2.5-mile double loop
Hiking time: 1.5–2 hours
Difficulty: Easy, with a short ascent
Trail surface: Natural
Best season: Fall through spring for smaller crowds
Other trail users: None
Canine compatibility: Dogs not allowed
Land status: Massachusetts state park

Fees and permits: Entrance fee required
Schedule: Hours vary with the seasons. The number of visitors is limited to 1,000 people at a time. The park will close when that limit is reached, which usually happens on hot summer weekends.
Maps: Walden Pond State Reservation
Trail contact: Walden Pond State Reservation, 915 Walden St., Concord, MA 01742; (978) 369-3254; mass.gov

Finding the trailhead: From exit 29B, Acton/Fitchburg, on I-95 west of downtown Boston, merge onto MA 2 west, Cambridge Turnpike. Continue 3.3 miles and turn west onto MA 2A, toward Littleton/Ayer. Follow 2A south for 1 mile to a traffic light. Turn left at the light onto MA 126 and drive 0.3 mile to the parking area, on your left. **Trailhead GPS:** N42 26.439' / W71 20.064'

The Hike

There aren't many combination scenic, historic, and literary hikes in the world, but this is one of them. Here at Walden Pond State Reservation, you can walk in the footsteps of Henry David Thoreau, visiting the place that inspired him to write *Walden*, his major work on nature and man. In 1837 the 20-year-old Thoreau had just graduated from Harvard when he returned home and joined his family's pencil-making business among other endeavors, such as carpentry, stone masonry, and teaching. As he worked his mind kept returning to Ralph Waldo Emerson's essay "Nature," which espoused the notion that engaging in the great outdoors can be spiritually fulfilling.

And just like with other young men, the reality of the daily grind of a job made Thoreau ask, "Is there more to life than this?" The question, combined with establishing a friendship with Ralph Waldo Emerson, further stoked his search for meaning in life.

The serene Walden Pond

This desire for purpose and meaning suddenly took on increased import when Thoreau's brother John passed away. In their youth the two had rambled the woods and waters of greater Concord, and John's birding passion had fueled his younger brother's interest in nature. By March 1845 Henry David Thoreau had cemented a plan to live out his theories. He wanted to live in the woods and become a writer. His friend Emerson offered Thoreau the use of a newly bought woodlot at Walden Pond, just outside Concord. Thoreau set about finding a spot for his one-room cabin and built it.

He moved in during the month of July. His friends wondered what he would do while ensconced in his lair. Thoreau wrote, studied Massachusetts natural history, kept a journal, and hoed a garden. Despite being in the woods, this was no isolation tank. Friends visited, and he visited Concord regularly, even employing himself as a surveyor.

After twenty-six months at Walden Pond, Thoreau returned to "normal life." He continued surveying and helping with the family pencil-making business. In 1854 he published *Walden*, which brought him wide acclaim. Thoreau succumbed to tuberculosis in 1862 at the too-young age of 44.

Part of Thoreau's thinking was that both rural and city dwellers need access to nature. He wrote, "I think that each tenant should have a park. . . . A common possession forever, for instruction and recreation." His own beloved Walden Pond became such a thing. As his writings circulated, readers wanted to see the place that inspired the man.

It didn't take long for them to come. In 1866 the Fitchburg Railroad company established a park along the shore near the railroad tracks. Here visitors swam, picnicked, and boated. In 1902 the park burned and was not rebuilt. However, the automobile age was upon the land, and drivers began to visit Walden Pond. The town of Concord built bathhouses on the waterside beach, increasing visitation.

► Walden Pond, where Henry David Thoreau resided and wrote for two years, was owned by none other than nature essayist and writer Ralph Waldo Emerson.

The pond became officially open to everyone in 1922 when the Emerson family and two other property owners donated 80 acres around the pond to the Commonwealth of Massachusetts to be preserved as a park, just as Thoreau imagined. Thoreau's former quiet haunt became extremely popular, seeing nearly 500,000 visitors during the summer of 1935! It is still popular today, with more than 600,000 visitors annually.

Walden Pond State Reservation offers hiking, swimming, picnicking, boating, and fishing, as well as nature study. If you are looking for a quiet experience, stay away during the warm season, especially on hot weekends, when the pond draws swimmers and sunbathers galore. The park does limit visitation to 1,000 visitors at a time; however, I prefer a weekday or winter visit for a quiet experience.

Before starting your hike, visit the bookstore and the replica of Thoreau's cabin near the parking area. You will then cross MA 126 and drop to the pond near the main beach. From there begin a counterclockwise loop on the Pond Path. Parallel the shore of this kettle hole lake, formed when a huge block of ice broke off a glacier and was surrounded by sediment. After the ice melted, a lake was formed. It is deep, clear, and bordered by sand, making it an alluring destination. However, the trail is fenced

Thoreau's Reasoning in His Own Hand

Henry David Thoreau's life and writing have been studied for more than a century and a half. Here, in his own words, is why he sojourned to Walden Pond: "I went to the woods because I wished to live deliberately, to front only the essential facts of life. And see if I could not learn what it had to teach and not, when I came to die, discover that I had not lived."

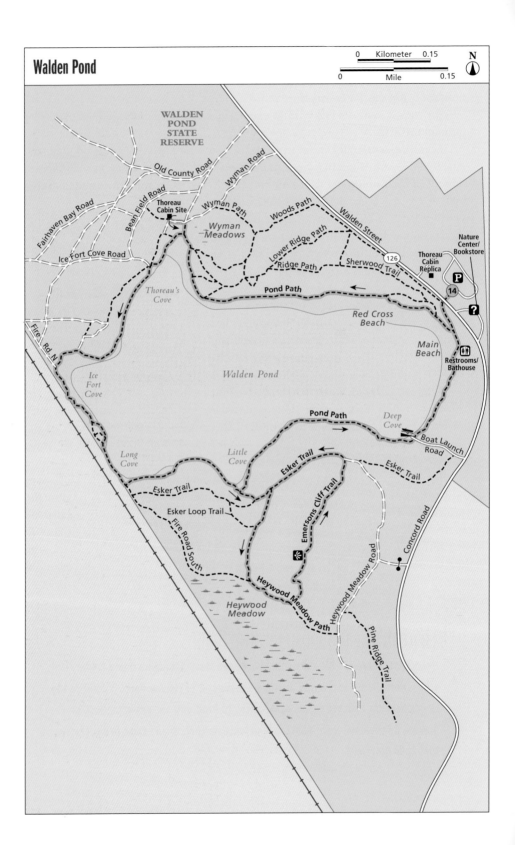

Walden Pond

WALDEN
POND
STATE
RESERVE

Old County Road

Wyman Road

Fairhaven Bay Road

Bean Field Road

Ice Fort Cove Road

Thoreau Cabin Site

Wyman Path

Wyman Meadows

Woods Path

Lower Ridge Path

Ridge Path

Sherwood Trail

Walden Street

126

Thoreau Cabin Replica

Nature Center/ Bookstore

P

14

Pond Path

Thoreau's Cove

Red Cross Beach

Fire Rd. N.

Ice Fort Cove

Walden Pond

Main Beach

Restrooms/ Bathouse

Pond Path

Deep Cove

Boat Launch Road

Long Cove

Little Cove

Esker Trail

Esker Trail

Esker Trail

Concord Road

Esker Loop Trail

Emersons Cliff Trail

Fire Road South

Heywood Meadow Road

Heywood Meadow Path

Heywood Meadow

Pine Ridge Trail

N

0   Kilometer   0.15

0   Mile   0.15

on both sides in very un-Thoreau-like fashion to protect the adjacent vegetation and keep people from creating erosive social trails. All the same, the wire fence detracts from the experience.

Visit the site of Thoreau's cabin, unearthed by Roland Wells Robbins and on the National Register of Historic Places. You can see the chimney foundation and the exact spot where the one-room dwelling stood. A huge rock pile next to it was started in 1872 when one of Thoreau's aging friends dropped a few stones to mark the spot of his cabin. You will see inscribed rocks and other mementos added to the pile.

After looping around most of the lake, take a spur to Emersons Cliff, passing Heywood Meadow, a glacially created wetland. Descend back to Walden Pond and complete your loop around this place that inspired a man who inspired millions.

Miles and Directions

0.0 Start from the parking area and cross MA 126 near the replica of Thoreau's cabin. Descend to the water and main park beach.

0.1 Turn right onto the Pond Path. Walden Pond stretches to your left. The trail is fenced in on both sides. The Sherwood Trail splits right.

0.4 Reach a trail intersection. A connector leads to other trails away from the lake. Turn into Thoreau's Cove. Pass another trail intersection and then bridge a wetland. Wyman Meadows is to your right.

0.5 Come to another trail intersection. Here the Pond Path leads left along Walden Pond. Turn right, climbing a gravel-and-log path to quickly turn left and reach Thoreau's cabin site. Check out the chimney foundation and the memorial rock pile. Look toward the pond through the trees. Backtrack and resume the Pond Path. Go by other connectors to the cabin site. Walk along the pond, bordered by a rock retaining wall.

0.7 Pass the connector with Ice Fort Cove Road. Turn into Ice Fort Cove on the Pond Path.

0.9 Come to Fire Road North near the railroad tracks. Keep sauntering along the pond, climbing a small bluff.

1.1 Pass the connector with Fire Road South in Long Cove. Stay along the pond.

1.3 Split right away from the Pond Path in Little Cove. Climb to the Esker Trail; head left and then quickly turn back right on the Esker Loop Trail.

1.4 Turn left at an intersection, dipping toward Heywood Meadow.

1.5 Stay left on the Heywood Meadow Path. The wetland is to your right.

1.6 Head left on the Emersons Cliff Trail. Ascend steeply.

1.7 Top out and grab a partial view to the northwest.

1.8 Return to the Esker Trail. Turn left.

1.9 After finishing the mini-loop, sally forth back to Walden Pond. Amble beside the water on the Pond Path.

2.3 Reach the boat ramp. Keep along the shore toward the beach changing station. Complete the lake circuit and then backtrack to the parking area.

2.5 Arrive back at the trailhead.

15 Great Brook Farm

This trail-heavy state park, centered by a working farm, presents a chance to explore history mixed with modern farming techniques. First visit the farm, then wander field and forest. View the cellar holes from mill workers' houses, the defensive Garrison House site, and the Farnham Cabin. Walk along Adams Mill, a dammed pond used for milling since 1730. After you are done, cool off with some tasty ice cream at the on-site creamery!

Start: State park interpretive center
Distance: 4.9-mile loop
Hiking time: 3–3.5 hours
Difficulty: Moderate
Trail surface: Mostly natural
Best season: Summer for ice cream
Other trail users: Bicyclists, equestrians
Canine compatibility: Leashed dogs allowed

Land status: Massachusetts state park
Fees and permits: Entrance fee required
Schedule: Open sunrise to sunset year-round
Maps: Great Brook Farm Summer Use trail map
Trail contact: Great Brook Farm State Park, 165 North Rd., Carlisle, MA 01741; (978) 369-6312; mass.gov

Finding the trailhead: From exit 34 off I-495 south in Lowell, Massachusetts, take MA 110 west for Chelmsford for 0.7 mile. Join MA 4 south for Bedford and continue south for 1 mile before angling right onto Concord. Follow Concord for 2 miles and turn left into Great Brook Farm State Park. From here follow North Road for 0.3 mile, turning left into a large parking lot and the main trailhead. **Trailhead GPS:** N42 33.449' / W71 20.907'

The Hike

Agriculture was integral to life in Massachusetts as the first colonists spread west from the coast. There were no stores; people had to grow food to live. Later, people farmed for a living, serving the city dwellers. Farmers diversified, with some specializing in dairy—what they do here at Great Brook Farm State Park. Today you can tour an ongoing dairy operation in conjunction with enjoying some of the park's 20 miles of trails.

Our hike explores a mix of environments; sometimes farm fields, at other times extremely rocky and hilly pinewoods. Elsewhere we traverse swamps and travel alongside quiet ponds. This land has been occupied a long time, and the thread of history is ever-present. Massachusetts natives had their own Grinding Rock, where they ground corn for meal. When the English settled here, they dammed River Meadow Brook and some of its tributaries to create millponds, generating power to operate mills for grinding flour and sawing lumber. In the mid-1600s the area residents—you can see the cellar holes of their former dwellings in what is now forest—banded together and built the Garrison House, a defensive structure to shield themselves

A hiker pauses to look down on the machinery at Adams Mill Dam.

against hostile natives. Ironically, the native's Grinding Rock is located close to the Garrison House.

Over the centuries the land went through changes of usage and owners. In the late 1930s William Farnham built a cabin on the Adams Mill Pond, settling on 8 acres. He ended up purchasing more than 1,000 adjacent acres, establishing the Great

Brook Farm. Farnham then brought in dairy cows. In 1974 he deeded the land over to the Commonwealth of Massachusetts for a state park.

The original working farm was no more. Then the state leased out the park's farm and a state-of-the-art dairy operation was established. Today you can tour the facility, usually on weekend afternoons, and view and feed farm critters. A trip to the ice-cream bar, located in the old milking barn, is a highlight. End your hike with a generous scoop or two of the many flavors offered at this creamery. It brings the dairy farm experience full circle.

The trail system is an intricate network of paths shared with bicyclists and equestrians. Trail intersections are frequent. Most are marked with a number corresponding to the Great Brook Farm State Park Summer Use trail map, available online and at the interpretive center. However, not all intersections are numbered. Do not leave the trailhead without a map.

Miles and Directions

0.0 Start from the interpretive center, following the signs for the ice-cream bar. This may be the only time in your life you follow hiking trail signs to a creamery. Pass the intersection with the Litchfield Loop and then follow a gravel path lined with big rocks up to the farm and ice-cream bar. Children can visit the farm animals, but save your ice cream for the end of the hike. Backtrack and join the Lantern Loop, the wide gravel track leading northwest.

0.2 Reach trail intersection #4. Head right on the Litchfield Loop. Pass alongside a field.

0.3 Stay left as the Litchfield Loop splits. Soon enter rocky woods.

0.4 Come to trail intersection #5. Stay left on the Hill Slide Trail and curve around a field.

0.7 Pass the connector leading right toward the Litchfield Loop. Stay left alongside the woods.

0.8 Reach trail intersection #6 after passing through a strip of swampy woods. Head left on the Stone Row Trail, a singletrack path coursing under pine-oak woods interspersed with rocks galore. See old rock fencerows and rock piles as wells as structures of recent origin. Wind past big boulders and over hills. Beware of unmarked user-created trails in this area; stay with the blazes.

1.2 Reach intersection #32. Stay left, still on the Stone Row Trail. Pass more interesting rock piles. Come near the Woodchuck Trail.

1.6 Intersect the Woodchuck Trail. Angle left and then immediately reach trail intersection #8 at the edge of a field. Go right here, southbound along the field.

1.7 At trail intersection #9, go left on the East Farm Trail, circling around the field.

1.8 Split right and descend into woods. Just ahead, cross a bridge over River Meadow Brook and reach trail intersection #10. Keep left here, rejoining the Woodchuck Trail.

2.0 A user-created trail splits left to private property. Stay with the Woodchuck Trail.

2.2 Pass cellar holes on your right. These once lay below the dwellings of settlers who lived and worked near mills on the property. Just ahead, a trail comes in on your right. Stay straight.

2.3 Reach trail intersection #11. Head left here on the Deer Run Trail.

2.4 At trail intersection #30, angle right and downhill as a loop of the Deer Run Trail curves left. Soon dip to a wetland and cross it on a boardwalk.

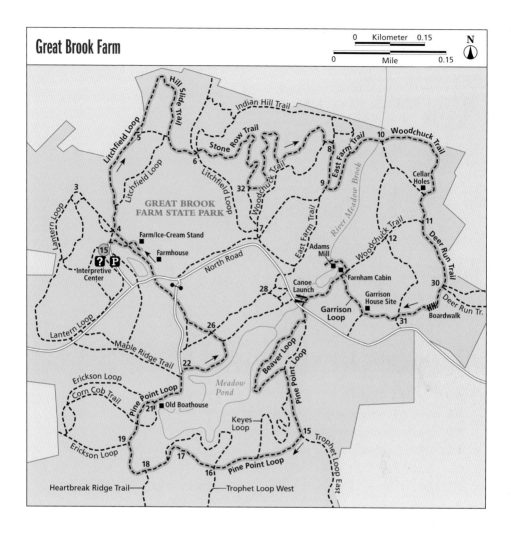

2.5 Rise to an intersection and the Garrison Loop. Split left and quickly reach trail intersection #31. Here a short trail leads left to North Road. Continue right on the Garrison Loop. Pass several rock walls of former inhabited terrain, now woods.

2.6 Arrive at the site of the Garrison House, a former defensive structure whose foundation is still visible. Another trail splits left to North Road. Stay right on the Garrison Loop. The Grinding Rock is in this vicinity.

2.7 Come to a flat and trail intersection. Visit the Farnham Cabin, though it is closed and decaying. As you face the cabin, follow the trail around the cabin to the right and cross two bridges atop the Adams Millpond dam. This mill was in use since 1730, a reason for settlers to live near the Garrison House. After exploring the area, backtrack to the front of the Farnham Cabin and then walk southwest toward North Road, passing over a small bridge.

3.0 Reach and cross North Road. Look left and join the wide Pine Point Loop.

3.1 Split right with the singletrack Beaver Loop. Wander hilly pine woods astride Meadow Pond and then curve back north.

A hiker/history buff peers into the cellar hole of the Garrison House.

3.3 Rejoin the Pine Point Loop, turning right. Walk an easy track.

3.4 Pass the first intersection with the Keyes Loop.

3.5 Reach intersection #15. Stay straight as the Trophet Loop East leaves left.

3.6 Pass the second intersection with the Keyes Loop.

3.7 Come to intersection #16. Keep straight on the Pine Point Loop as the Trophet Trail comes in from your left and another path leaves right for Meadow Pond.

3.8 Reach trail intersection #17. A path leaves right toward Meadow Pond. Continue straight.

3.9 At trail intersection #18, the Heartbreak Ridge Trail leaves left. Stay with the Pine Point Loop.

4.0 Reach trail intersection #19. Stay straight here as the Erickson Loop leaves left. Come along a field and pass the Corn Cob Trail.

4.1 Pass trail intersection #21, then dip. Turn right and check out the old boathouse. Resume the Pine Point Loop. Ahead, bridge River Meadow Brook then open onto a field.

4.2 Reach trail intersection #22. Here the Maple Ridge Trail goes left and a gravel road goes straight. The hike heads right on a grassy path along Meadow Pond.

4.4 Come to a trail in a small meadow after turning away from Meadow Pond. Stay straight and climb to reach four-way trail intersection #26. Keep straight here, aiming for the farm. Shortly, another path comes in on your left.

4.7 Cross the gravel road connecting to North Road. Keep straight and soon cross North Road near the farm. Follow the gravel trail by the farm pond—then go get ice cream!

4.9 Arrive back at the trailhead.

16 Halibut Point State Park

This hike explores a former coastal granite quarry operation at a superlatively scenic preserve on the Massachusetts coast. Walk to a converted World War II observation tower, affording incredible views of the quarry below and the expanse of the Atlantic Ocean beyond, clear to Maine. From there, circle the quarry, exploring the workings of the operation. Detour to an elevated panorama from Halibut Point and then drop to explore the rocky seacoast. From there hike more of the quarry and the rugged shore before returning to the trailhead.

Start: Halibut Point parking area
Distance: 1.9-mile loop with spurs
Hiking time: 1.5–2 hours, including exploring
Difficulty: Easy
Trail surface: Gravel, natural
Best season: Summer
Other trail users: None
Canine compatibility: Leashed dogs only

Land status: Massachusetts state park
Fees and permits: Entrance fee required
Schedule: Open 8 a.m. to 9 p.m. daily from Memorial Day through Labor Day
Maps: Halibut Point State Park
Trail contact: Halibut Point State Park, 5 Gott Ave., Rockport, MA 01966; (978) 546-2997; mass.gov

Finding the trailhead: From the first rotary in Gloucester at the east end of divided highway MA 128, join and follow MA 127 left as it winds through small villages and changes street names. Reach the left turn for Halibut State Park and Gott Avenue after a total of 5.8 miles. Follow Gott Avenue just a short distance and turn right into the state park. **Trailhead GPS:** N42 41.210' / W70 37.859'

The Hike

The scenery at Halibut Point State Park stacks up against anywhere on the Massachusetts coast. It is so pretty I wonder how the employees of the former Babcock Farm Quarry got any work done! Halibut Point is strategically located on the north flank of greater Boston Harbor, the tip of Cape Ann. The jutting peninsula has a commanding view of the ocean. The tower you climb at the park was a former World War II observation post erected to help aim guns at German ships. The name Halibut Point is a misnomer, for it originated from sailing ships having to tack their sails to get around the point. Another term for tacking is "hauling about," which somehow morphed into "halibut." You know how thick some New England accents can be.

This granite-covered shoreline with its superlative views was once home to the Pawtucket Indians, who came here to spend their summers fishing, much as tourists do today, flocking to greater Cape Ann when the days are long and the weather warms.

The disguised observation tower, now visitor center, overlooks Babson Farm Quarry.

In 1702 Samuel Gott, a local weaver, built his home here. The private residence still stands. Gott also left his name on the avenue that accesses Halibut Point State Park. Somewhere around the 1840s, a couple of locals got the idea to mine the attractive high-quality granite outcrops that created picture-postcard scenes along the coast. Cape Ann granite weighed 168 pounds per cubic foot! That is some high-quality stuff. The granite of Halibut Point had another strategic advantage—it was directly beside the Atlantic Ocean. That made shipping the stone cost-effective. However, for the first six decades, the quarrying was done on a small scale. Granite was broken up using hand tools—chisels, shims, and flat wedges. Later, round drills were used, but even these were forced into the granite by hand. Blocks of granite were moved by derricks, large block-and-tackle systems attached to the quarry edge. These early derricks were powered by oxen or men.

Around 1900 a full-scale operation was put into place at what became known as Babson Farm Quarry. Nearby Rockland Granite Company invested in the latest equipment—steam-powered drills, water pumps, and derricks. A coal-fired steam plant was installed on-site to power the machinery. This increased production increased shipping needs. A short train line was installed to move the granite from the quarry to the pier at nearby Folly Cove, where it was shipped off in boats specially designed to carry the incredibly heavy granite.

Wet and Dry Quarry

Today Babson Farm Quarry is full of water, filled by seeping springs exposed when the granite was dug as well as rainwater. Originally quarries like this were kept dry by removing the water bucket by bucket. Sometimes animals were used to haul the water. Additionally, windmills powered pumps. Later the quarry was kept dry with steam-powered pumps. It's hard to imagine the rock-lined pool ever being devoid of water. By the way, swimming is not allowed in Babson Farm Quarry.

In its heyday Babson Farm Quarry employed over 800 men, though around 500 was the average. In the late 1920s a prolonged strike quieted the mine. Cut blocks and other evidences of work were left just as they were the day the men walked off the job. Then the Great Depression hit; Babson Farm Quarry was never to reopen. The sound of the crashing sea and the squawk of shorebirds once again reigned as the rumble and hiss of the steam plant and the crashing of rock came to an end.

During World War II the strategic location of Halibut Point once again became evident, this time from a defensive perspective. Late in the war, a tower was built to help protect Boston Harbor. The building was deliberated constructed to look like a church in order to disguise its true purpose. The lower part of the building resembles a simple wooden chapel. Above it rises a concrete tower with slit-like windows facing to the sea, presenting a sweeping panorama of the New England coastline. A small steeple was added to complete the ruse. Up close, it would fool no one, but to German aircraft high in the sky, the disguise could prove effective. Today the building is used as Halibut State Park's visitor center. You can learn a lot from the interesting displays. Steep steps lead to the top of the tower. Climbing it is a must!

Halibut Point later saw other military uses, playing a role in the development of radar before the locale was left to us civilians. The Commonwealth of Massachusetts established a state park on the site, protecting the history of the area as well as the important ecosystem along the coast—wind-sculpted seaside heath and the rest of the coastal environment. An adjacent 15-acre property is owned by The Trustees of Reservations. The trail system here extends to that property, Halibut Point Reservation, allowing you to not only explore Babson Farm Quarry via a self-guided trail but also hike additional pathways through the woods, heaths, and outcrops of Halibut Point, the park's natural side.

This hike takes you first to the visitor center/tower, where you can learn about the quarry and other park history. Grab a view from atop the tower and then take the self-guided quarry tour. The vistas from the quarry edge will keep you busy taking pictures! Take a side detour to the giant grout pile, with more outstanding views from

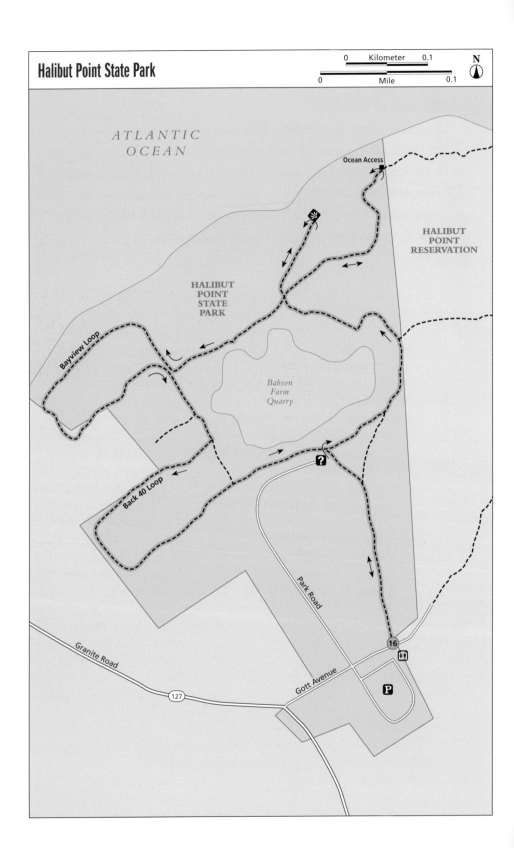

Halibut Point State Park

ATLANTIC OCEAN

HALIBUT POINT STATE PARK

HALIBUT POINT RESERVATION

Ocean Access

Bayview Loop

Back 40 Loop

Babson Farm Quarry

Granite Road

Park Road

Gott Avenue

127

16

0   Kilometer   0.1

0   Mile   0.1

N

this colossal heap of excess granite blocks. Then descend through forest transitioning into coastal heath. Next explore the rocky Atlantic Coast. Finally, continue touring the quarry, making a couple of spur loops to experience more of this gorgeous headland—a worthy hiking destination from both historic and scenic perspectives.

Miles and Directions

0.0 Start from the Halibut Point State Park parking area, crossing quiet Gott Avenue; join a tree-roofed mulch trail.

0.2 Reach a trail intersection. Head left toward the visitor center. Be sure to climb the tower here and absorb the interpretive information. Enjoy overlooks of Babson Farm Quarry and the Atlantic beyond. Begin the self-guided quarry tour. The numbered stops are painted on granite. Circle the quarry counterclockwise, stopping to learn about the quarrying process, rejoining the main wide gravel loop.

0.3 A narrower trail leads right, into the Halibut Point Reservation. Keep straight, circling the quarry.

0.4 Come to a four-way intersection. First head out to the grout pile and the sweeping overlook of Halibut Point and beyond. Backtrack to the four-way intersection and head down to the ocean, leaving forest for coastal heath. Pass a small quarry area, where visitors create artwork with small broken stone in a de facto granite playground. Explore the coast before backtracking.

0.9 Continue the tour after returning from the ocean. Loop around the quarry.

1.0 Turn right on the Bayview Loop. Walk along the coastline then circle back.

1.3 Resume the main loop.

1.4 Turn right onto the Back 40 Loop. Pass old stone fences from agricultural days.

1.7 Return to the tower/visitor center area, completing the self-guided tour. Backtrack toward the parking area.

1.9 Arrive back at the trailhead.

17 Borderland State Park

This hike explores the primary estate and contiguous natural lands and waters of an early twentieth-century New England "power couple," Oakes and Blanche Ames. You can first visit their fireproof granite home, dubbed "Borderland." From there visit their forests, fields, and ponds, managed for wildlife under the Ameses' direction. Stop by a standing farmhouse and then move on to the site of a farm, once an Ames dwelling, from the early 1800s. View a stone lodge before completing your circuit through this popular state park.

Start: Borderland Visitor Center
Distance: 3.3-mile loop
Hiking time: 1.5–2.5 hours
Difficulty: Easy to moderate
Trail surface: Gravel, natural
Best season: Year-round
Other trail users: Bicyclists and equestrians on some trails

Canine compatibility: Dogs allowed
Land status: Massachusetts state park
Fees and permits: Parking fee required
Schedule: Open 8 a.m. to sunset year-round
Maps: Borderland State Park
Trail contact: Borderland State Park, 259 Massapoag Ave., North Easton, MA; (508) 238-6566; mass.gov

Finding the trailhead: From exit 10 off I-495 northwest of Taunton, Massachusetts, take MA 123 north for 3 miles. Turn right onto MA 106 east and continue 0.5 mile to Poquanticut Avenue. Turn left and follow Poquanticut Avenue north for 1.3 miles. Turn left onto Massapoag Avenue and continue 2 miles. Make a right turn into the park and follow the main road to the visitor center. **Trailhead GPS:** N42 3.751'/W71 9.912'

The Hike

What do you get when you combine two leading Massachusetts families of colonial Yankee stock—with former governors on both sides—in a marital union where the man and woman are as accomplished as their forebearers? You get the story of couple who developed a home and grounds on 1,700 acres in southeastern Massachusetts—land now left as a legacy of love honoring their marriage, their careers, their causes, and the place they cherished. Their estate, Borderland, is on the National Register of Historic Places.

Blanche and Oakes Ames were wed in 1900. Oakes Ames, son of Governor Oliver Ames of the famous Ames shovels, from which part of the family's wealth was derived, was a Harvard professor who later became a leading orchid botanist. Blanche, a graduate of Smith College, was a suffragette whose political cartoons made their way onto the national stage and furthered the cause of women being able to vote.

It is against this backdrop that we find them acquiring land for their own homesite on the boundary of Sharon and Easton, Massachusetts, which they were later to name Borderland. Blanche and Oakes cobbled together small farms in the Poquanti-cut Brook valley—a mix of fields, bogs, hills, and granite outcrops.

This land, first settled in the early 1700s, had long been in use. One impound-ment, Puds Pond, was created in 1746 by Jedidiah Willis, who used the waterpower for a sawmill. Downstream, a nail factory and a pair of textile mills also ran off power from this stream. Leach Pond, also on the property, was dammed in the 1820s to ensure a constant water supply for an ironworks that operates even now.

The Ames family initially moved into a wooden homestead on the property, the Tisdale House, erected in 1810. However, this dwelling wouldn't do for the Ameses. Oakes was acquiring a significant botanical library, and fear of fire led Blanche to design the steel-reinforced stone-and-concrete structure—fireproof for certain—that we see today. Ironically, the Tisdale house later burned; all that's left is the foundation.

After building Borderland, Blanche and Oakes set about developing the property as a combination farm and game and forest preserve in their spare time between writ-ing books, drawing, painting, and managing their three other homes in Gloucester,

The Borderland House is on the National Register of Historic Places.

Massachusetts; Ormond Beach, Florida; and Boston. And did I mention they were raising four children too?

A large staff at Borderland executed the couple's plans. Under the Ameses' direction, the employees first repaired and then expanded the dams on the property's ponds. There are a total of six ponds among the fields, hills, and wetlands of Borderland. The pair practiced forestry and built the basic infrastructure of carriage roads and trails that are in place today. They also did a little farming. Oakes implemented a scientific approach to agriculture. One of his professorial specialties was economic plant research and how agriculture had affected culture and civilization. He was one of the first to advance the notion that culture was a by-product of advancement in agriculture, leading to spare time in which man could develop culture. He also studied orchids and became a world-renowned specialist in them. Blanche, with her talent for drawing, illustrated his writings on orchids. They also raised turkeys and gardened at Borderland.

▶ In 1971 Borderland was acquired by the Commonwealth of Massachusetts and turned into a state park.

This active, talented couple grew to love Borderland and spent most of their time there, managing the land, entertaining friends, and later hosting their grandchildren. Oakes passed away in 1950, but Blanche lived on the estate another nineteen years.

Today we can explore the over 1,700 acres of preserved land. After leaving the visitor center, you can check out the Ames Mansion up close. Tours are held on specific days, so if you want to see the impressive library and perhaps some of Blanche's paintings, check ahead for tour dates and times. Otherwise you will have to be satisfied with viewing the house from the outside and visiting the gardens. From there, join the Pond Walk carriage road. Eventually come along Leach Pond, where blooming water lilies shade bass and perch. A mix of forest and field pays homage to the agricultural history of the land. Stop and see the Smith Farm, where Oakes Ames implemented his agricultural theories.

Continue the hike to visit Puds Pond, a serene still-water spot that belies its industrial history. The hike briefly joins Mountain Street and then stops at the site of the Tisdale House, where Blanche and Oakes first lived at Borderland. Walk along Upper Leach Pond and come near still other ponds and granite outcrops. Return to Leach Pond, stopping by a stone lodge overlooking the impoundment. Don't be surprised if you see wildlife here—I have spotted deer and turkeys on the property. Additional miles of trails explore other parts of this legacy left by that early twentieth-century New England power couple—Blanche and Oakes Ames.

Miles and Directions

0.0 Start from the visitor center and walk the wide gravel carriage road toward the Ames Mansion.

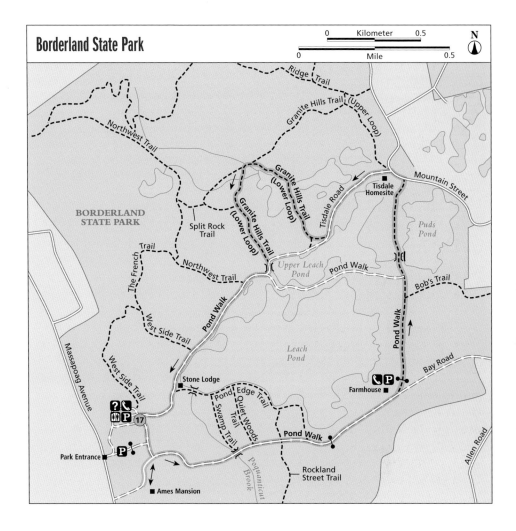

Borderland State Park

0   Kilometer   0.5

0   Mile   0.5

N

0.2   Reach the Ames Mansion. Explore the grounds and then head left as you face the stone dwelling, dropping off a small hill and entering woods on the Pond Walk. A road comes in on your right from the rear of the mansion. Cross Poquanticut Brook on a bridge.

0.5   Keep straight on the Pond Walk as the Swamp Trail leaves left.

0.6   Keep straight as the Quiet Woods Trail leaves left.

0.8   Keep straight as the Rockland Street Trail leaves right.

0.9   Keep straight as the Pond Edge Trail enters on your left. Come alongside Leach Pond; enjoy aquatic views.

1.0   Pass through a normally open gate and temporarily leave Leach Pond. Enter the fields of the Smith Farm, part of greater Borderland.

1.2   Come to the 1880 home of the Smith Farm. Turn left just beyond the wooden dwelling on the Pond Walk as Bay Road Lane keeps straight. The dwelling was originally the abode of

Civil War veteran and doctor Asabeil Smith. The place was later purchased by Oakes Ames for agricultural experiments.

1.5 Reach a trail intersection in a field. Here the more heavily used Pond Walk veers left. Stay straight toward Puds Pond on a grassy track.

1.6 Bridge the outflow of and cross the dam of bucolic Puds Pond. Keep straight through a blend of field and forest.

1.9 Come to Mountain Street. Turn left onto the paved road and walk just a short distance. Leave the road and reach the Tisdale homesite, where the Ameses first lived on this parcel. The Upper Loop Trail heads right here, but stay with the old Tisdale Road—a wide track paralleling the northwest shore of Upper Leach Pond, created by the Ameses in 1939. Pass granite outcrops on your right.

2.4 Pass the upper end of the Granite Hills Loop.

2.5 Pass the lower end of the Granite Hills Loop.

2.6 The Pond Walk comes in on your left. Note the wooden bridge over the outflow of Upper Leach Pond. Keep right on the Pond Walk.

2.7 Pass the Northwest Trail leaving right. Leach Pond is to your left.

3.0 The West Side Trail leaves right.

3.1 Come to the lodge, a stone structure overlooking Leach Pond. Stay right here, climbing a bit away from the pond. Pass a couple of paths splitting from the Pond Walk.

3.3 Arrive back at the visitor center.

18 Blackstone Canal at Uxbridge

This trek examines the meshing of early American agricultural and transportation history. Start at a Revolutionary War–era farm. Visit the barn-turned–visitor center with its exhibits. Next walk the old towpath of the Blackstone Canal. Head to an arched stone bridge and then stroll along the canal to find an intact mill representing the birthplace of industry in New England.

Start: River Bend Farm at Blackstone River and Canal Heritage State Park
Distance: 2.5 miles out and back
Hiking time: 1.5–2 hours
Difficulty: Easy
Trail surface: Pea gravel
Best season: Year-round
Other trail users: Bicyclists, joggers
Canine compatibility: Dogs allowed

Land status: Massachusetts state park
Fees and permits: No fees or permits required
Schedule: Open 8 a.m. to sunset year-round
Maps: Blackstone River and Canal Heritage State Park
Trail contact: Blackstone River and Canal Heritage State Park, 287 Oak St., Uxbridge, MA 01569; (508) 278-7604; mass.gov

Finding the trailhead: From exit 20 off I-495 near Milford, Massachusetts, take MA 85 south for 1.2 miles; turn right onto MA 16 west. Follow MA 16 west for 4.6 miles. Turn right onto Hartford Avenue and continue 3.1 miles. Turn left onto Oak Street to reach River Bend Farm Visitor Center on your left after 0.25 mile. **Trailhead GPS:** N42 5.677'/W71 37.410'

The Hike

The starting place for this hike, River Bend Farm, was established in the 1760s. Originally located along the Blackstone River for the fertile, flat soils Uxbridge offered, the farm's location helped it thrive at first and then survive later, harder times. The Blackstone Canal, though in operation for a mere twenty years, from 1828 to 1848, helped keep River Bend Farm afloat. River Bend's proximity to the canal allowed the farm to grow and ship produce to feed the mill workers in nearby towns. Production actually increased at this farm. Back then there were far more farmers than townspeople. New England was much more open, with fields plentiful and forests few. Today the reverse is true, including far more town dwellers than farmers.

In the mid-1900s River Bend Farm grew into a large dairy operation, functioning until 1974 before becoming part of the Massachusetts state park system. The visitor center for the Blackstone River and Canal Heritage State Park is located in the old dairy barn, where the Voss family had their main dairy operation. Don't worry; it was restored in 1995 and smells just fine now. The milking shed and silo were dismantled. The preserved barn is now a fascinating place. The basement serves as the visitor center entrance. Take steps up to the old barn hayloft. View the displays and artifacts

Hikers and paddlers encounter one another along the Blackstone Canal.

about River Bend Farm, the Blackstone Canal, and the history of the Blackstone River Valley. The visitor center is open year-round, but during warm months the rear shed to the hayloft is opened, providing an overlook of the canal waters, the hiker bridge over the canal, and the bottomlands beyond.

The actual house that was River Bend Farm is now in private hands and is across the street. However, a large parcel of land on the east side of Oak Street and across the canal is Massachusetts state parkland. North of Hartford Avenue, where this hike turns around, is more park property with hiking trails, a portion of which follow the old Blackstone Canal towpath. Therefore there are additional hiking opportunities. Picnic areas are located at the trailhead and both turnaround points of this hike.

You may want to bring your canoe or kayak on this hike. Between the canal and the Blackstone River, canoeists and kayakers can make a loop paddle. They can start at River Bend Farm, paddle up toward Hartford Avenue and the Rice City Pond Dam on the canal, then portage over the dam and float down the Blackstone River. After that, paddlers can portage back to the canal and then paddle back up to the visitor center for a roughly 3-mile adventure. How about that!

The hiking here isn't too shabby either, and you can see many effects of the canal and the changes it brought. First leave the River Bend Farm area, crossing the Blackstone Canal on a bridge. From here you will head north, tracing the old towpath to

More Hiking from River Bend

Beyond this trek, you can also hike two nearby trails. From the River Bend Farm visitor center, head north on the old towpath for 0.25 mile and cross Hartford Avenue. Here you can join the Goat Hill Trail and visit the Goat Hill Lock, typical of the Blackstone Canal. Return via Goat Hill and enjoy a panorama of the valley on a 6.0-mile hike. The King Philip Trail starts on Hartford Avenue and then meanders along Rice City Pond before climbing to Lookout Rock and another view. This is about a 3.0-mile round-trip trek. There are plentiful other historical hiking opportunities all along the Blackstone River Valley National Heritage Corridor.

Hartford Avenue and the Rice City Pond Dam. This water-storage impoundment was created after the canal was abandoned. The canal water level was raised, ensuring that what became Stanley Mill, downstream, would have a steady supply of water to power the mill. The Rice City Pond Dam was destroyed by a hurricane in 1955 and then rebuilt 5 feet lower than its previous elevation. The earlier, higher dam provided more volume and height for the water to fall, giving it more power to turn the mill's turbines.

Here you can also see the photo-worthy stone arch bridge on Hartford Avenue. The hike then turns south, passing alongside the canal and widened pond areas on a level trail. Ahead, the partly shaded gravel path takes you by what is left of the Widow Willard Bridge. What became the canal property had been taken by eminent domain, but the Blackstone Canal Company had to compensate landowners. In this case the canal builders had to build Widow Willard a bridge over the canal or pay her $125 so that she could have one built. Widow Willard needed the bridge. Her barns and livestock were on one side of the canal and her pasturage was on the other side. This is but one of more than fifty such farm bridges the company had to build along the canal right-of-way.

▶ By 1860 more than 80 percent of New England had been cleared for cropland and pasturage. The wood was mostly used for construction and fuel.

Finally you will arrive at the Mendon Street trailhead and the Stanley Woolen Mill, which still stands, albeit as silent as the still waters of the canal. Moses Taft started this operation in 1853. It was typical of the textile mills that once dotted the Blackstone River Valley from Worcester, Massachusetts, to the river's tidal waters in Rhode Island. Taft picked this site in order to siphon waters from the old Blackstone Canal. He used these water rights to power turbines to process wool from its raw state. He then dyed the wool, ultimately creating finished fabrics ready for market. During the Civil War,

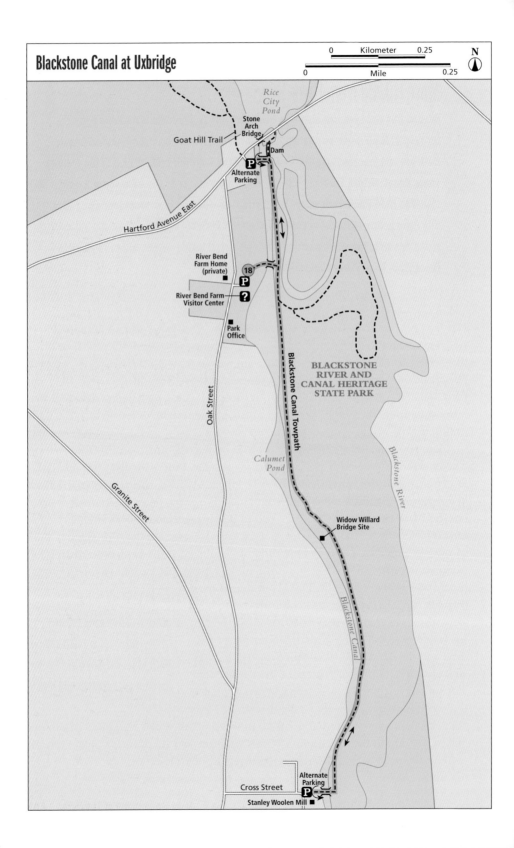

Blackstone Canal at Uxbridge

0   Kilometer   0.25

0   Mile   0.25

N

Rice City Pond

Stone Arch Bridge

Goat Hill Trail

Dam

P

Alternate Parking

Hartford Avenue East

River Bend Farm Home (private)

18

P

River Bend Farm Visitor Center

?

Park Office

Oak Street

Blackstone Canal Towpath

BLACKSTONE RIVER AND CANAL HERITAGE STATE PARK

Blackstone River

Calumet Pond

Granite Street

Widow Willard Bridge Site

Blackstone Canal

Alternate Parking

P

Cross Street

Stanley Woolen Mill

uniforms for the Union Army were made here. The mill continued the tradition of supplying the military, making soldiers' clothes during World War I, World War II, and the Korean War. The mill continued operating until 1987, one of the longest-lasting mills in the Blackstone River Valley. Today you can stand on the bridge over the Blackstone Canal, gaze upon the now-quiet mill with its smokeless smokestack and shut water-intake valve, look into the shuttered windows, and see the passage of history.

Miles and Directions

0.0 Start from the visitor center and walk toward the Blackstone Canal. Cross a stone bridge and reach the historic canal towpath. Turn left (north) toward Hartford Avenue.

0.2 Come to the Rice City Pond dam and Hartford Avenue. The canal and the free-flowing Blackstone River are very close together. The river upstream is stilled by the Rice City Pond dam. Be sure to walk toward the road to gain a view of the graceful arched stone bridge over the old canal. Picnic tables provide a break spot. Backtrack.

0.4 Return to the bridge linking the towpath to River Bend Farm. Continue south, passing a loop trail leading left to grassy former farmland in the Black River Valley. Keep straight on the gravel towpath.

1.0 Come to the Widow Willard Bridge remnants. Continue straight on the old towpath.

1.2 The towpath and canal bend to the right.

1.5 Reach the Stanley Woolen Mill and a bridge linking to the Menden Avenue parking area. Backtrack to the trailhead.

2.5 Cross the bridge over the canal and arrive back at the River Bend Farm trailhead.

19 Moore State Park

This hike is centered on a mill village–turned–country estate along Turkey Hill Brook. The stream drops 90 feet in 0.25 mile, providing waterpower for mills during a 180-year span. See the falls, a restored millhouse, the site of a mill village, a quarry, and some incredible flower gardens, planted by an estate owner who lived here after the mill era ended. An additional walk loops you through a quiet part of the park on a rock-lined country lane.

Start: Moore State Park trailhead
Distance: 2.7-mile double loop
Hiking time: 1.5–2 hours
Difficulty: Easy
Trail surface: Natural
Best season: May and June for gardens in bloom
Other trail users: None

Canine compatibility: Dogs allowed
Land status: Massachusetts state park
Fees and permits: No fees or permits required
Schedule: Open sunrise to sunset
Maps: Moore State Park
Trail contact: Moore State Park, 1 Sawmill Rd., Paxton, MA 01612; (508) 792-3969; mass.gov

Finding the trailhead: From exit 5 off I-95 near Worcester, Massachusetts, take MA 140 west for 0.2 mile then turn left onto Legg Road. Follow Legg Road for 1.7 miles to a T intersection. Turn right onto Manning Road and follow it 2 miles to another T intersection. Turn left onto MA 31 south and continue 8 miles, passing through the village of Paxton. Turn right onto Sawmill Road and enter Moore State Park. Travel 0.1 mile and turn left into the parking area. **Trailhead GPS:** N42 18.620'/W71 57.297'

The Hike

While settling New England, the early colonials had to be resourceful. They not only had to choose advantageous locales but then also draw from the land and water for their livelihood. The section of the stream that came to be known as Turkey Hill Brook descended 90 feet through a small gorge, ideal for setting up a mill. Water turned the wheels of the mill, which in turn provided power to grind corn or wheat or turn a saw blade to cut wood. Forests were needed for construction and firewood. Stone was needed to make the foundations of buildings and the mill. The land currently occupied by Moore State Park had all that.

Upstream of the mill and falls, what became Eames Pond was dammed, ensuring a constant water supply. As with many mill sites, a community grew here. Local farmers and subsistence agriculturalists brought their grain to be ground. The mill became a trading center, which led to a store being built. Over time, no fewer than five separate mills were constructed on this site, establishing the falls of Turkey Mill Brook as a power source and hub of activity.

The historic Moore State Park mill as seen from Artist Point.

A tavern was built a stone's throw away. This became home to the Eames family, for whom the pond is named. A one-room schoolhouse was constructed, adding to the mill village. The mill and the area around it are now listed on the National Register of Historic Places as the Moore State Park Historic District.

By 1930 the era of the mill village was over. The last mill here powered a saw, cutting lumber, but even that proved unprofitable. However, the mill building remains; you can see it perched at one of the three small dams along a short stretch of Turkey Mill Brook.

Residents sought greener pastures. The mill and adjacent property were sold to Glen and Florence Morton, who morphed the locale into a country estate. Mrs. Morton, an avid gardener, began planting varieties of rhododendron, azalea, and mountain laurel all along Turkey Hill Brook and throughout the property. The blooms were spectacular! The color and assortment of flowers brought spring alive at Eames Pond—and do to this day.

In 1946 the Mortons sold their place to the Spaulding family of nearby Worcester. Connie Spaulding was so taken by the blooming gardens that she named the estate "Enchanta." The Spauldings owned a profitable department store in Worcester and plowed more money and blooming shrubs into Enchanta. They transformed the site's one-room schoolhouse into their home, situated between Eames Pond and the falls of Turkey Hill Brook. In 1965 the Spauldings sold their property to the Commonwealth of Massachusetts, and Moore State Park came to be.

Today you can see the nexus of historic mill village and country estate while hiking here. It makes for a rewarding amalgamation of natural beauty and Massachusetts history. The hike first leads you down old Blackhill Road and then joins the Azalea Path—the beginning of a flowery wonderland if you visit during May or June. (Call the park ahead of time for precise blooming conditions.) Curve near the current Blackhill Road and then join the rhododendron-lined driveway of Enchanta. You can even see the old post where the "Enchanta" sign hung. The hike then splits left and goes to Artist Point. Here the restored mill forms a backdrop as Turkey Hill Brook cascades over stone ledges flanked by evergreens. Visit the trip-hammer (a mill-powered pounding device) site below and then head upstream. Come to the heart of the historic district. Visit the mill close up. Check out the rockwork along the stream and the dams built to force the water through narrow power-delivering chutes. The Eames House/tavern site is nearby. Walk by the lower millpond and then come to the Spaulding House, part of which was once the one-room school.

▶ **The first mill along Turkey Hill Brook was established in 1747.**

The hike then passes the upper dam, which holds back Eames Pond and makes its own scenic spill. The bridge over the dam has a gazebo built within it—a popular point of repose, where the still waters of the pond reflect the New England sky. From here the hike explores the park's informal gardens. Walk along a narrow path nestled by evergreens. Loop through a peninsula jutting into Eames Pond, then head for the hills. The Stairway Loop Trail leads past a cliff line, where rock was quarried to erect the buildings of the historic district. Stroll through the heart of the historic district one more time; enjoy the Enchanta Trail, passing the foundations of an old chalet

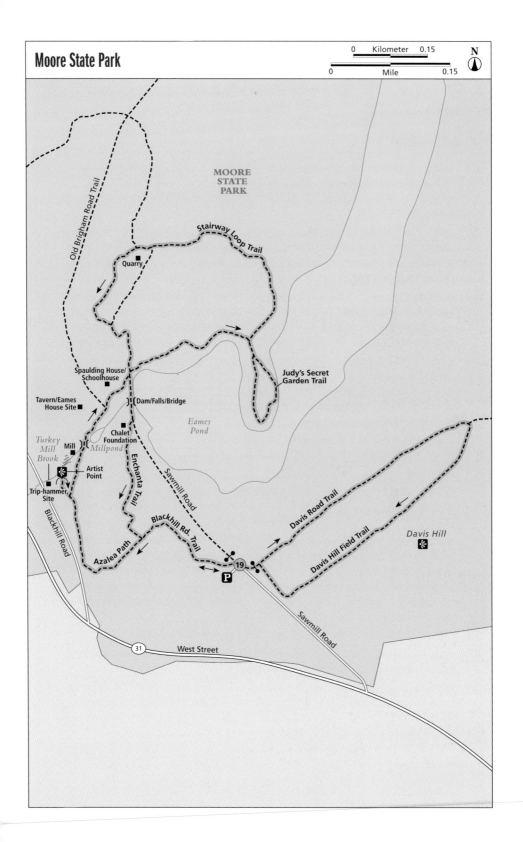

Moore State Park

MOORE
STATE
PARK

Old Brigham Road Trail

Stairway Loop Trail

Quarry

Spaulding House/
Schoolhouse

Tavern/Eames
House Site

Dam/Falls/Bridge

Chalet
Foundation

Judy's Secret
Garden Trail

Turkey
Mill
Brook

Mill

Millpond

*Eames
Pond*

Artist
Point

Enchanta Trail

Sawmill Road

Trip-hammer
Site

Blackhill Road

Azalea Path

Blackhill Rd. Trail

Davis Road Trail

Davis Hill Field Trail

Davis Hill

19

P

Sawmill Road

31   West Street

before returning to the trailhead. From here you can take the tree-canopied Davis Road Trail along old stone walls. Ascend and then turn into an open field, passing over the high point of Davis Hill. Grab a view to the southeast and then return to the trailhead, having explored more New England history.

Miles and Directions

0.0 Start from the trailhead kiosk on the Blackhill Road Trail. Pass through a field bordered by a chestnut research orchard, where American chestnuts are being studied in order to combat the chestnut blight that decimated these trees throughout the United States. Soon enter woods.

0.2 Reach a trail junction. Here the Enchanta Trail (your return route) leaves right. For now keep straight, joining the Azalea Path. Continue descending. Break through a rock wall, coming very near current Blackhill Road. Join the old estate driveway, passing the post that once held an "Enchanta" sign.

0.4 Come within earshot of Turkey Hill Brook. Split left toward the Artist Overlook. Here you can grab a view of the falls and mill. Backtrack; then head along the right bank of the stream up to the mill site. Bridge Turkey Hill Brook and begin exploring the heart of the historic district. Continue up the left bank of Turkey Hill Brook, passing a serene dammed millpond.

0.6 Reach Eames Pond after passing the Spaulding House, a converted one-room schoolhouse. The dam of Eames Pond spills in a curtain below a gazebo, creating a scenic spot. Head away from the gazebo and then split right on the Stairway Loop Trail. Sally forth amid blooming azaleas, mountain laurel, and rhododendron.

0.8 Reach the intersection with Judy's Secret Garden Trail. Split right here and make a loop on a peninsula. Return to and continue the Stairway Loop Trail.

1.1 Come to a saddle alongside an intact rock wall, heading left through hilly woods.

1.3 Come to an intersection. The trail left leads below a cliff line where stone was quarried for the mill community. Head right, climbing some steps to reach another intersection. Stay left here, walking above the cliff line as the trail leading right heads toward Old Brigham Road Trail.

1.4 Reach the other end of the trail going below the cliff line. Continue descending and return to Eames Pond. This time, cross the dam, passing through the gazebo. Re-explore the historic district if you please. Otherwise, reach Sawmill Road, an asphalt road closed to public vehicles. Walk a few steps left on Sawmill Road and then split right, passing the foundation of a forgotten chalet. Enter a mix of tall pines and planted flowering plants on the Enchanta Trail.

1.8 Intersect and turn left on the Blackhill Road Trail. Backtrack to the trailhead.

2.0 Reach the trailhead and then cross Sawmill Road to join the gated Davis Road Trail. Stroll a canopied gravel track bordered by stone walls.

2.4 Turn right, leaving Davis Road Trail. Join a mown path cutting over Davis Hill. Surmount the grassy knoll. Grab a view to the southeast and then descend. Turn right at the bottom of the hill.

2.7 Arrive back at the trailhead.

20 Summit House at Skinner State Park

This hike explores Mount Holyoke, an early tourist mecca offering an exceptional panorama from the Summit House, an 1800s mountaintop hotel. On your way up, pass the Devil's Football, a geological formation. Stop at Halfway House to view the engine of New England's first mountain tram. Next, steeply climb to the restored Summit House. Break off from the crowds. Pass more vistas and then trace a mountain stream en route to the trailhead.

Start: Lower Mountain Road trailhead

Distance: 4.9-mile loop

Hiking time: 3–3.5 hours

Difficulty: Moderate due to a 700-foot climb

Trail surface: Natural

Best season: Whenever skies are clear; weekends for Summit House tours

Other trail users: Nominally bicyclists and equestrians

Canine compatibility: Dogs allowed

Land status: Massachusetts state park

Fees and permits: No fees or permits required

Schedule: Open 8 a.m. to sunset

Maps: Joseph Allen Skinner and Mount Holyoke Range State Parks

Trail contact: Joseph Allen Skinner State Park, 10 Skinner State Park Rd., Hadley, MA 01035; mass.gov

Finding the trailhead: From exit 19 off I-91 near Northampton, Massachusetts, take MA 9 east for 1 mile to a traffic light and Bay Road. Turn right onto Bay Road and follow it 1.1 miles; keep straight, joining MA 47. Stay with MA 47 for 3.6 miles and turn left onto Old Mountain Road. Follow Old Mountain Road for 0.3 mile to the trailhead on your left, just before the sharp left turn to climb Mount Holyoke. **Trailhead GPS:** N42 17.729'/W72 35.861'

The Hike

Mount Holyoke, rising above the Connecticut River, was one of America's earliest tourist draws. At one time it was second in visitation only to Niagara Falls. Here's a quote from a yesteryear brochure about Mount Holyoke: "Many other peaks have a higher altitude and offer wilder and more unmixed natural scenery—but no other blends in its wide prospect so much that is rich in soil and cultivation, or presents so much agricultural wealth of beauty, mingled with so much that is wildly majestic, grand and inspiring."

That vacation ad is true. Your wide panorama of the Connecticut River Valley is much as it was then—the river and agricultural fields in the foreground; towns rising in the distance coupled with wild mountain lands as a backdrop. You can drive to the Summit House these days, but don't—the effort of hiking it enhances the view.

Hikers started climbing Mount Holyoke in the early 1800s. They could stand upon its crest, gazing from Connecticut to New Hampshire and outward to Massachusetts's highest peak—Mount Greylock. In 1821 a group of local Northampton

Gazing down to the Connecticut River Valley from Mount Holyoke.

businessmen built a cabin at the peak. Thus began the history of a structure atop Mount Holyoke. In the following years around 3,000 visitors a year summited the mountain. In 1849 John and Fanny French purchased the mountaintop along with 10 adjacent acres. They built a hotel and were in business by 1851. Visitors flocked to the mountaintop—leaving the train station in nearby Northampton, taking a steamboat across the Connecticut River, and then heading to Mount Holyoke.

Over the years the Summit House grew and changed. It was first expanded in 1861. The Frenches sold the enterprise to New York businessman John Dwight in 1871 and then ran Summit House for him. In the 1890s the Summit House was enlarged yet again.

In 1908 the Summit House came into the hands of Joseph Skinner. A local who loved Mount Holyoke, he wanted both the hotel and the mountain preserved. Skinner modernized the hotel with electricity and indoor plumbing. He even had a road built to the top of the mountain. But vacation travel patterns were changing as the automobile came into widespread use. The halcyon days of the Summit House were over.

The Great Depression, coupled with partial destruction of the hotel during the 1938 hurricane, spelled the end of the hotel as a business. Skinner offered to sell the

New England's First Mountain Tram

The last part of the journey to the top of Mount Holyoke became an adventure itself when owner John French installed a tram to get supplies up the mountain. He quickly realized the attraction of hauling tourists up the tram too, and New England's first mountain tram was born. Initially French used horsepower for the wheeled cart and then later installed a steam engine, which you can see today. Back then visitors could ascend the last part of the mountain three ways: via the tram, which started at the Halfway House; up 522 steps that ran along the tramline; or by horse and carriage. A ride cost 25 cents; children rode for half price.

The tramway stayed in use, evolving from an open cart to being enclosed with walls and a roof. The tram was further upgraded in the 1920s, when the steam engine was replaced with an electric engine and the hauling rope was replaced with a steel cable. In the early 1940s the electric engine burned out and was not repaired due to supply shortages during World War II. The line later became demolished by snows. In 1965 the Massachusetts state park service burned what remained of the tram.

hotel and property to the Commonwealth of Massachusetts, which wouldn't buy the property but did accept it as a donation. The Summit House and the lands around it became Skinner State Park.

The Summit House you see today was restored to its late-1800s appearance during a renovation project in 1988. If it's closed, you can peer into the building through its many windows. The views from the wraparound porch are truly stunning. Tours of the Summit House are held on warm season weekends and into fall. Visit the park website for exact tour dates and times.

This hike visits not only the Summit House but also natural features on Mount Holyoke via a fine trail system. Starting on the shoulder of Mount Holyoke, view the Devil's Football, a huge rock resembling what its name implies. Descend to a lesser visited part of the mountain and then work your way back up via the Tramway Trail to reach the Halfway House. Make a steep climb to the Summit House. Join the Metacomet-Monadnock Trail (M&M Trail) and run the rocky crest of the Holyoke Range. Soak in views from outcrops before dropping off the mountain's south side on quiet, lesser used paths. Enjoy a southward view from Black Rock. Enter the Dry Brook valley, traversing deep woods and interesting volcanic formations. Emerge onto lower Old Mountain Road and then walk a short piece back to the trailhead.

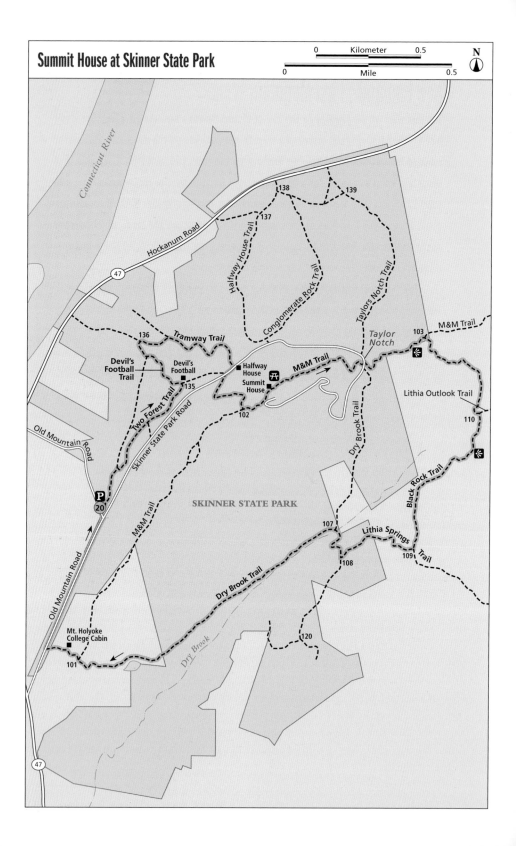

Summit House at Skinner State Park

0   Kilometer   0.5

0   Mile   0.5

N

Connecticut River

Hockanum Road

47

138

139

137

Halfway House Trail

Conglomerate Rock Trail

Taylors Notch Trail

Taylor Notch

M&M Trail

103

136

Tramway Trail

Devil's Football Trail

Devil's Football

135

Halfway House

Summit House

M&M Trail

Lithia Outlook Trail

110

Two Forest Trail

Skinner State Park Road

102

Dry Brook Trail

Black Rock Trail

Old Mountain Road

P
20

SKINNER STATE PARK

M&M Trail

107

Lithia Springs Trail

108

109

Old Mountain Road

Dry Brook Trail

120

Mt. Holyoke College Cabin

101

Dry Brook

47

Miles and Directions

0.0 Start from the trailhead kiosk on the Two Forest Trail toward the Halfway House area. Enter woods on the north slope of Mount Holyoke. Ahead a trail keeps forward, but stay with the blazed path switchbacking uphill.

0.3 Reach a trail intersection where a wide path cuts right to the summit road. Stay straight on a narrower path toward the Devil's Football.

0.5 Reach trail intersection #135 and the Devil's Football, a giant tan rock resembling a football half buried in the ground. The Two Forest Trail keeps straight and is the most popular way to the Halfway House, but turn left here and join the Devil's Football Trail, descending in deep woods.

0.7 A trail enters from your left, tracing an old roadbed. Turn right here and soon reach trail intersection #136. Make another right here. Quickly join the Tramway Trail, heading uphill on a wide path.

1.1 Emerge onto the Summit House access road at the Halfway House area. Explore the area, including the display of the tram steam engine. Continue the hike by turning right on the road and then taking the Halfway Trail steeply uphill.

1.3 Reach trail intersection #102. Go left and keep ascending.

1.4 Emerge onto a rock outcrop and the Summit House. Savor spectacular views from the porch of the Summit House. Head east to and through the picnic area, joining the M&M Trail. More views open in the picnic area. Enter woods and then descend a stony trail.

1.8 Cross the mountain road at Taylor Notch. Stay straight on the M&M Trail while the Dry Brook Trail leaves right. Climb sharply, passing outcrops with vistas.

2.1 Reach trail intersection #103 in a gap. Turn right here on the Black Rock Trail; descend then rise a bit, then resume descending. Stay with the blazes.

2.5 Reach trail intersection #110. Stay right with Black Rock Trail. Climb to an easterly view to the south and then saunter southwest through quiet woods.

3.0 Reach trail intersection #109. Turn right here, climbing then bisecting a flat.

3.3 Reach trail intersection #108. Turn right here. Cross normally dry Dry Brook.

3.4 Reach trail intersection #107. Stay left here on the Dry Brook Trail. Descend the valley on an old roadbed. Pass under a power line.

4.1 Cross a dry feeder stream that has cut a narrow gorge across the path. Admire the rock formations here.

4.2 Pass a pond to your left while wandering wooded knolls.

4.4 Reach trail intersection #101. Rejoin the M&M Trail, descending past the Mount Holyoke College Cabin.

4.5 Return to Old Mountain Road, turning right on the dirt road.

4.9 Arrive back at the trailhead.

21 Chester-Blandford State Forest

This hike presents an ideal combination of history and beauty in the Berkshire Mountains of western Massachusetts. Hike up Sanderson Brook on a trail system developed by the Civilian Conservation Corps to visit 60-foot Sanderson Brook Falls. From there climb toward Observation Hill. Detour by an old mica mine and then loop your way back to the trailhead, stopping for an incredible view from Observation Hill.

Start: Sanderson Brook Road trailhead
Distance: 5.4-mile lollipop
Hiking time: 3–3.5 hours
Difficulty: Moderate to difficult
Trail surface: Natural
Best season: Spring for bold waterfall
Other trail users: Bicyclists, equestrians; illegal ATVs
Canine compatibility: Dogs allowed

Land status: Massachusetts state forest
Fees and permits: No fees or permits required
Schedule: Open sunrise to sunset
Maps: Chester-Blandford State Forest
Trail contact: Chester-Blandford State Forest, PO Box 105, Chester, MA 01011; (413) 354-6347 (summer); (413) 269-6002 (winter); mass.gov

Finding the trailhead: Take exit 3 off I-90 near Westfield, Massachusetts. Bear right after the tolls and follow MA 10/202 south for 3 miles into downtown Westfield. Turn right onto US 20 west and follow it 16 miles to the Sanderson Brook Falls trailhead on your left. **Trailhead GPS:** N42 15.347'/W72 56.819'

The Hike

The Great Depression hit worldwide in 1929, eventually making it all the way to Chester, Massachusetts. There it took the form of the Civilian Conservation Corps—a group of young men employed by the US government, ostensibly to create jobs where there were none. The 113th CCC Company was situated in a flat along the Westfield River, just below a tract of land that was to become Chester-Blandford State Forest. The hundred or so men set about to improve the forest, first combating the gypsy moths that were defoliating oak trees. They left an additional legacy, and you walk upon trails and roads they built, including the path to Sanderson Brook Falls. Besides being paid a wage, the young men also learned the value of teamwork and camaraderie.

Said one CCC boy: "All the time we grew closer together. In the winters, we froze together, and in the summers, we baked together. We were bruised with the same rocks and banged with the same picks. Sore backs soon became strong backs. Stringy bodies, iron bodies . . . and if you see some pal wiping his eyes as he goes out, don't say a thing because you will do the same when you go out."

The view from Observation Hill

Remember these fellows as you make your way up to Sanderson Brook Falls. From there you will enjoy more CCC handiwork, stopping by a still-standing chimney and then climbing a ski trail they built. Snow skiing had just become popular in New England, and the CCC crew added this path, which seems rather steep to me for skiing. Nevertheless, the ski trail takes you to Observation Hill Road. Enjoy a mountaintop trek to Mica Mine Road. Here you will drop into the Gold Mine Brook valley, where small mines yielded mica, emery, and corundum, as well as a little of that shiny yellow stuff. Yes, people prospected for gold in the Berkshires, and hobbyists do it today. Industrial mining still goes on in this range.

However, if you are looking for visual treasure, take the spur trail to a couple of old mica mines. Upon the ground of this spur trail, the shiny pliable stuff that peels off in layers and looks like broken mirrors will be scattered on the ground. The first mica mine opening is on the left. Water oozes from a rectangular opening in a sheer stone wall. Continue up the spur, passing irregular slag piles on your left before the trail dead-ends at another mine.

The hike then heads for a natural feature—the vista at the north tip of Observation Hill. The access trail is named for H. Newman Marsh. He was instrumental in developing the Jacob's Ladder Scenic Byway, the road passing below the state forest

Sanderson Brook Falls spills in stages

through the Berkshires. From Observation Hill you can see the scenic byway as it passes along the Westfield River, from which rise wooded mountains and is worth the trek.

Beyond here a steep path leads back down to Sanderson Brook. This path was originally developed by the CCC as a firebreak. Be prepared to keep your brakes on, and be grateful not to be hiking up this path. The return to Sanderson Brook trailhead is a simple backtrack to the trailhead.

The current state park map is inaccurate. However, it is not too hard to figure out where you are. For assurance, bring a topographic map downloaded onto a GPS. Forest personnel are having a hard time keeping off-road vehicles out of the forest, so please report any ATV activity.

If you still have some energy, stop by Boulder Park, a roadside trail system originally constructed by the CCC. It features much of their stonework and is now overlain with a universally accessible trail.

Miles and Directions

0.0 Start from the Sanderson Brook Road trailhead. Head up a wide gravel road built by the CCC and enter woods.

0.1 Pass around a pole gate and then bridge Sanderson Brook. Continue up the densely wooded mountain valley.

0.2 Meet the H. Newman Marsh Memorial Trail, which heads left, steeply up Observation Hill, and is your return route. Keep straight on Sanderson Brook Road, overlooking the crystalline mountain rill below as you ascend mildly among rocks, ferns, and mossy boulders beneath northern hardwoods.

0.6 Bridge Sanderson Brook again. You are now on the right bank, climbing a narrow part of the vale. This is a good wildflower area. Quickly bridge Sanderson Brook again.

0.9 Split right on a singletrack path toward Sanderson Brook Falls. Skirt a wetland to reach the cataract as it spills 60 feet in stages over a rock face. Backtrack and return to Sanderson Brook Road. Continue up an incline. Look for a view of Sanderson Brook Falls from the road.

1.3 Bridge a small tributary of Sanderson Brook. Keep working uphill.

1.4 Pass around a pole gate with a standing chimney to your right. Ahead, roads split left and right. Take a third track heading sharply left, the CCC Ski Trail. Soon pass a concrete spring box to the right of the trail. The climb sharpens as a small brook flows to your left.

2.0 Reach Observation Hill Road. Turn left on a level track. Wander through swampy woods.

2.4 A track leaves right to a dead end. Keep straight on Observation Hill Road, hiking parallel to a rock escarpment.

2.9 Come to a triangular trail intersection. Split right onto Mica Mine Road. (You will return to this junction later.) Descend a rocky path.

3.0 A spur trail goes right toward Gold Mine Brook. Stay straight, still descending.

3.2 Mica Mine Road keeps straight. The spur to the mica mines leaves left; take this trail. You will know you have missed the turn to the mica mines if you reach a ford of Gold Mine Brook. Following the spur to the mica mines, you quickly come to the visible mine opening on your left with water oozing out. Look for the mica layers on the ground. Keep forward to pass overgrown slag piles and another mine to the left before dead-ending. Backtrack and then continue back up Mica Mine Road.

3.7 Return to the three-way trail intersection. Go straight on Mica Mine Road.

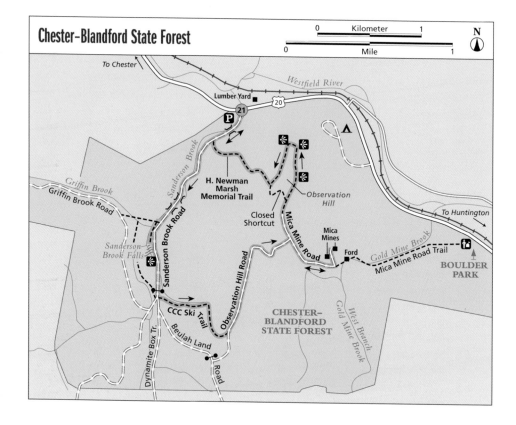

Chester-Blandford State Forest

3.9 Join the H. Newman Marsh Memorial Trail, a blazed singletrack path at the end of Mica Mine Road. Begin bending around the narrow north ridge of Observation Hill. The land drops sharply off to your right. Views open through the trees. A closed shortcut leaves left.

4.3 Open to a prominent vista on a piney rock outcrop, enhanced by mountain laurel. Look below for the Westfield River and US 20, the Jacob's Ladder Scenic Byway. Fayes Hill and Gobble Mountain frame the valley. From here curve south, gently ascending.

4.7 Turn sharply right and begin stepping downhill near a streamlet. This is where the old shortcut entered.

4.8 Rock-hop the streamlet. You are now on the left bank. Keep descending steeply, dropping a total of 600 feet in 0.4 mile. Keep your brakes on. Stone steps aid the drop.

5.2 Return to Sanderson Brook Road and backtrack to the trailhead.

5.4 Arrive back at the trailhead.

22 Mount Greylock

Hike from the highest point in Massachusetts, Mount Greylock, at its oldest state preserve. Explore the memorial tower and visit the CCC-built lodge. Soak in the incredible views before striking out on the Appalachian Trail. Head northbound on the AT and then spur off to visit Robinson's Point. The Overlook Trail leads to a vista, and then you take the AT up the south slope of Mount Greylock, enjoying more highland forest at the historic park.

Start: Mount Greylock parking area
Distance: 3.1-mile loop with short out-and-back
Hiking time: 2–2.5 hours
Difficulty: Moderate due to rocky, slow trails
Trail surface: Natural
Best season: Whenever skies are clear
Other trail users: None
Canine compatibility: Dogs allowed

Land status: Massachusetts state park
Fees and permits: Parking permit required
Schedule: Open late May through Nov 1, only when road to tower is open
Maps: Mount Greylock State Reservation
Trail contact: Mount Greylock State Reservation, 30 Rockwell Rd.; Lanesborough, MA 01237; (413) 499-4262; mass.gov

Finding the trailhead: From the intersection of Main Street and US 7 in Lanesborough, Massachusetts, take Main Street east for 0.6 mile. Turn right onto Greylock Road, reaching the visitor center in 0.9 mile. From there follow the scenic byway (Rockwell Road) 8 miles to the top of Mount Greylock. **Trailhead GPS:** N42 38.225' / W73 10.049'

The Hike

The citizens of Massachusetts hold their high point, Mount Greylock, in high regard. After all, they chose the place for their first designated wilderness reservation. Moreover, it is special—not only is it the highest point in the state at 3,491 feet, but a mountaintop tower built in the 1930s is the state's official memorial to its war veterans. From a natural perspective, the reservation contains the state's only spruce-fir boreal forest, among other God-given attributes.

For more than one hundred years, people have been flocking to Massachusetts's oldest state park to enjoy the magnificent views, smell the evergreens cloaking the mountainsides, and escape the daily grind. The commissioners first in charge of Mount Greylock Reservation put it succinctly back in 1898: "We are to bear in mind that the utility of the reservation is primarily spiritual, not physical; but the highest purpose is always best attained with some wise reference to lower objects. There will always remain in the reservation large areas in which the freedom and boldness of nature will constitute the primary impression, and render the chief service."

Today's citizenry can seek that same renewal of spirit atop Mount Greylock—and find some interesting history as well. Rising high in western Massachusetts, the mountain first attracted visitors in the late 1700s. Farmers had settled the adjacent valleys and were working their way up the slopes, clearing land for pasturage and wood. In 1830 the faculty and students at nearby Williams College cut what had become known as the Hopper Trail up the mountain to study its unique climate and

The memorial to Massachusetts war veterans graces Mount Greylock.

vegetation. They also erected a pair of observation towers. Our hike traces a portion of the Hopper Trail, a trail college students still use to ascend Mount Greylock on their annual Mountain Day. Later in 1863, a Williams College professor founded the Alpine Club, ostensibly the first hiking club in the country.

The origin of the name Mount Greylock is now muddled, but the peak clearly became established as a New England icon. With views extending up to 70 miles and the ability to see five states on a clear day, why wouldn't it be? Newly laid rail lines brought visitors from Boston and beyond. At the same time, glassmaking, iron smelting, and textile industries were being established in adjacent towns, gobbling up wood from Mount Greylock's hillsides. That, combined with wood, paper, and charcoal businesses—also using wood—alarmed locals. Subsequent fires and floods on Greylock heightened concerns about the future of Massachusetts's master peak.

▶ **Mount Greylock Reservation harbors Massachusetts's only boreal forest.**

In 1885 a band of citizens formed the Greylock Park Association and purchased 400 acres atop the mountain. This small mountaintop preserve became the heart of what we see today. Seeking to enhance preservation through recreation, the Greylock Park Association constructed a road to the mountain peak and an iron observation tower. A toll was established to pay for the improvements, but the revenue proved too little. Eventually the association became overwhelmed and turned to the state for financial help.

In June 1898 the Commonwealth of Massachusetts established the state's first public lands atop Mount Greylock. The state eventually increased the 400-acre preserve to the 12,000 acres we behold today. That is what makes hiking here so special—among all the lands in the state, we can explore the very first place chosen as a preserve.

Mount Greylock was chosen first again as the site for the official memorial to the state's war veterans. Initially planned for Boston, the memorial now stands as an imposing and inspiring granite tower topped with a light that can be seen from 70 miles away at night. The 93-foot bastion, quarried from Massachusetts stone, was completed in 1932 and forms the centerpiece of the Mount Greylock experience. You can climb the tower during restricted hours and dates; check the website for details. Gravel paths circle the tower and lead to inspiring views.

More changes were to come in the 1930s. The Civilian Conservation Corps came to Mount Greylock, building trails and backcountry lean-tos, and completed the Bascom Lodge, a rustic building of native stone and wood. The lodge is located just below the high point and offers overnight accommodations as well as dining. The CCC also erected the nearby Thunderbolt Shelter, a ski warming hut to go along with the Thunderbolt Ski Trail they cut out. These mountaintop structures are on the National Register of Historic Places.

Looking into the Hopper from Robinson's Point

This hike starts atop Mount Greylock. You will want to wander around, heading to the war memorial tower and walking up it if possible. Even if you cannot climb the tower, extensive panoramas can be had from the ground—five states in all: Massachusetts, New York, Vermont, New Hampshire, and Connecticut. As you walk the nature trails atop the mountain, note the inscribed rocks that have been placed about. They contain inspiring writings about the wonders of creation. Admire the Bascom Lodge, well integrated into the landscape. The views from the dining area will distract from whatever you are eating.

After settling down, start your hike at the metal relief map of Mount Greylock. Set out on the Appalachian Trail, cut into the state reservation back in 1930. It takes you by the stone Thunderbolt Shelter. After joining the Robinson's Point Trail, find a rock outcrop overlooking a valley known as The Hopper. Pick up the Overlook Trail, traversing spruce, fir, and northern hardwoods. Grab another view from a clearing. Your circuit around Mount Greylock takes you to the historic Hopper Trail, opened so long ago by college students. Rejoin the Appalachian Trail for your final ascent back to the top of Mount Greylock.

Note: The road to the top is open seasonally; check before you come. Also check beforehand to see if the tower is open.

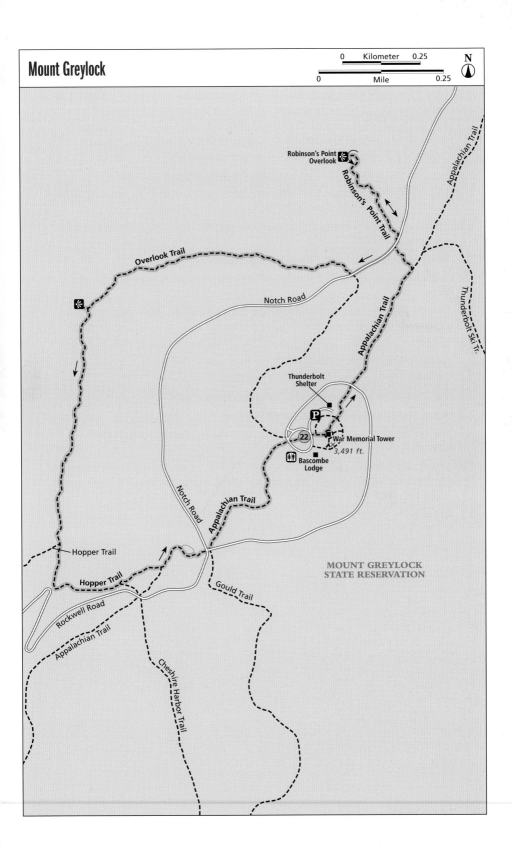

Mount Greylock

Kilometer
0   0.25

Mile
0   0.25

N

Appalachian Trail

Robinson's Point
Overlook

Robinson's Point Trail

Thunderbolt Ski Tr.

Overlook Trail

Notch Road

Appalachian Trail

Thunderbolt
Shelter

P

22

War Memorial Tower
3,491 ft.

Bascombe
Lodge

Notch Road

Appalachian Trail

Hopper Trail

Hopper Trail

Gould Trail

MOUNT GREYLOCK
STATE RESERVATION

Rockwell Road

Appalachian Trail

Cheshire Harbor Trail

Miles and Directions

0.0 Start at the metal relief map of Mount Greylock, located between the parking area and the war memorial tower. Follow the Appalachian Trail northbound directly to the tower. At the tower angle left, staying with the AT as other paths spoke away from the tower. Descend into woods. Just ahead, split left and return to the edge of the parking area. Pass the Thunderbolt Shelter. Keep descending on the wide and rocky AT.

0.4 Reach an intersection. Take the signed Robinson's Point Trail as it splits left.

0.5 Meet Notch Road. Walk right a few steps; cross the road and resume the Robinson's Point Trail. Descend steeply amid evergreens, moss, rocks, and hardwoods.

0.8 Emerge at Robinson's Point. Look down on the rugged wooded valley of The Hopper. Backtrack to Notch Road.

1.1 Reach Notch Road. Turn right here and walk along the road.

1.2 Join the Overlook Trail, which has come from atop Mount Greylock. Head downhill on a slope.

1.8 Take the short spur right to an overlook of the Taconic Mountains above Green River Valley. Resume the Overlook Trail.

2.3 Meet the historic Hopper Trail just after passing a closed trail leading right and crossing Hopper Brook. Turn left, uphill, on the Hopper Trail.

2.4 Come near Rockwell Road. Turn away, still ascending.

2.5 The Cheshire Harbor Trail leaves right. Stay with the Hopper Trail.

2.6 Reach a trail intersection. Join the Appalachian Trail.

2.7 Come alongside a highland pond, with frogs and tadpoles aplenty during the warm seasons.

2.8 Emerge at a three-way road intersection. Cross Notch Road and stay with the AT, ascending. The Gould Trail leaves right here from a gravel parking area. Make the final push up Mount Greylock.

3.1 Return to the Mount Greylock crest area, passing a maintenance facility and restrooms. Cut through woods and arrive back at the metal relief map.

Vermont

Stone relics of a now-forgotten sawmill line the stream that once provided the mill's power (hike 28).

23 The Stone House of Robert Frost

Take a hike to the one-time farm, now a museum, of New England poet Robert Frost. Start astride Lake Paran, taking in mountain views in rolling meadows. Cross Paran Creek and then walk through land that once was Frost's farm. Traverse a pine grove planted by Frost himself. Wander by stone walls before reaching the historic home dedicated to the poet who wrote some of his most famous passages within its walls.

Start: Lake Paran Park
Distance: 3.7 miles out and back with figure-eight loop
Hiking time: 2–2.5 hours
Difficulty: Moderate
Trail surface: Natural
Best season: May through Oct to visit the Stone House Museum
Other trail users: None
Canine compatibility: Dogs allowed

Land status: North Bennington town property
Fees and permits: No fees or permits required
Schedule: Trail open sunrise to sunset; museum open 10 a.m. to 5 p.m. Wed through Sun
Maps: Robert Frost Trail
Trail contact: The Fund for North Bennington, Inc., PO Box 803, North Bennington, VT 05257; northbennington.org; frostfriends.org

Finding the trailhead: From the intersection of VT 7 and VT 7A in North Bennington, Vermont, on Main Street, take Houghton Street east for 0.2 mile, crossing a pair of railroad tracks. Just after the second crossing, turn right into Lake Paran Park. Follow the park road and soon reach a large parking area. From here walk downhill toward the picnic shelter and snack bar. Follow the concrete sidewalk toward the park swim area and reach the trailhead. **Trailhead GPS:** N42 55.997' / W73 14.219'

The Hike

"...And miles to go before I sleep, and miles to go before I sleep." These are the final two lines of Robert Frost's famous poem "Stopping by Woods on a Snowy Evening." This hike leads to the very house where he wrote those memorable words and many others, including parts of *New Hampshire*, his Pulitzer-winning poem collection. He wrote "Stopping by Woods on a Snowy Evening" in June of 1923, ironically during summer, yet you can easily imagine Frost traveling the winter landscape of South Shaftsbury, the location of this farm where he lived from 1920 to 1929. The house itself is significant; built in 1769, it's a colonial-style home unusually constructed primarily of stone. The house today remains much as it did during Frost's stay. His farm once stretched over 80 acres, where he and his family grew apples among other endeavors.

Both this house and the events that transpired inside are historic.

The trail to reach what is known today as the Robert Frost Stone House Museum is much newer. Following seven years of land acquisition and planning, the Robert Frost Trail opened in 2011 and is operated under the auspices of a land trust in North Bennington, Vermont. Even though the trail leads to the stone house, the trail and museum are not affiliated. There is a fee to visit the museum, and hours are restricted.

At the stone house you can see the very room where Frost wrote "Stopping by Woods on a Snowy Evening." The entire room is dedicated to that poem. Other Frost exhibits lend insight into the New England farmer-turned-writer who became arguably America's most notable twentieth-century poet.

Frost took a roundabout way to get to this farm. Born in San Francisco, the famed rural New Englander didn't even reach the East until he was 12 years old. His family landed in Lawrence, Massachusetts, where he graduated from high school and then went on to Dartmouth. By then writing was in his blood, and it stayed there after his first poem, "My Butterfly: an Elegy," was published. He married his high school sweetheart, Elinor, and they began a family. Frost bounced around, ending up on a farm in New Hampshire, where he adapted to, then embraced, and ultimately wrote about the rural life. His poems reflected this immersion in a way of life New

Robert Frost Stone House Museum

Englanders had lived since before this country was a country—the life of the farmer trying to make his way despite the rocky soils, the droughts, the insects, and the cold, yet appreciating the beauty of the place and time.

Wide-ranging success in the writing field eluded him until he moved to England, where he thought publishers would be more open to his writings. Frost was right. His association with and encouragement from writer Ezra Pound helped too. There he published two poetry collections, *A Boys Will* and *North of Boston*. World War I drove him and his family back to America in 1915, where he returned to New Hampshire an acclaimed poet. Publishers now sought him, including *Atlantic Monthly* magazine, which had previously turned down his submissions. When they requested material from him, Frost sent the very same poems they had rejected! Frost also had plenty of offers to teach at universities, which he did throughout his life.

In 1920 Frost moved to the stone house in Vermont, seeking a warmer climate in the lowlands of Vermont as opposed to the highlands of New Hampshire. He was looking for more success in the agricultural arena, particularly to cultivate his apples. Frost lived to be one of America's most-venerated poets, winning four Pulitzer Prizes. He was appointed Vermont's poet laureate in 1961 and passed away in 1963, at age 88. Robert Frost is buried in nearby Bennington.

The aptly named Robert Frost Trail starts at Lake Paran Park in North Bennington. It parallels the shore of Lake Paran and then splits, with the Shore Trail continuing along Lake Paran. On the way out, take the Robert Frost Trail. It takes the higher road—perhaps the road less traveled by—affording views into Massachusetts, New York, and Vermont's own Green Mountains. You then drop to Paran Creek, a dark rill feeding Lake Paran. The path cuts through the slender gorge of Paran Creek, passing rock outcrops before climbing to a field. Now you turn back into woods, entering the land that was Frost's 80-acre farm. Roll through woods before dropping to wetlands. The trail crosses the wetland on an elevated causeway used by cattle to graze both sides of the marsh. Enter the red pine grove planted by Frost and his son Carol. They laid out 1,000 pines as part of Vermont's soil conservation program. These evergreens are approaching the century mark. The hike then works around woods and beside mossy stone fences that were likely exposed in Frost's day. Emerge at the stone house museum. See the old barn and apple trees planted by Frost, in addition to his house.

Try to time your hike with a trip to the museum, though the museum can be accessed by automobile. ***Note:*** Trail parking is available at the museum but is not recommended, since the museum is open seasonally and the gates to the museum are closed promptly at 4:30 p.m. Towing is enforced.

Miles and Directions

0.0 Start from the swim area sidewalk access on the Robert Frost Trail and enter woods on a level singletrack path. Lake Paran is to your right. Cross a boardwalk over a sloped grassy wetland.

0.3 Reach a trail intersection. Here the Shore Trail splits right; this is your return route. For now go left, climbing on the Robert Frost Trail. Rise to grassy overlooks of the lake and mountains beyond. Traverse a mix of meadow and trees.

0.7 Come to a four-way trail intersection. Briefly reunite with the Shore Trail. Stay left here, still on the Robert Frost Trail. Climb to a level field.

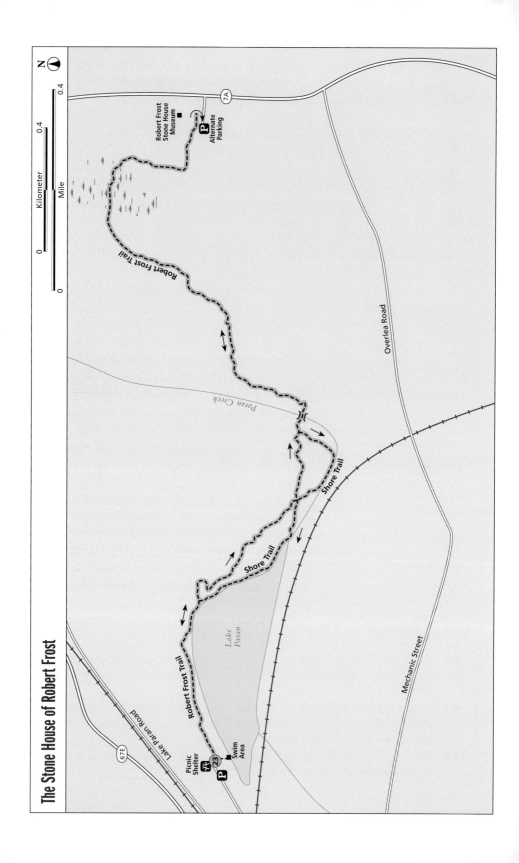

The Stone House of Robert Frost

N

Kilometer
0   0.4

Mile
0   0.4

Robert Frost Stone House Museum

Alternate Parking

7A

Robert Frost Trail

Paran Creek

Shore Trail

Shore Trail

Robert Frost Trail

Lake Paran

Overlea Road

Mechanic Street

Picnic Shelter

Swim Area

67E

Lake Paran Road

23

0.8 Reach a confusing intersection. Here a doubletrack keeps straight while the singletrack Robert Frost Trail dives right into woods. Follow the blazed Frost Trail right.

0.9 Meet the Shore Trail again at Paran Creek. Cross the stream, enjoying the covered seating in the middle of the span. Reenter woods, turning up the Paran Creek valley. Walls of the gorge rise on your right.

1.2 Emerge on the edge of a field. Hike parallel to the woods edge.

1.3 Turn left back into woods, entering land that was once part of Robert Frost's farm.

1.6 Reach a wetland. Head east across a causeway built to allow cattle to graze the western parts of the farm.

1.7 Leave the wetland and reenter woods. Pass through the grove of red pines. Begin running alongside mossy, broken down stone walls.

2.0 Reach the Robert Frost Stone House Museum. Explore and then backtrack to the bridge over Paran Creek.

2.9 Cross the bridge and stay left on the Shore Trail. Continue along the creek and then the lake.

3.2 Return to the four-way intersection. Stay left, still on the Shore Trail. Remain close to Lake Paran.

3.4 Turn left on the Robert Frost Trail toward the trailhead.

3.7 Arrive back at the swim access and picnic shelter.

24 West River Trail

This hike traces an old railroad grade through the scenic West River gorge. Start at the Salmon Hole at Jamaica State Park, site of a 1740s battle, then trace a travel route first used by Abenaki Indians. Later a rail line was blasted through the forbidding terrain. You will take an easy albeit beautiful hike on the converted rail grade and then spur onto a foot trail, entering Hamilton Falls State Natural Area. Ascend along Cobb Brook to reach 120-foot Hamilton Falls, a rewarding destination.

Start: Jamaica State Park
Distance: 6.0 miles out and back
Hiking time: 3–3.5 hours
Difficulty: Moderate with a 500-foot climb
Trail surface: Pea gravel, natural
Best season: Early May through Columbus Day
Other trail users: Bicyclists
Canine compatibility: Dogs allowed
Land status: Vermont state park

Fees and permits: Entrance fee required
Schedule: Open 10 a.m. to sunset early May through Columbus Day weekend
Maps: Jamaica State Park Recreational Trails Guide
Trail contact: Jamaica State Park, 48 Salmon Hole Ln., Jamaica, VT 05343; (802) 874-4600; vtstateparks.com

Finding the trailhead: From the intersection of VT 30 and VT 100 in East Jamaica, Vermont, take VT 30/VT 100 north for 3 miles to the town of Jamaica. Turn right on Depot Street and follow it 0.3 mile, bridging the West River. Just after the bridge, turn left into the state park. Follow the main park road to dead-end at the Salmon Hole and playground. **Trailhead GPS:** N43 6.561'/W72 46.505'

The Hike

This hike travels through the yawning valley of the West River, deep in the Green Mountains. The waterway has been used as a travel corridor for centuries, linking the Connecticut River Valley with Lake Champlain and points west. In pre-Columbian days it was tough traveling through the gorge of the river as it sliced through the Green Mountains. Going down West River toward the Connecticut River in a canoe wasn't as bad, though the Abenaki faced challenging rapids. Getting back upriver was hardest. Thus the Abenaki called the West River the "Waters of the Lonely Way." They also consumed the resources of the river. The very spot where you start this hike—the Salmon Hole—was an important seasonal camp. It is believed the natives had been using what came to be Jamaica, Vermont, and Jamaica State Park for untold centuries. An archaeological dig at the Salmon Hole in 2010 unearthed thousands of artifacts, from spear points to stone tools.

By the 1700s European powers were vying for what would later be called New England. The Spaniards had all but given up on the upper East Coast, but the French

Hamilton Falls

and the English penetrated farther and farther from the Atlantic, heading inland to establish relations with the local Indians, to establish forts for defense, and to validate territorial claims. That was the setting in 1748, when a troop of British soldiers found themselves at the Salmon Hole, resting and trying to shoot salmon from the West River for dinner. The French and Indians who were pursuing them heard the shots and ambushed the British at their waterside camp, killing several. This skirmish later became known as the Salmon Hole Massacre.

Today the state park and waterside facilities belie the historic nature of the Salmon Hole. However, the still waters of the West River attract swimmers and anglers to this day. With the campground nearby and even a playground, the flat astride the Salmon Hole exudes a completely different aura. On other stretches of the river, paddlers seek whitewater thrills. An annual September water release from the upstream Ball Mountain Dam turns the West River into a foamy froth, attracting whitewater boaters from all points of New England.

The Green Mountains have always been a point of pride for Vermonters, but they can't deny the challenge in getting through and around them, even now. After the Civil War, railroad lines spread their tentacles throughout the country as communities realized they would reap economic benefits from a rail line passing through their town. The idea was born to snake a rail through the Green Mountains using the historical route along the West River. By 1879 the West River Railroad was worming from Brattleboro to South Londonderry, stopping at communities like Jamaica along the way. The rugged terrain, prone to slides, and the narrow gauge of the railroad, leaving cars subject to toppling, created an unreliable track. Floods and snows didn't help either. The West River Railroad became known as "36 miles of trouble." A newspaper editorial dubbed the line the "try-daily—they go down in the morning and try to get back at night."

The line remained silent for decades until the Friends of the West River Line was formed with the idea to transform the rail right-of-way into a multiuse trail. Through their ongoing efforts, we now have the West River Trail—ultimately to once again link Brattleboro and South Londonderry. Today stretches of the path are open, including the section heading upriver from Jamaica State Park, beginning at the Salmon Hole. Stay tuned as the rail trail, one of the few in southern Vermont, expands.

▶ By 1936 the West River Railroad had been abandoned—one final flood had left the line repairs too costly to continue.

By the way, bring more than shoes for this hike. If you are inclined to swim, fish, or camp, Jamaica State Park is an ideal getaway, with all the activities concentrated in one place. This hike picks up the West River Trail at the park. The path scoots around the upper part of the state park campground and then gloms onto the West River Railroad bed. The scenery is immediately noteworthy—the rushing West River singing its way through rapids, broken by slower segments; the steep walls of Little Ball Mountain rising to your right, deep in forest cover with ferns and mosses growing where imposing boulders are not. At times you are squeezed in by the blasted bluff on one side and the West River on the other.

The walking is easy on the wide former rail bed. Pass The Dumplings, a spot where enormous boulders clog the West River, creating both a scenic sight and a challenge for paddlers. Picnic tables make stopping along the trail a breeze. Tributaries

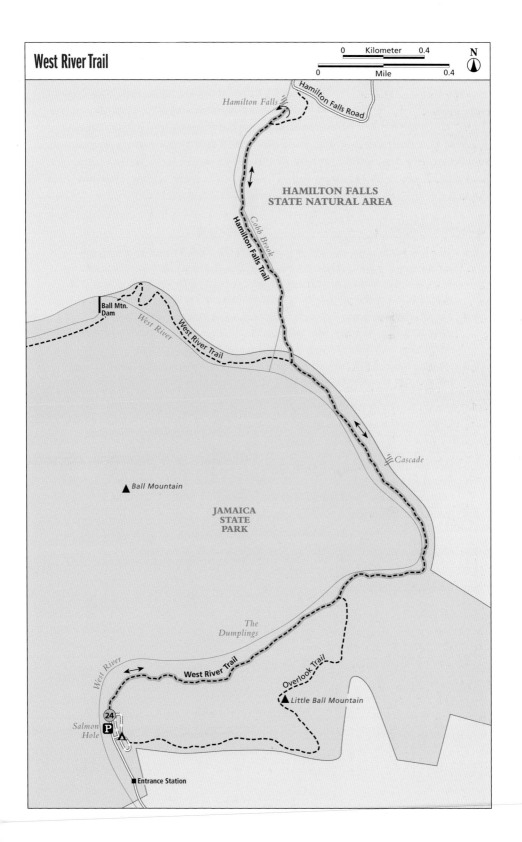

West River Trail

0 Kilometer 0.4
0 Mile 0.4

N

Hamilton Falls

Hamilton Falls Road

HAMILTON FALLS
STATE NATURAL AREA

Cobb Brook

Hamilton Falls Trail

Ball Mtn.
Dam

West River

West River Trail

▲ Ball Mountain

JAMAICA
STATE
PARK

≋ *Cascade*

*The
Dumplings*

West River

West River Trail

Overlook Trail

▲ Little Ball Mountain

24

P

*Salmon
Hole*

■ Entrance Station

flow under the trail after creating warm-up cascades for your final destination—Hamilton Falls. The hike splits away from the former rail line and then joins an old wagon road for a climb up the Cobb Brook valley in the Hamilton Falls State Natural Area, a Vermont state preserve. As you climb among the everywhere-you-look splendor, Cobb Brook tumbles below in cataracts and pools. A side trail leads to the base of 120-foot Hamilton Falls, gushing white over a rock face, barely forming a pool at its base before speeding onward to the West River. Just so you know, at least ten people have died climbing up Hamilton Falls. Don't do it. Instead take the Hamilton Falls Trail up past the falls and gain a top-down vista of the cataract.

Miles and Directions

0.0   Start from the main day-use parking area. Pass through the children's playground and join a wide trail entering woods. Bisect a picnic area. The West River flows to your left. The wide trail makes for easy walking under a canopy of evergreens and hardwoods. Stop at occasional interpretive signs detailing the human and natural history of the valley.

0.4   A curve of the river opens views north of the mountains. Continue uptrail. Pass the first of a few trailside picnic tables. Spur trails lead to small riverside beaches and swim holes. Ahead, view the boulder-strewn part of the river known as The Dumplings.

0.9   Meet the Overlook Trail. The hiker-only path leads 0.5 mile to vistas atop Little Ball Mountain and then returns to the state park campground. Continue upstream on the West River Trail.

1.2   The trail and river bend left as a stream comes in on your right.

1.7   The trail passes over a stream. Look right for an unnamed cascade tumbling through rocks.

2.0   Meet the Hamilton Falls Trail. Thus far you have gained 160 feet in 2.0 miles. You are fixing to gain 470 feet in 1.0 mile. Join the Hamilton Falls Trail up an old wagon road along Cobb Brook, entering the Hamilton Falls State Natural Area.

2.4   The ascent briefly eases.

2.9   Turn left onto the spur trail to Hamilton Falls. Descend into dark evergreen woods.

3.0   Reach the base of 120-foot Hamilton Falls. Backtrack down Cobb Brook.

4.0   Rejoin the West River Trail; head downriver.

6.0   Arrive back at the trailhead.

25 Deer Leap Loop

This hike first explores the old-growth forest of Gifford Woods then joins the Appalachian Trail (AT). Climb to the Deer Leap, a rock from which you can gaze upon a sea of mountains, then drop to Maine Junction, the intersection of Vermont's historic Long Trail and the equally historic AT. After contemplating the histories of these two paths, take the AT north to complete the loop before returning to Gifford Woods.

Start: Gifford Woods State Park office
Distance: 5.7-mile lollipop
Hiking time: 3–4.5 hours
Difficulty: Moderate to difficult
Trail surface: Natural
Best season: Summer
Other trail users: None
Canine compatibility: Dogs allowed

Land status: Vermont state park, national forest
Fees and permits: State park entrance fee required
Schedule: Open mid-May through late Oct
Maps: Hiking from Gifford Woods State Park
Trail contact: Gifford Woods State Park, 34 Gifford Woods Rd., Killington, VT 05751; (802) 775-5354; vtstateparks.com

Finding the trailhead: From Woodstock, Vermont, take US 4 west 14 miles to intersect VT 100. Stay with US 4 west /VT 100 north for 6.2 miles; split right with VT 100 north for 0.6 mile and turn left into Gifford Woods State Park. Park in the lot below the office. **Trailhead GPS:** N43 40.576' /W72 48.665'

The Hike

This hike reflects how the United States and its citizens came to regard the wealth of outdoor treasures within its bounds. When young America was simply thirteen states, the country was a scattering of small towns enveloped by an endless wilderness that needed to be tamed. As we spread westward and settled in the fertile lands beyond the Appalachian Range, there was still more wilderness to conquer. At the dawn of the 1800s, Thomas Jefferson already realized the country was destined to stretch from the Atlantic to the Pacific.

Americans kept moving westward. Less and less of the country seemed a howling wilderness. Then there came a shift: It seemed that we didn't need to tame all the wild places but rather protect and preserve some of them for future generations. Later, men like Henry David Thoreau and Aldo Leopold espoused the importance of interacting with nature and planted the concept of man's role in preserving our special places into the American conscience. By the late 1800s the concept of a national park had come to fruition with the establishment of Yellowstone. Individual states began to develop parks of their own, to reserve special places and provide recreation for all to enjoy. Later came James P. Taylor and Benton MacKaye. Their idea was to link

Hikers look at mountains beyond from the Deer Leap.

preserved lands via footpath, an extensive trail, a long trail, where citizens of nearby communities could access the natural pathways. Thus Vermont's Long Trail (Taylor's idea) and the Appalachian Trail (MacKaye's idea) were conceived. However, it took a lot of effort from a lot of people to make them what we see today.

Meanwhile, New England was a growing land of farms and manufacturing centers. A surprising amount of forest was cut down for fuel, crops, and pasturage. In Vermont the sheep industry was booming. Wool was in demand. The urban textile mills needed raw material to process. Sheep coated open mountainsides, gobbling up pasturage. By 1875 only 20 percent of Vermont was forested. Suddenly, wildernesses were few and far between and patches of old-growth woods were a rare and notable site. And so it was that Walter Barrows began to notice people stopping by the forest on his farm to admire the big trees that grew near Kent Pond, in the shadow of Deer Leap Mountain. Concerned that his forest would be cut down one day, Barrows gave this 13-acre tract to the State of Vermont, and in 1931 Gifford Woods State Park was established. The original 13 acres were subsequently developed by the Civilian Conservation Corps. They built the park office and picnic area, as well as the Upper Camping Loop and trails. Later, more land was purchased, and today the park comprises 285 acres.

Our hike explores this confluence of outdoor recreation and preservation, starting at Gifford Woods State Park. First you leave the park office and follow the Old Growth Interpretive Trail to admire the large maples, hemlocks, and birches. Join the Kent Brook Trail to meet the Appalachian Trail and ascend the slope of Deer Leap Mountain. Take the spur to the wide-open outcrop of Deer Leap Overlook, from which you can see the expanse of the once-again-forested Green Mountains. The trail then curves around Deer Leap Mountain and drops to Maine Junction, the point where the Long Trail and Appalachian Trail diverge—or meet, depending on your hiking direction. At this spot you can stand in Willard Gap and reflect on how these long-distance pathways demonstrate the value of preserving and interacting with the natural beauty found in New England and beyond. Consider how the ideas and actions of leaders in outdoor thought brought about paths through wildernesses where we can engage in restorative activities that offset our hectic, electronic-centered lives.

▶ Vermont's Long Trail, extending from the Massachusetts state line north to Canada, was completed in 1930. The Appalachian Trail, stretching from Maine to Georgia, was completed in 1937. Both have been repeatedly rerouted and improved.

Miles and Directions

0.0 Start at the CCC-built Gifford Woods office. Climb the stairs to the office and then head left to join the Old Growth Interpretive Trail. Walk through deep woods past picnic areas. Ahead, split right, walking toward the Kent Brook Trail.

0.1 Meet the Kent Brook Trail. Head left here, winding through rocky woods of birch, hemlock, and maple. Cross occasional mucky areas and seasonal streams. Stay with the blazes.

0.3 Come within sight of the Upper Camping Loop of Gifford Woods State Park. Turn away, working mostly uphill in thick forest.

0.7 Meet the Appalachian Trail. Turn right, joining the world's longest marked footpath southbound toward Georgia, its southern terminus. Climb irregularly on a rocky, rooty track. Enter the Green Mountain National Forest.

0.9 The trail passes between a pair of small boulders.

1.2 Level off in spruce woods. The slope falls sharply to your left, down toward US 4 and Sherburne Pass.

1.3 A short spur left leads to a partial view of Pico and Killington Peaks. Resume climbing.

1.6 Reach a trail intersection. The Sherburne Pass Trail leaves left, downhill, for Sherburne Pass and US 4. Stay right here with the AT. Just ahead, reach a second trail intersection. Turn left here on the Deer Leap Trail, toward Deer Leap Overlook, beginning the loop portion of the hike. The AT goes straight and will be your return route. Work through evergreens interspersed with white paper birch.

1.9 Reach another trail intersection. Leave the Deer Leap Trail and head left toward Deer Leap Overlook. The path works through spruce woods, over rock faces, on boardwalks, and even uses a stairway as it heads south for the outcrop of Deer Leap.

Deer Leap Loop

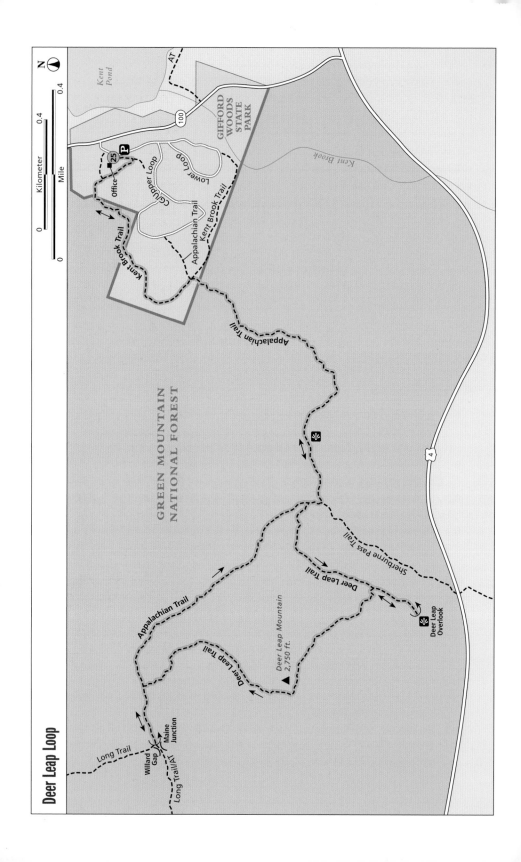

N

Kilometer
0   0.4   0.4
Mile
0   0.4

Kent Pond

AT

100

GIFFORD
WOODS
STATE
PARK

P
25
Office

CG Upper Loop

Lower Loop

Appalachian Trail

Kent Brook Trail

Kent Brook Trail

Kent Brook

GREEN MOUNTAIN
NATIONAL FOREST

Appalachian Trail

4

Sherburne Pass Trail

Deer Leap Trail

Deer Leap
Overlook

Deer Leap Mountain
2,750 ft.

Appalachian Trail

Deer Leap Trail

Long Trail

Willard
Gap

Maine
Junction

Long Trail/AT

Long Trail

2.1 Come to the Deer Leap. Here a large sloping rock outcrop opens to Pico Peak and its ski slopes, as well as a ski village below. Blue Ridge Mountain rises to the west, Killington Peak stands to the southeast, and a host of wooded lands completes the panorama. Soak in the scene and then backtrack to the main trail.

2.3 Arrive back at the Deer Leap Trail. Descend left, working off stone ledges.

2.4 Cross a streamlet and begin ascending steeply on Deer Leap Mountain.

2.6 Top out on Deer Leap Mountain. Obscured views open to the northwest. Begin descending.

3.1 Reconnect with the Appalachian Trail. Head left, still southbound.

3.3 Come to Willard Gap and historic Maine Junction, where two long trails link. Here the AT splits left for Georgia and the Long Trail goes right to Canada. Begin backtracking, northbound, on the AT. It is 489 miles to Mount Katahdin in Maine, the trail's northern terminus. Head north on the AT toward Maine, but we are only going to Gifford Woods.

3.5 Pass the Deer Leap Trail to your right. Begin covering new ground on the AT.

4.1 Reach the other end of the Deer Leap Trail. You have been here before. Backtrack on the AT, still toward Gifford Woods State Park. Just ahead, pass the Sherburne Pass Trail and stay with the AT.

5.0 Reach the Kent Brook Trail. The AT goes straight toward the Upper Camping Loop. Turn left with the Kent Brook Trail.

5.7 Arrive back at the Gifford Woods office.

26 Mount Tom

This hike heads to Mount Tom, overlooking the town of Woodstock, Vermont, at Marsh-Billings-Rockefeller National Historical Park. First visit the home and gardens of an estate where several conservation-minded owners used forestry techniques and sound farming as a role model for future land use. A series of carriage roads takes you through this recovered land. Your return hike is via the narrow, aptly named, Precipice Trail.

Start: Billings Farm and Museum visitor center
Distance: 3.7-mile lollipop
Hiking time: 2–2.5 hours
Difficulty: Moderate
Trail surface: Natural
Best season: Fall for colors
Other trail users: None
Canine compatibility: Dogs allowed
Land status: National Park Service

Fees and permits: No fees or permits required; fee required to visit Billings Farm
Schedule: Trails open to hiking spring through fall
Maps: Marsh-Billings-Rockefeller NHP; Walk Woodstock!
Trail contact: Marsh-Billings-Rockefeller National Historical Park, 54 Elm St., Woodstock, VT 05091; (802) 457-3368; nps.gov/mabi

Finding the trailhead: From the intersection of VT 12 and US 4 in downtown Woodstock, near the town green, take VT 12 north (Elm Street) for 0.3 mile to reach the right turn into the Billings Farm and Museum. Park here; there is no public parking at the national historical park. The trail to the national historical park starts to the right of the Billings Farm and Museum visitor center.
Trailhead GPS: N43 37.909' / W72 30.952'

The Hike

Marsh-Billings-Rockefeller National Historical Park—Vermont's only national park—tells the story of three families and their dedication to conservation, all centered on a farm and estate adjacent to Woodstock. Back in 1805 the Marsh estate was built, and young George Perkins Marsh explored the woods and family farm, gaining an indelible appreciation for Vermont's natural beauty. As an adult Marsh went off to Washington, representing his slice of Vermont in Congress, then joined the diplomatic corps in Italy. It was there he saw how thousands of years of abuse of the land had rendered part of the Mediterranean coast as barren as the moon. This cemented his notions of land stewardship and led to his classic book, *Man and Nature*. His own beloved Green Mountain State was being recklessly timbered and over-farmed, causing erosive damage to the land and the rivers that flowed through it. Marsh passed away before his ideas could be fully implemented.

A Vermonter named Frederick Billings later bought the Marsh property, returning after cashing in on the California gold rush. Billings had missed the verdant mountains and valleys of his home state, but he returned to find devastation. In 1869 Billings planted trees by the thousands on the denuded slopes of Mount Tom, using scientific forest management techniques and establishing sound practices on his Jersey cow farm. The land around the estate began to heal, and once more Mount Tom proudly wore the fall colors for which it had been known.

The Billings offspring continued the tradition of conservation-minded farming and land management at the farm and estate. Billings's granddaughter, Mary French, married Laurance Rockefeller, and they lived at the manse beneath Mount Tom. The Rockefeller family had already donated money and property to establish and improve more than twenty national parks, so it was only "natural" that in 1992 Mary and Laurance donated the estate and the adjacent 550-acre forest to the National Park Service to establish a preserve—the only park in the country dedicated to historical conservation. The couple donated their farm to a separate entity, but the farm and estate are part of the same experience.

The estate mansion and its gardens

Today you can visit the site where these three families lived and carried out their dreams for a more conservation-minded Vermont. You can not only check out the grounds—from the farmhouse–turned–visitor center to the mansion to the gardens—but also roam some of the 20 miles of carriage road (closed to vehicles) and footpaths that wander the slopes of Mount Tom, rising above the estate. Entrance to the Billings Farm requires a fee. The farm is not run by the National Park Service, despite the fact that the farm and national park share the same parking lot. Confusing, eh? It won't be when you get here.

▶ George Perkins Marsh's seminal book, *Man and Nature*, was released in 1864.

Our hike leads from the shared parking lot and heads to the national park, where you should stop by the visitor center and then at least circle by the estate and gardens, as well as the pool and greenhouse area. From there walk past the horse shed to eventually join Mountain Road, which leads up the wooded slopes of Mount Tom and along Pogue Brook. From there Mount Tom Road leads through open pastures and woodlots. Look for stone fences on impossibly steep slopes from the bad old days of erosive agriculture. By the way, forestry management is an ongoing process at the national historical park. Eventually you will open onto the south peak of Mount Tom, where generations of Woodstock residents have hiked, to see the view of the Ottauquechee River valley and the town of Woodstock below. You can even see the chimneys of the Mash-Billings-Rockefeller estate as well as the fields of the Billings Farm. Beyond rises a wooded wonderment of mountains—Vermont as we all know and love it.

Your return hike is drastically different. Leave the panoramas of Mount Tom, joining the Precipice Trail. Walk a slim footpath on a steep slope protected by wire cable. Drop via switchbacks, skitter along cliff lines, and twist among boulders on the declivitous southeast slope of Mount Tom. A half mile of excitement leads you back into the system of carriage roads and a chance to view the estate grounds a second time. Upon returning to the Billings Farm and the parking area, consider touring the first-rate agricultural facility.

Miles and Directions

0.0 Start from the Billings Farm visitor center. Head right on an asphalt path to immediately cross VT 12 and enter Marsh-Billings-Rockefeller NHP. Pick up a gravel road and take it left to the NHP Carriage Barn visitor center. Continue to visit the brick mansion and gardens. At the site of the pool, split right, uphill, toward the Horse Shed.

0.4 Come to the Horse Shed and some big pines. Cemetery Road splits left; stay right on the Upper Meadow Road, passing a wooden gate. Ascend into woods. Pass a spur leading right back to the main building complex.

0.6 The Precipice Trail leaves left. This is your return route. Stay straight on the Upper Meadow Road.

0.8 Join Mountain Road. Climb.

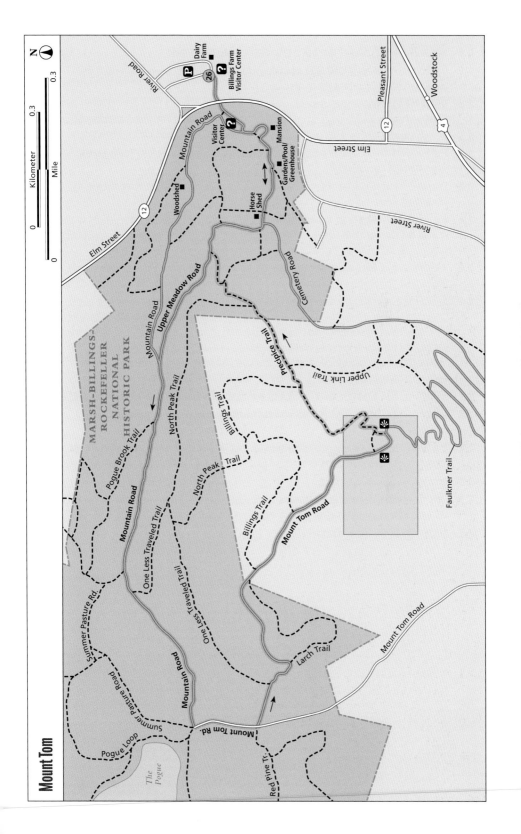

Mount Tom

MARSH-BILLINGS-
ROCKEFELLER
NATIONAL
HISTORIC PARK

N

Kilometer
0   0.3   0.3

Mile
0   0.3

River Road

Dairy Farm

P

26

Billings Farm Visitor Center

Mountain Road

Visitor Center

Mansion

Gardens/Pool Greenhouse

Horse Shed

Woodshed

Elm Street

12

Pleasant Street

Woodstock

12

4

Elm Street

River Street

Cemetery Road

Upper Meadow Road

Mountain Road

Pogue Brook Trail

North Peak Trail

North Peak Trail

Billings Trail

Precipice Trail

Upper Link Trail

Billings Trail

Faulkner Trail

Mount Tom Road

Mountain Road

One Less Traveled Trail

One Less Traveled Trail

Summer Pasture Rd.

Pogue Pasture Road

Summer Pasture Road

Mountain Road

Pogue Loop

The Pogue

Mount Tom Rd.

Larch Trail

Mount Tom Road

Red Pine Tr.

0.9 Pogue Brook Trail leaves right, but stay straight on Mountain Road.

1.2 Pass Summer Pasture Road after crossing Pogue Brook. Ahead, One Less Traveled Trail leaves left. Again, stay straight on Mountain Road.

1.5 Reach a major intersection. Here Mountain Road ends, the Pogue Loop goes straight, and Summer Pasture Road comes in on your right. Go left on Mount Tom Road, crossing an arched stone bridge over Pogue Brook. Ascend through a mix of pasture and woods.

1.7 The Red Pine Trail and an unnamed road leave right. Stay on Mount Tom Road, gaining views through the meadows.

1.8 One Less Traveled Trail comes in left. Ahead, the Larch Trail leaves right. Keep ascending Mount Tom Road.

2.0 The Larch Trail enters right. Ahead, the Billings Trail climbs left. Look for stone fences to the right of the road on ultra-steep, now-wooded terrain. Work around the north peak of Mount Tom.

2.2 A spur trail rises left to meet the Billings Trail. Continue on the wide carriage road, passing over a built-up section of road.

2.4 Reach the overlook at the south peak of Mount Tom. Vistas open to the southwest of the Ottauquechee River valley below and the Green Mountains beyond. Curve past a second view, this one of Woodstock below, even the chimney of the mansion and the Billings Farm fields. Note the sitting benches and large lighted star. Here join the singletrack Precipice Trail left. It starts below the overlook. The Faulkner Trail leaves right. Immediately switch-back on a narrow path bordered with cables, slipping along a cliff line.

2.7 The Billings Trail comes in on your left. You can hear the sounds of the city below.

2.8 The Upper Link Trail leaves right. Keep straight with the Precipice Trail, passing mossy outcrops.

2.9 The North Peak Trail leaves left. Join a carriage road and keep straight, ending the rugged section of the Precipice Trail. Descend.

3.0 An unnamed spur leaves right.

3.1 Return to Upper Meadow Road, completing the loop portion of the hike. Backtrack to the trailhead. This is your chance to explore the grounds a second time.

3.7 Arrive back at the trailhead.

27 Dalley Loop

This hike exudes history from first step to the last. Explore a former farm community via old roads that visit no fewer than a dozen homesites. Learn about 1800s subsistence farmers living on the slopes of Ricker Mountain. See home foundations, stone walls, cemeteries, barn sites, even one house still standing. Trailside interpretive information, along with the home vestiges, conveys a fascinating story of a way of life gone by.

Start: Dalley Loop History Hike trailhead
Distance: 4.1-mile loop
Hiking time: 2.5–3.5 hours; more for exploring homesites
Difficulty: Moderate due to 700-foot climb
Trail surface: Gravel
Best season: Summer
Other trail users: Bicyclists, equestrians
Canine compatibility: Dogs allowed

Land status: Vermont state park
Fees and permits: Entrance fee required
Schedule: Open 8 a.m. to sunset, mid-May through Columbus Day weekend
Maps: Little River State Park
Trail contact: Little River State Park, 3444 Little River Rd., Waterbury, VT 05676; (802) 244-7103; vtstateparks.com

Finding the trailhead: From exit 10 on I-95 near Waterbury, Vermont, take VT 100 south for 0.5 mile and turn right on US 2 west. Follow US 2 west for 1.3 miles and turn right on Little River Road. Continue 3.4 miles to the Little River State Park entrance station. From here curve left, aiming for the B Loop of the campground. Drive for 0.6 mile and turn right into the lot marked "History Hike Parking." **Trailhead GPS:** N44 23.589′ / W72 45.978′

The Hike

The rocky, wooded slopes of Ricker Mountain don't seem attractive for farming here in the twenty-first century. However, back in the 1820s a fellow named Joseph Ricker settled on this raggedy land above the Little River. Ricker was what we now call a subsistence farmer. He grew crops and raised livestock for his family's use, to survive, to grow enough to make it through the winter—then do it all over again. A typical subsistence farmer might have a couple of pigs, some chickens, a few cows, sheep, and at least one horse for transportation and farm work. A vegetable garden always got the best spot and was close to the house. Fruit trees graced the yard. Row crops such as corn, rye, oats, and barley were grown to consume over the winter. Nothing went to waste.

If a Vermont farmer was to make a little money, he was going to do it from the trees on his property. He could cut timber for the sawmills or to make lye soap or tannic acid. In late winter he could tap the maple trees to make syrup or sugar. Getting

The Ricker Cemetery

these products to market was difficult, but the hard-earned cash could in turn purchase coffee, whiskey, or other things he couldn't get from the land itself.

Joseph Ricker had most of the mountain to himself until the mid-1800s, when the railroad came to Waterbury. Settlers followed. They made their way up the Little River valley, homesteading above Stevenson Brook, from which Ricker Mountain rises. As such things happen, one man recruits his friends and family to join him. A sizable group of Irish settled here, as well as others who were offspring of the original residents.

However, there was more bad land than good. Thin mountain soil was quickly exhausted. Life was harder for the children of the original residents. They wanted more than just the hardscrabble day-to-day, month-to-month, year-to-year endurance challenge on Ricker Mountain. Yet there were folks like Almeron Goodell, who bought his farm in 1863, settled along a tributary of Stevenson Brook, and subsisted until he passed away in 1910. Unlike Goodell, most residents and their offspring began to wander slowly away, heading for the flatter, more productive, and free land that was promised west of the Mississippi. The community of Ricker Mountain drifted out of existence.

The twentieth century moved on. A terrible flood came to the Green Mountain State, 1927 it was, and the Little River burst from its banks, killing many and causing wide-ranging property damage. A second deadly flood in the 1930s brought about the construction of Waterbury Dam. The US Army Corps of Engineers, along with the Civilian Conservation Corps, completed the dam in 1938. This isolated the few remaining residents of Ricker Mountain, and their properties were sold to establish Mount Mansfield State Forest, now comprising 37,000 acres.

In 1962 Little River State Park was carved from the forest. The Dalley Loop Trail was established, and interpretive information was added. As you head up the trail, each homesite is marked. Walk around to see the stone fences and home and barn foundations, as well as metal relics like barrel staves, farming implements, even old maple tapping buckets. Please leave these vestiges of history for others to discover.

▶ The Dalley Loop was named for Dan Dalley, a Civil War veteran who survived sixteen battles and escaped after being captured. He lived here fifteen years.

As you walk, imagine living here, where over a winter you might burn 40 cords of wood to keep your house warm. Imagine building the rock walls that served as property dividers or livestock fences. Imagine having the snowy county road sporadically cleared by horse-drawn plows. Imagine burying your family members in cemeteries you plotted. Imagine the good times—tasting the first fruits of your garden, working with your neighbors to build a shed, listening to your child recite what he or she learned at the school down the lane. Imagine life as it was on Ricker Mountain.

Miles and Directions

0.0 Start from the parking area, crossing the road and ascending the Dalley Loop. Pass around a pole gate, working up Ricker Mountain.

0.1 The trail splits. Stay left and begin the loop portion of the Dalley Loop.

0.3 Reach the David Hill Farm site. A foundation stands here. He wasn't here long, soon leaving to work a sawmill.

0.5 Stay straight as the Cutoff Trail heads left for Stevenson Brook. The Bert Goodell Farm site is on your right. He tore down this house and used the wood to build another.

1.1 Cross a tributary at the High Bridge. You can see the smallish bridge to your right—a rock structure that isn't high.

1.2 Come to the Almeron Goodell Place. This is the only standing farmhouse left on Ricker Mountain. He made the wood roof shingles himself. Imagine spending your entire adult life here.

1.4 Open to a meadow. Apple trees stand on the perimeter. The relatively flat Patsy Herbert Farm site is ahead. The Irishman was wealthy by local standards, with his 500 acres of land, thirty cattle, four horses, and three hogs.

1.5 The Sawmill Loop leaves left and heads to the sawmill that planed wood for World War I and was out of business by 1922. Stay straight with the Dalley Loop.

1.6 The other end of the Sawmill Loop comes in left and visits other homesites. Stay right here on the Dalley Loop.

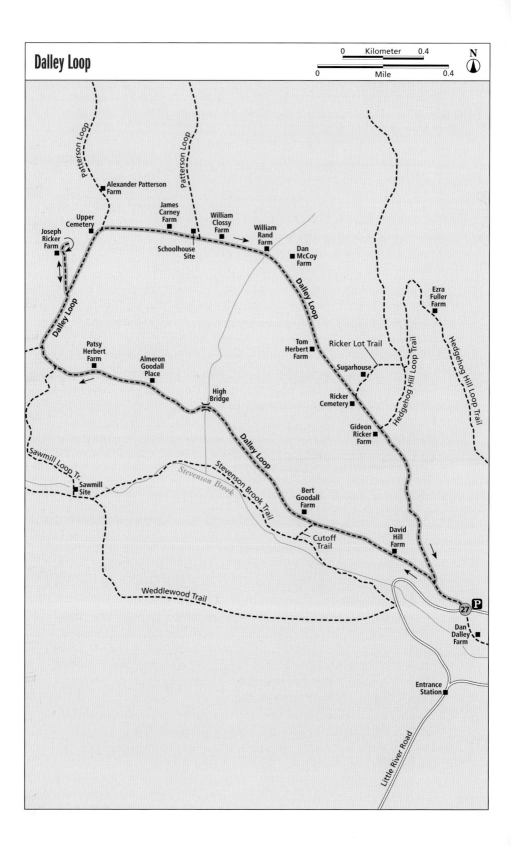

Dalley Loop

0 Kilometer 0.4
0 Mile 0.4

N

Patterson Loop

Patterson Loop

Alexander Patterson Farm

James Carney Farm

William Clossy Farm

William Rand Farm

Upper Cemetery

Joseph Ricker Farm

Schoolhouse Site

Dan McCoy Farm

Dalley Loop

Dalley Loop

Patsy Herbert Farm

Almeron Goodall Place

Tom Herbert Farm

Ricker Lot Trail

Ezra Fuller Farm

Sugarhouse

Hedgehog Hill Loop Trail

Hedgehog Hill Loop Trail

High Bridge

Ricker Cemetery

Gideon Ricker Farm

Sawmill Loop Tr.

Sawmill Site

Stevenson Brook Trail

Stevenson Brook

Dalley Loop

Bert Goodall Farm

Cutoff Trail

David Hill Farm

P

27

Weddlewood Trail

Dan Dalley Farm

Entrance Station

Little River Road

1.8 Split left uphill for the Joseph Ricker Farm. He was the original settler here on the mountain named for him. Check out the metal maple tapping buckets in the now-exposed home cellar. A meadow is nearby. Investigate some largely intact walls and foundation of Ricker's outbuildings. Backtrack to the Dalley Loop.

2.3 Reach the Upper Cemetery and the Patterson Loop. This area was once known as Rickers Corners. The Upper Cemetery is one of several internments on the mountain. Keep curving around the Dalley Loop, having topped out in elevation.

2.6 Pass the James Carney Farm. He once had over 700 maple trees tapped for sugar during the late 1880s.

2.7 Come to the site of the District 10 Schoolhouse and the other end of the Patterson Loop. The school opened and closed over the years, as the number of school-age children waxed and waned.

2.7 Find the William Clossy Farm. His was a sad story. He bought the farm sight unseen, moving East. He died here, homesick and a farming failure. His ashes were buried against an old rock wall by his wife. Rock walls abound for the next trail segment.

2.9 Reach the William Rand Farm. His was a success story. He made money in the California gold rush, returned home to Vermont, bought this farm, and then acquired additional acreage, leasing it out to tenant farmers.

3.2 The Tom Herbert Farm site is on your right. Here you can check out his stone-lined well and home foundation.

3.4 The Ricker Lot Trail leaves left. Stay straight, descending; pass the Ricker Cemetery, with many marked graves. Keep descending.

3.5 Reach the Gideon Ricker Farm site and the Hedgehog Hill Loop Trail, which leaves left. See the circular silo foundation, the large barn foundation, and his homesite. View the numerous metal artifacts. Three generations of his family lived here. Keep straight, rapidly descending.

3.8 Cross a pretty mountain stream on a stone bridge.

4.0 Complete the Dalley Loop. Backtrack to the trailhead.

4.1 Arrive back at the trailhead.

28 Groton Forest Hike

This hike exudes natural beauty while exploring Groton State Forest's past. Start along Osmore Pond at a Civilian Conservation Corps picnic shelter, then walk trails developed back during the Great Depression. Climb Little Deer Mountain, where a view of Lake Groton and forestland spreads beyond. Hike to the lake and return along Coldwater Brook, where you see the stone remains of a long-abandoned sawmill.

Start: Osmore Pond picnic shelter
Distance: 6.7-mile loop with spur
Hiking time: 4–4.5 hours
Difficulty: Moderate to difficult due to rocky trails
Trail surface: Natural
Best season: Fall for colors
Other trail users: Equestrians on limited sections
Canine compatibility: Dogs allowed
Land status: Vermont state forest

Fees and permits: Entrance fee required
Schedule: Open 10 a.m. to sunset Memorial Day weekend through Columbus Day weekend
Maps: Groton State Forest Summer Trails Guide
Trail contact: New Discovery State Park, 4239 Vermont Route 232, Marshfield, VT 05658; (802) 426-3042; vtstateparks.com
Special considerations: The trails here are often rocky, so take your time and wear sturdy shoes.

Finding the trailhead: From downtown Marshfield, Vermont, take US 2 east for 1 mile then curve right on VT 232 for 4.2 miles to enter New Discovery State Park. Pass the entrance station and head for the B Loop of the campground. Veer right toward Osmore Pond to dead-end at the CCC picnic shelter and canoe access. **Trailhead GPS:** N44 18.566'/W72 16.913'

The Hike

What is now Groton State Forest has seen a lot of people and changes over the past few hundred years. Originally the Abenaki roamed through here, seasonally hunting and fishing. They used the network of ponds, rivers, and lakes as a paddle-and-portage route linking the Connecticut and Winooski River valleys. The area remained a wilderness until after the American Revolution, when war veterans claimed this untamed land we now call Vermont.

A small community grew around Ricker Pond, mainly involved in logging and developing wood products. Sawmills were found on almost every major Groton pond and brook. The Montpelier and Wells River Railroad came in 1873, allowing wood to be cheaply shipped out of the region. Logging boomed for the next half century. More mills sprang up. The old ones were enlarged. This is likely the period when the mill site you will see on Coldwater Brook came to be. The Coldwater Brook mill site is well located on a drop in the stream, behind which a small dam was built. The elevation drop provided the necessary power to operate the sawmill.

Lake Groton forms the centerpiece to extensive forestlands.

The railroad also brought the first campers to Groton. Each summer the railroad line would drop campers off at Rocky Point Flag Stop, along Lake Groton. The "station" was an old railroad coach opened on one side, its seats still intact. Camping from around July 4 to Labor Day, visitors would swim, boat, fish, hike, and pick berries from their waterside retreats. Imagine if we could camp for such lengths nowadays!

All the while, logging was continuing. Several forest fires, combined with the extensive tree removal, threw the ecosystem out of balance. In 1919 the State of Vermont bought its first tract here, establishing the state forest, which now comprises over 26,000 acres. Today Groton State Forest is a haven for flora and fauna, as well as a place of respite and renewal for its two-legged visitors. Nothing much happened here until the CCC arrived in the 1930s, with kids from New York and Rhode Island ready to work. They built the well-preserved picnic shelter you see at the trailhead and constructed most of the paths this hike utilizes. They also built some of the campgrounds and other outbuildings and planted trees that began the reforestation process we appreciate today.

Though the CCC history is evident only in structures and some of the fire pits along your hike, realize that most footsteps you take were originally cleared by these young men more than four generations ago. Start the adventure by walking the shoreline of Osmore Pond. The stone-pocked trail leads you to the spur up Little Deer Mountain. An open outcrop presents extensive southward panoramas overlooking the state forest centered by Lake Groton. By the way, the area got its name because so many original settlers moved up here from Groton, Massachusetts, which in turn was named for the English estate of Massachusetts governor John Winthrop. Just to confuse matters further, Lake Groton has gone by other names—Lunds Pond, Wells River Pond, even Long Pond. Name aside, the view is stellar, and you can see why early campers took trains to this spot and stayed for over a month at a time.

The hike then leaves south along gurgling Hosmer Brook to Lake Groton. Reach the Groton Nature Center, a place to take a break, get water, or learn a few things. The Little Loop Trail takes you to Coldwater Brook. Next you will come to the sawmill site. Here huge, irregularly cut blocks of stone are arranged to channel Coldwater Brook just below an approximately 10-foot-drop in the creek. On the far side of the stream, you will discover a wall of the mill, standing about 5 feet high and stretching a pretty good ways. All the metal workings of the mill were taken out when the operation ceased. The scene is now cloaked in forest. It can be hard to imagine the men and noise in a once-cleared area. All you hear today is water song from Coldwater Brook.

Beyond the mill site, climb the slope of Big Deer Mountain before dropping to Osmore Pond. Hike along its east bank and make a complete circle of the pond, finishing the trek.

I suggest completing your historic hike with a camping trip in the tradition of Vermont tourists from the late 1800s. There are four campgrounds within the confines of the state forest. Camping here rounded out my own Groton State Forest experience.

Miles and Directions

0.0 Start from the Osmore Pond parking area. Descend past the historic CCC shelter then split right on the Osmore Pond Loop just before reaching the canoe launch area. Enter rocky woods, passing CCC-built picnic areas and a couple of walk-in campsites with shelters.

0.7 Reach a trail intersection on the southwest side of the pond. Head right on the Little Deer Mountain Trail. Quickly cross the Telephone Line Trail. Trace a singletrack path through woods. Ascend.

1.1 Open onto the outcrop atop Little Deer Mountain. Enjoy extensive panoramas of Lake Groton and adjacent forests. Boulder Beach is visible below. Backtrack to the Osmore Pond Loop.

1.5 Continue the loop, bridging Hosmer Brook. Quickly reach a four-way trail intersection and turn right onto the Hosmer Brook Trail. Descend along the attractive stream. The path is rocky and slow.

2.6 Join the wide Telephone Line Trail, heading left.

2.7 Pass a pair of spurs leading right to the Big Deer Campground. Stay left on a wide undulating track.

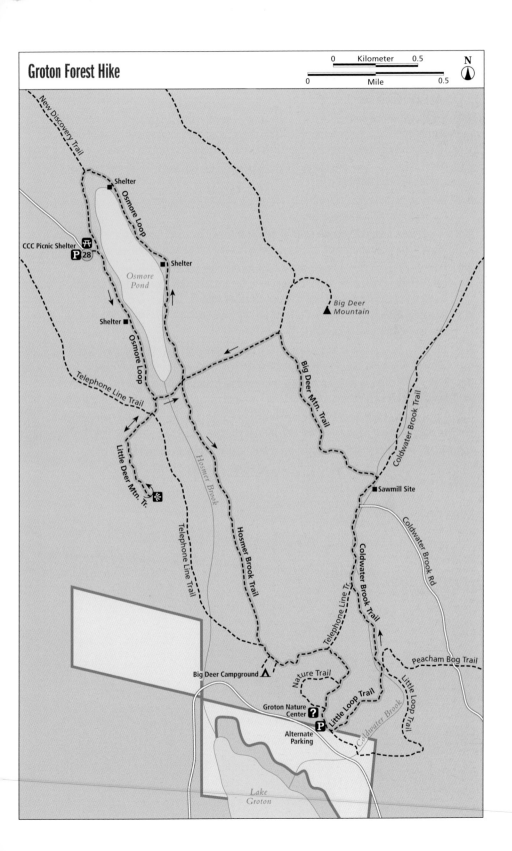

Groton Forest Hike

0   Kilometer   0.5

0   Mile   0.5

N

New Discovery Trail

Shelter

Osmore Loop

CCC Picnic Shelter

P 28

Osmore Pond

Shelter

Big Deer Mountain

Telephone Line Trail

Shelter

Osmore Loop

Big Deer Mtn. Trail

Coldwater Brook Trail

Little Deer Mtn. Tr.

Hosmer Brook

Sawmill Site

Coldwater Brook Rd

Telephone Line Trail

Hosmer Brook Trail

Telephone Line Tr.

Coldwater Brook Trail

Peacham Bog Trail

Big Deer Campground

Nature Trail

Little Loop Trail

Little Loop Trail

Groton Nature Center

P

Alternate Parking

Coldwater Brook

Lake Groton

2.9 Leave the wide trail onto a singletrack path, the continuation of the Hosmer Brook Trail, heading toward Groton Nature Center. Curve over irregular terrain.

3.1 Meet the Nature Trail. Turn right here.

3.2 Leave right on the spur to Groton Nature Center. Descend to a grassy area and the nature center. From the nature center, head left to the adjacent parking area and come to the Little Loop Trail. Stay left on the Little Loop Trail as it immediately splits. Climb.

3.6 Reach a four-way trail intersection. Head left here on the Coldwater Brook Trail. Ascend to a bluff above Coldwater Brook.

4.0 The wide multiuse Telephone Line Trail comes in here. Keep straight as this segment of the Coldwater Brook Trail widens too.

4.2 Find a wide, heavy-duty bridge leaving right. It crosses Coldwater Brook to meet Coldwater Brook Road. Stay straight on the Coldwater Brook Trail, again a singletrack footpath.

4.4 Come to the sawmill site on your right. Look for the huge boulders stretched in a line below a sloping cascade on Coldwater Brook. The tall and wide mossy wall of the mill building lies behind this now completely reforested spot.

4.5 Reach an intersection. Head left here on the Big Deer Mountain Trail. Gently rise through woods and step over a streamlet.

5.1 The 0.8-mile spur trail to the summit of Big Deer Mountain leaves right. Stay left on the Big Deer Mountain Trail, shortly topping a ridge then descending to Osmore Pond.

5.5 Return to a four-way intersection. You have been here before. Turn right on the Osmore Pond Loop. Ahead, pass a couple of lakeside camps on a stony track.

6.4 At the north end of the pond, the New Discovery Trail leads right for the state park campground. Turn south along the west side of Osmore Pond.

6.7 Arrive back at the trailhead after passing a couple of remote picnic sites.

New Hampshire

The Pliny Range reflects off Cherry Pond (hike 33).

29 Smarts Mountain

This hike visits the mountaintop site of an old ranger cabin and fire-watching tower. Take the former tower access jeep road to meet the Appalachian Trail and climb to the peak of Smarts Mountain. Ascend the metal observation tower and then visit the once-lonely quarters of the ranger cabin, now an Appalachian Trail shelter. Soak in incredible views. Return via the AT, grabbing more vistas of the mountains and of the fire tower atop Smarts Mountain while descending rocky Lambert Ridge.

Start: Dorchester Road Appalachian Trail crossing
Distance: 7.2-mile loop
Hiking time: 4.5–5.5 hours
Difficulty: Difficult due to 2,100-foot climb
Trail surface: Natural
Best season: Any time skies are clear
Other trail users: None
Canine compatibility: Dogs allowed

Land status: National Park Service
Fees and permits: No fees or permits required
Schedule: Open 24 hours a day year-round
Maps: National Geographic #740, White Mountain National Forest West
Trail contact: National Park Service, Appalachian Trail Park Office, PO Box 50, Harpers Ferry, WV 25425; (304) 535-6278; nps.gov/appa

Finding the trailhead: From the intersection of NH 10 and Dorchester Road on the east end of the town green in Lyme, New Hampshire, take Dorchester Road east, looking for the sign that says "Dartmouth Skiway." Follow Dorchester Road for 2.9 miles, then veer left as Dorchester Road becomes gravel. (The road going straight heads to the Dartmouth Skiway.) At 1.7 miles come to the trailhead on your left, just before bridging Grant Brook. **Trailhead GPS:** N43 47.820' / W72 4.297'

The Hike

From the 1920s until the 1970s, state and national forests used fire towers and stationary wardens manning them, scanning the horizon for conflagrations. It was a lonely job. These fire towers were situated atop peaks that offered 360-degree views. After a site was selected, a road was constructed to the peak and supplies were driven up on what now seem impossible grades and declivitous terrain. Ranger quarters were built too. The quarters were small, with limited facilities, and usually used rain runoff for water. In New Hampshire's Appalachian Range, that meant putting up with incredibly windy conditions, not to mention rain, snow, and cold.

Rangers usually were linked to the outside world via telephone line so that they could report fires. The ongoing maintenance of the towers, ranger cabins, and telephone lines led forestry officials to reconsider their options and ultimately switch to fire watching by air, launching planes during heightened forest fire conditions. Most fire towers were dismantled, but not the one atop Smarts Mountain. And when the Appalachian Trail was routed over the mountain, the wooden warden's cabin was turned into a hiker trail shelter. Unlike most trail shelters, this shelter is completely enclosed. Inside you can see where the old pot-bellied stove once warmed the cool nights. A sink still stands in the corner. Windows light the inside.

As lonely as it was for the fire warden, the Smarts Mountain shelter is a welcome sight for Appalachian Trail thru-hikers seeking refuge from the elements. And the views from the nearby metal observation tower attract day hikers who want an astronomical panorama of New Hampshire's highlands, beyond to Vermont, and seemingly all the way to Boston on a clear day. An additional southward view can be reached via foot, for those disinclined to climb the narrow flights of tower stairs that take you above the evergreen mantle cloaking Smarts Mountain.

▶ The current 41-foot-high Smarts Mountain Tower was constructed in 1939, replacing the original two log towers erected in 1915.

This hike is more than just the view at the top. Start out tracing the old ranger road, which has transformed into a rough trail from decades of non-maintenance. The

This former ranger quarters is now an Appalachian Trail shelter.

The bulk of Smarts Mountain looms above Lambert Ridge.

first part seems viable for a jeep, but then you cross a stream and the path morphs into a rocky track with an amazing amount of open rock slabs over which water flows, making the footing a challenge in places, much less traction for a jeep. Climb into evergreens and meet the Appalachian Trail. From here the AT ascends sharply up Smarts Mountain, at one point using metal rungs to scale a wet rock slab. The crest is surprisingly level; you can stroll around to visit the natural view, campsites, and the ranger cabin and then climb the tower—if you dare.

Your return trip uses the AT. Wander along Lambert Ridge through deep rocky forests. The last part of the hike traverses open rock slabs through mini-meadows. Some of these slabs offer panoramas of the first order, with views into the Connecticut Valley and Vermont to the west, Smarts Mountain tower to the east, and a host of hills in all directions. Save this hike for a clear day and you will be well rewarded. **Note:** The loop can be wet and slick after rains, so come on a dry, clear day if you can.

Miles and Directions

0.0   Start from the Dorchester Road parking area, heading right on the Smarts Ranger Trail. Grant Brook flows to your right. You will be heading up the valley of this unnamed stream for a while. Ascend an old jeep road that is often wet and rocky and barely recalls a road. Drainages flowing off Lambert Ridge bisect the trail. In places, a path parallels the road-bed when the bed has been overtaken by water.

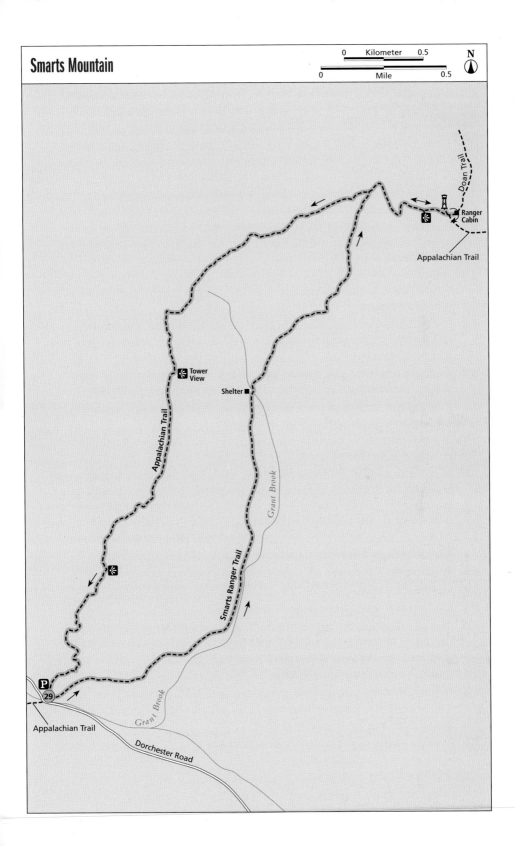

Smarts Mountain

0   Kilometer   0.5

0   Mile   0.5

N

Doan Trail

Ranger Cabin

Appalachian Trail

Tower View

Shelter

Grant Brook

Appalachian Trail

Smarts Ranger Trail

P

29

Appalachian Trail

Grant Brook

Dorchester Road

0.3 Come alongside a stone fence from former subsistence farming days. Old roads split off, but the correct trail is evident.

0.6 Span a small brook on a short relic bridge. Rise to a bluff above the stream to your right.

0.8 Come alongside Grant Brook. Watch for large white pines in the trailside woods.

1.3 Reach what is known as a corduroy road. Here logs were laid side by side perpendicular to the route of travel, making passable a wet section of roadbed. A corduroy road is bumpy but better than slogging through mud. Corduroy roads were often used during the Civil War to wheel cannons and other heavy equipment over slushy terrain.

1.8 Come to a three-sided trail shelter, open to the front. Rock-hop Grant Brook. The trail becomes more primitive. Curve northeasterly.

2.2 Cross back over Grant Brook. The ascent up Smarts Mountain steepens. Work up a stony, wet track broken by open rock slabs, some of which are slick. Spruce and balsam become more prevalent.

2.3 Pass an erect pole around which stones are laid. This is a remnant of a transmission line that once led to Smarts Mountain tower and enabled rangers to report forest fires. Pass over more rock slabs.

2.6 Find another trailside transmission pole. Ahead you will see more rock piles that once steadied these poles in windy conditions. The steep trail seems very unlikely as a jeep road, but it once was.

2.9 The Smarts Ranger Trail ends. Meet the Appalachian Trail, coming in from your left. Stay straight, northbound, on the AT, which now follows the old jeep road; the trail steepens.

3.0 Climb log steps and then work your way up metal bars inlaid to help hikers surmount a wet slab.

3.3 Level out on the crest of Smarts Mountain amid spruce and balsam. Ahead, a spur leaves right to a view. Pass another spur to a privy.

3.4 Reach the short trail left to the metal observation tower. Climb the tower for fantastic views in all directions. Just ahead, the AT leaves right; you go left a short distance to reach the old ranger cabin, now an AT trail shelter. The Doan Trail descends north from the ranger cabin. Backtrack, now southbound on the AT.

3.9 Return to the intersection with the Smarts Ranger Trail. Stay with the AT, still southbound, and continue a sharp decline over more open rock slabs, now on Lambert Ridge.

4.3 The path levels out. Traverse a mossy, ferny, evergreen wonderland pocked with wetlands.

4.9 Step over a tiny brook.

5.1 Begin an uptick along Lambert Ridge. The trail undulates.

5.3 Open onto a rock slab that presents vistas of Smarts Mountain tower to the east. More slabs ahead afford views east and south to the horizon and west to the Connecticut River Valley. Rock cairns help you navigate open rock slabs.

5.9 Continue descending from Lambert Ridge.

6.4 An open stone ledge delivers a first-rate panorama to the southeast. Dip into oaks, cherries, and pines, curving between small ledges. Cut through an old rock fence from farming days on a decidedly unproductive rocky slope.

7.2 Drop back into the parking area and arrive at the trailhead.

30 The Flume

First discovered in 1805 by a 93-year-old woman while fishing, The Flume is a geological wonder—a slot gorge where whitewater crashes through a slim defile. The Flume quickly became a tourist attraction. You will not only pass through The Flume but also visit two historic covered bridges and learn about how this slice of the White Mountains was saved in perpetuity.

Start: The Flume Visitor Center
Distance: 2.1-mile loop
Hiking time: 1 to 2 hours
Difficulty: Easy to moderate
Trail surface: Gravel, some asphalt and boardwalk
Best season: Summer
Other trail users: None
Canine compatibility: Dogs not allowed

Land status: New Hampshire state park
Fees and permits: Entrance fee required
Schedule: Open when the visitor center is open, 9:00–5:30 during summer
Maps: Franconia Notch State Park–Flume Gorge
Trail contact: Franconia Notch State Park, 9 Franconia Notch Pkwy., Franconia, NH 03580; (603) 745-8391; nhstateparks.org

Finding the trailhead: From exit 33 on I-93, just north of North Woodstock, New Hampshire, take US 3 north for 2.3 miles to the Flume Gorge & Visitor Center at Franconia Notch State Park. Buy a ticket for the Flume Gorge Trail at the visitor center before you begin the hike. **Trailhead GPS:** N44 5.834' / W71 40.790'

The Hike

Back in 1805, "Aunt Jess" Guernsey was fishing the Pemigewasset River, a crashing mountain stream cutting through the White Mountains. On her way home, the 93 year old was crossing a tributary of the Pemigewasset when curiosity got the best of her. She headed up the tributary, searching for likely holes where a trout might be lurking. Instead she found a whale of a geological wonder that became known as The Flume. The stream she was walking along had carved an amazing canyon through the rock, creating the sheer-sided gorge now protected under the auspices of Franconia Notch State Park.

During Aunt Jess's day, the land had not been long settled. Her relative Dave Guernsey had built a blockhouse—an elevated fort of sorts—just a mile south of The Flume as a defensive stronghold against Indian attacks, which were still occurring as late as 1812. Settlers trickled into this mountainous terrain, officially dubbed the township of Clinton, though "many portions of the township seem to have been designed by nature as a residence for creatures of habits different than from those of man's." In other words, this place was more suited for wild animals than even New Hampshire mountaineers.

The Flume Gorge

However, time and civilization have a way of marching on. And what was dubbed Franconia Notch became known for its raging beauty. By 1848 the Flume House hotel was open for business. Stagecoach, then railroad, lines enabled tourists to reach The Flume and other area attractions, where they would spend the summer exploring the valley of the Pemigewasset River. For it wasn't just The Flume that brought

The Philosopher of the Pool

By the 1850s, the Flume Gorge had become a full-blown tourist attraction, and one man capitalized on that. In 1853 Professor John Merrill brought a boat down to The Pool, on the Pemigewasset River below the Sentinel Pine Bridge (which wasn't there in Merrill's day), and would give visitors to Franconia Notch a little ride. His tour was short, as The Pool isn't big, but his oratory brought him notoriety—and tips. Merrill remained popular and kept coming back every summer for thirty years. Merrill had a now-forgotten theory about the origin of the universe, and his postulating led him to be dubbed "The Philosopher of the Pool." To this day, you can see the pin and ring used to tie up his boat embedded in the granite wall of The Pool.

them here but also the Old Man of the Mountain—the huge, life-like natural profile worn into the side of Cannon Mountain. (The perilous overhanging Old Man of the Mountain collapsed and sloughed off the mountain in 2003.)

Over the years, tourism grew at Franconia Notch, and so did the Flume House. Other hotels were built, including the Profile House, named for the silhouette of the Old Man of the Mountain. The lands that housed these attractions were under private ownership, and timber companies saw value in the trees, not the geological formations. As the threat grew to strip Franconia Notch of its green mantle, the Society for the Protection of New Hampshire Forests and other groups began an innovative marketing campaign: "Buy a Tree. Help Save the Notch." For a dollar, regular folks could "purchase" a tree to save in Franconia Notch. Along with monies from the New Hampshire legislature and philanthropic contributions from some wealthy donors, Franconia Notch State Park came to be. Aunt Jess Guernsey's discovery was preserved.

Today an entire visitor center is dedicated to the Flume Gorge. It offers interpretive displays and is also where you purchase your ticket to hike The Flume. A short bus ride from the visitor center to the bottom of the gorge takes people of lesser abilities for a fee to ease their walk to The Flume. Expect to take your time and soak in the beauty, interpretive displays, and other natural features within the 2.0-mile walk.

After leaving the visitor center, you reach the Big Boulder, part of the extensive glacial legacy of Franconia Notch. The hike then drops to the Pemigewasset River, where you stop by The Flume Covered Bridge, built in 1886. The trek then leads by the Boulder House, another historic structure, part of yesteryear's tourism facilities. Enter The Flume—where you will get your money's worth out of the entrance fee. Bridges and boardwalks allow you to traverse the slender slit carved by Flume Brook.

The Flume Covered Bridge

Avalanche Falls puts an exclamation point on your trip through The Flume. However, the highlights are far from over. Stop by Bear Cave. Descend to Cascade Brook and view the waterfall coursing through Liberty Gorge. Reach the Sentinel Pine Bridge, named for an old-growth evergreen that fell in the 1938 hurricane and was incorporated into a covered bridge the next year. The covered hiker bridge takes you back across the Pemigewasset River, where a trip through the Wolf Den awaits, as well as a vantage of the Pool, a deep slowing of water amid the crashing waterway. Finally wander through the Boulder Garden, a glacier-deposited rock menagerie. The sights here are so fantastic you will understand why Aunt Jess's relatives initially didn't believe her when she told them of The Flume.

Miles and Directions

0.0 Start by purchasing a ticket at the visitor center and head left, ascending steps. Trace an asphalt path to cross a closed park road. Pick up the gravel path on the far side of the road.

0.1 Reach the loop portion of the hike at the Big Boulder, a large glacial rock. Split right on the Flume Path and descend toward the Pemigewasset River.

0.3 Reach the Flume Covered Bridge. Originally built in 1886, it has been rebuilt numerous times. Ascend from the Pemigewasset River.

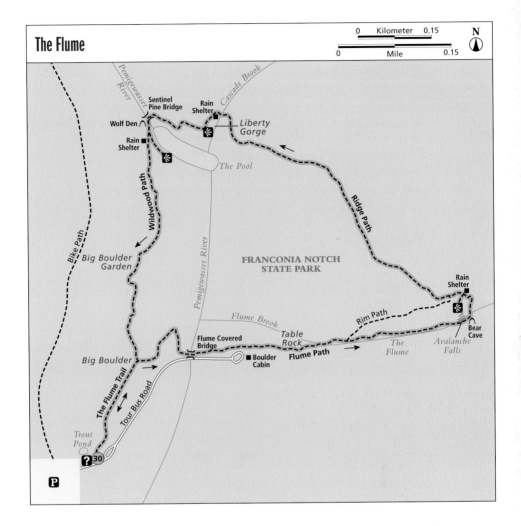

0.4 Come to the Boulder Cabin, an old building on your right. It contains historic displays, restrooms, and souvenirs.

0.5 Come alongside Table Rock, a wide granite slab over which Flume Brook flows. Look for displays showing visitors to Flume Gorge from days gone by. Ascend along Flume Brook, which narrows considerably. The valley displays everywhere-you-look beauty. Ahead, the Rim Path leaves left and rises above The Flume.

0.6 Enter The Flume. The canyon walls rise and narrow and the Flume Path ascends using natural surface trails, boardwalks, and bridges. The gorge is a sight to behold. At high flows, mist rises from the cascades.

0.8 Reach 45-foot high Avalanche Falls. It can really dish out the spray as you pass by on a boardwalk. The Flume opens; pass Bear Cave, a bouldery overhang. Cross Flume Brook and come to a rain shelter. Here a spur path heads to an overlook of Avalanche Falls, a top-down view. Backtrack from the overlook and join the Ridge Path. Head mostly downhill.

1.3 Bridge Cascade Brook and reach another rain shelter. Here Cascade Brook crashes in a series of cataracts through Liberty Gorge below. Take the spur trail to an overlook of the cascades of Cascade Brook.

1.5 Come to an overlook of The Pool and the Pine Sentinel Covered Bridge. This historic covered pedestrian bridge was built using an ancient storm-toppled pine.

1.6 After crossing the Sentinel Pine Bridge, come to the Wolf Den Trail, which sneaks up a rock slit and then slips under a boulder pile to emerge on the other side. Try the trail and then stay left to an overlook of The Pool, a glacially scoured parcel of still water in the crashing Pemigewasset River. Backtrack to join the southbound Wildwood Path.

1.8 Pass through a glacially deposited garden of massive boulders.

2.0 Complete the loop portion of the hike. Turn right and backtrack to the trailhead.

2.1 Arrive back at the visitor center.

31 Lincoln Woods Trail

This hike traces an old railroad bed—replete with hundreds of ties and several bridges—deep into the East Branch Pemigewasset Valley of White Mountain National Forest. Beyond the old rail, views are inspiring of the river and the mountains that rise from it. Make your way to Franconia Creek, where you find the most expansive old railroad bridge, then head up Franconia Creek to view Franconia Falls—a long, multi-faced cascade crashing among granite slabs.

Start: Lincoln Woods Visitor Center
Distance: 6.4 miles out and back
Hiking time: 3.5–4 hours
Difficulty: Moderate
Trail surface: Gravel, railroad ties, some natural
Best season: Late spring through early summer for boldest waterfall
Other trail users: Bicyclists
Canine compatibility: Dogs allowed

Land status: National forest
Fees and permits: Parking fee required
Schedule: Open 24 hours a day year-round
Maps: National Geographic #740, White Mountain National Forest West
Trail contact: White Mountain National Forest, 71 White Mountain Dr., Campton, NH 03223; (603) 536-6100; fs.usda.gov/main/whitemountain/home

Finding the trailhead: From exit 32 on I-93 near Lincoln, New Hampshire, take NH 112 east for 5.5 miles to the Lincoln Woods Visitor Center, on your left just after bridging East Branch Pemigewasset River. **Trailhead GPS:** N44 3.838'/W71 35.263'

The Hike

It's a good thing when you can combine a hike through history with a hike through a beautiful place. Such is the case in this parcel of the White Mountain National Forest, where the East Branch Pemigewasset River carves a dramatic valley deep between imposing peaks. Moreover, the East Branch is quite striking itself—crashing silvery-white between boulders, slowing in dark tea-colored pools. A verdant forest of balsam, spruce, pine, and hardwoods rises along its banks and upward. Ferns crowd the forest floor among silent boulders. Bears, moose, and deer ramble through the woods. Chipmunks skitter along the forest floor.

But it wasn't always this way.

In the late nineteenth century, lumber baron J. D. Henry based a logging operation out of nearby Lincoln, down on the main stem of the Pemigewasset River. He stretched railroad tracks up the adjoining mountain valleys—miles of steel, spike, and wood—to harvest the wealth of trees that rose upon the Appalachian Range. Henry set up twenty-four lumber camps along these rail lines, including the East Branch Pemigewasset, where this hike takes place. Over 400 men were scattered in the camps,

The author walks atop the old ties along the Lincoln Woods Trail.

felling, stripping, and loading trees; using horsepower to move the timber from the mountainside to the railcars and then taking the wooden gold to the yard in Lincoln.

These lumbermen lived a rough and tumble life—a hazardous one too. Men were on the job six days a week. Despite their families being just a few miles distant in Lincoln, it was often months before fathers saw their wives and children, or grooms locked eyes with their brides. However, they had Sunday off—except for the camp cook. On the Lord's Day some read their Bibles. Others played cards. Still others just plain rested, preparing for another round of tackling timber in the ever-changing weather of these verdant highlands. Yes, they worked in winter too. The frozen ground made operating in swampy areas much easier. At least in winter, they didn't have the mosquitoes, gnats, and flies tormenting their every step.

The hike through Lincoln Woods to Franconia Falls is much less arduous than that of the life of the New Hampshire lumberman. You climb only 250 feet over the first 2.8 miles while tracing the railroad grade and then ascend 70 feet the next 0.4 mile to the falls. Start at the Lincoln Woods Visitor Center, housed in a log cabin, and absorb some information before striking out. From there, drop to the East Branch Pemigewasset River, crossing it on a hiker bridge that presents stupendous views of the waterway and the highlands from which it flows. I dare anyone to stand on that bridge and not take a picture—the scenery is that gorgeous.

From the bridge, work up the west side of the valley. It won't be long before you notice the railroad ties embedded into the ground at your feet. Then you will see several exposed ties in a row. Eventually the ties transform from fascinating tangible historical evidence of New Hampshire's logging past to a near nuisance that you have to continually dodge. Nevertheless, the ties are cool. You may even spot an iron rail that wasn't hauled off. The resplendent gushing Pemi', as it is affectionately known, will capture your eye too. And when you can't see it, you will hear it.

En route, check out the stonework of the railroad bridges that span the tributaries of the East Branch, still standing after decades of mountain floods and freezes. The most impressive span is at Franconia Creek, where stone abutments over which tons

Lincoln Then and Now

Today Lincoln, New Hampshire is a mountain-based tourist town, catering to summer and winter visitors recreating in the White Mountains. Interestingly, the logging railroad created Lincoln. In 1890 what became Lincoln was just the homesite of a loner in the mountains. Four years later, James E. Henry built his logging railroad and sawmill, basing it out of the area. The East Branch & Lincoln Railroad became the largest logging railroad in New England and one of the longest lasting, extending into 1948. By then Lincoln had not only the rail line and sawmill but also a pulp mill. It is hard to believe what an industrial town it was when you look at Lincoln today, with its ice-cream shops, kayak and ski rentals, resort hotels, and other businesses catering to tourists.

East Branch Pemigewasset River charges from the wilderness of the same name.

of timber passed now support hikers entering the Pemigewasset Wilderness. After checking out the bridge, leave the railroad grade and take a rooty footpath to Franconia Falls. This multi-tiered cascade stretches over a hundred yards or so, first dropping in multiple chutes, then gathering for a slide over a sheet of granite, and then spilling more in braids. And it doesn't slow down much after that.

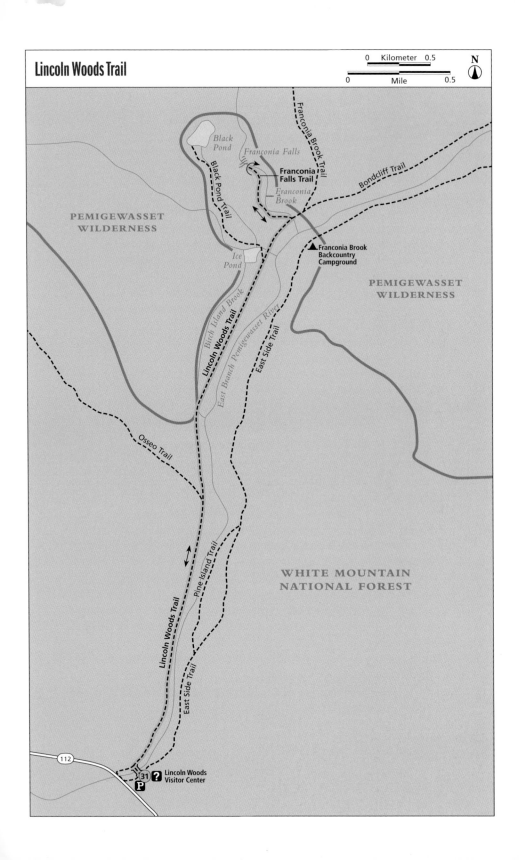

Lincoln Woods Trail

0   Kilometer   0.5

0   Mile   0.5

N

PEMIGEWASSET
WILDERNESS

Black
Pond

Franconia Falls

Franconia
Falls Trail

Franconia Brook Trail

Bondcliff Trail

Franconia
Brook

Black Pond Trail

Ice
Pond

Franconia Brook
Backcountry
Campground

PEMIGEWASSET
WILDERNESS

Birch Island Brook

Lincoln Woods Trail

East Branch Pemigewasset River

East Side Trail

East Side Trail

Osseo Trail

Pine Island Trail

WHITE MOUNTAIN
NATIONAL FOREST

Lincoln Woods Trail

East Side Trail

112

31

P

Lincoln Woods
Visitor Center

The cataract offers different faces in different seasons, as does the Lincoln Woods Trail. Franconia Falls can freeze over in winter, gush in roaring rumbles in spring, or become more rock than water in late summer and fall. The Lincoln Woods Trail is popular year-round. Its very gentle grade attracts snow skiers and snowshoers. The East Branch Pemigewasset will freeze over too. And all will be still on a New England winter day, when the sun barely reaches the valley, much like it was back in the loggers' day.

Miles and Directions

0.0 Start from the log Lincoln Woods Visitor Center. Descend on a set of stairs and head left, passing a couple of picnic tables. Reach and cross the pedestrian bridge over the East Branch Pemigewasset as an all-access trail keeps downstream and uses the road bridge to cross the river. Soak in the wonderful mountain views upstream from the bridge.

0.1 Reach a trail intersection just across the bridge. The all-access path comes in from the left. Stay right on the Lincoln Woods Trail, a wide path. Head into forest with the river on your right. You are tracing the old railroad grade. Look for ties and spikes.

0.7 Bridge a small stream on an old railroad span. Pass a washed-out area that opens river views.

0.9 Cross a stream flowing down from Mount Flume, using part of a railroad bridge. Ahead, look for a pile of railroad ties on trail right.

1.4 Reach the Osseo Trail. Keep straight on the Lincoln Woods Trail.

1.8 Pass near the river. Look for an embedded steel railroad line.

1.9 Bridge Birch Island Brook. Railroad ties continue to be embedded in the wide pathway.

2.1 Note the stone foundation of a building from a logging camp on trail left.

2.6 Reach a trail intersection in a flat with a stone fence line. Here the Black Pond Trail leaves left. Stay straight on the Lincoln Woods Trail.

2.9 Come to Franconia Brook. Here a hiker bridge keeps straight, crossing Franconia Brook using the stone abutments of the railroad line. The Pemigewasset Wilderness is on the other side. Cross the bridge and check it out. Walk under it too, considering its now-primitive construction. Head left up Franconia Falls Trail on a rooty footpath. Franconia Brook is to your right.

3.2 Come to Franconia Falls. It is a multi-tiered cascade that stretches over 100 yards or so, not a singular drop. The falls starts below where Franconia Brook curves left. Several spur trails descend to the water here. The official trail dead-ends at the cataract. Backtrack to Lincoln Woods Trail.

3.6 Arrive back at the Lincoln Woods Trail. Begin the gentle downgrade along the former rail line.

6.3 Return to the pedestrian bridge over the East Branch Pemigewasset. Walk the scenic span across the mountain river

6.4 Arrive back at the trailhead.

32 Willey House Loop

This hike takes you through the heart of Crawford Notch State Park, between two ultra-steep and rugged mountains, where in 1826 nine people died in an avalanche under somewhat mysterious circumstances. First view an old stone railroad stop, visit Ripley Falls, and then take the Appalachian Trail (AT) up Mount Willey. Next descend past huge views, experiencing firsthand the sharp, avalanche-prone slopes. Drop to the Willey House site and then turn down the Saco River to experience aquatic beauty and montane vistas.

Start: Willey House Station parking area
Distance: 4.7-mile loop with spur
Hiking time: 3–3.5 hours
Difficulty: Moderate to difficult due to steep sections, irregular trail
Trail surface: Natural
Best season: Summer through fall
Other trail users: None
Canine compatibility: Dogs allowed
Land status: New Hampshire state park
Fees and permits: No fees or permits required

Schedule: Open sunrise to sunset year-round
Maps: Crawford Notch State Park Hiking Trails and Summits
Trail contact: Crawford Notch State Park, 1464 US Route 302; Harts Location, NH 03812; (603) 374-2272; nhstateparks.org
Special considerations: This hike has some steep sections and may be slow going, but the moderate overall distance makes the hike very doable. Just take your time.

Finding the trailhead: From exit 35 on I-93 north of North Woodstock, New Hampshire, take US 3 north for 10 miles to US 302. Turn right and take US 302 east to reach Crawford Notch State Park at 8.9 miles. Continue through the park, passing the Willey House site on your right, and travel a total of 12.2 miles on US 302. Turn right onto Willey Station Road and continue for 0.2 mile to dead-end at the Ripley Falls trailhead. **Trailhead GPS:** N44 10.025'/W71 23.158'

The Hike

Have you ever heard the saying "It gives me the Willies," describing something that makes one scared? Read on and you may find a new reason for using the phrase. The Willey House story starts in 1771, when a moose hunter by the name of Nash stumbled through a pass in the White Mountains. Excited about the potential for the pass opening settlement and trade, Nash went straight to the New Hampshire governor, who worked out a deal: If Nash would build a road through the pass, the governor would hand out a generous land grant. So a "road" was opened through the pass. Nash got his land grant, then moved on. Exit Mr. Nash from the story. In the late 1790s Abel Crawford opened a tavern as a way station for travelers on Nash's road, at the base of steep crags. Thus the pass became known as Crawford Notch.

In 1825 Samuel Willey, his wife, five children, and two hired hands moved to the tavern, located near the Saco River. They expanded the locale and improved

Hikers gather below Ripley Falls.

accommodations. The following June a terrible landslide crashed down behind the Willey House from the mountain, a mountain destined to receive the Willey name. The nighttime roar of dirt, trees, and rock terrified the Willey family. They resolved to move, but Willey later built a stone shelter to help them survive another potential slide. Drought came to the White Mountains that summer until late August, when the south winds brought a storm men see once in their lifetimes. Incessant rains flooded the parched soil. The Saco River rose more than 20 feet! The Willey family awakened that night to find the river at their doorstep. They were not to be crushed by a landslide but drowned by the Saco! The nine of them dashed from the kitchen, where they had gathered to pray and read the Bible, and walked uphill, where the river wouldn't go.

Then came that sick rumble from above. Down roared a deadly mix of rock, soil, water, and trees, ripping the mountainside to bare rock and aiming directly for the Willey House. By some miracle, the landslide divided above their house, splitting around a ledge and then into the raging Saco River.

After the flood subsided, a passerby stopped at the Willey House. Nary a soul could be found. Strangely, the beds were flung open, nightclothes strewn about, and the family Bible lay open on the table. The body of a hired hand was found, then Mr. and Mrs. Willey, mixed in with the debris below their home, where the Saco had raged. Even after an all-out search, three of the Willey children were never found.

What happened? Why did they flee into the black stormy night rather than stay in the house or head to their shelter? Newspapers and periodicals made the story a national legend. Renowned New England writer Nathaniel Hawthorne wrote a short story based on the tragedy, *The Ambitious Guest*. Subsequently the White Mountains gained fame, beginning their rise as a tourist destination.

The Willey House continued as an inn. Additions were made, and the Willey House itself became a tourist attraction. Unfortunately the house and inn burned in 1898. In 1913 the land became part of Crawford Notch State Park. A cluster of log buildings was built around the Willey homesite for dining and lodging. A few of these rustic spruce structures stand today.

Now Mounts Webster and Willey stand above the chasm of the Saco River, guarding the secret of that night in 1826. On this hike you can visit the Willey House site; but first stop by the Willey House Station, a former stop on a still-active railroad line, laid in 1875 and arguably spawned by the tourist demand following the Willey tragedy. Next visit a natural destination—Ripley Falls. This 120-foot cataract on Avalanche Creek dashes white over a tan stone slope. Then follow the Appalachian Trail up the side of Mount Willey. After gaining altitude, you will descend the declivitous slope on the Kedron Book Trail. Parts of this path will make you understand how slides can occur on such a steep incline and will allow you to look across at the slide-riddled slopes of Mount Webster.

Reach the Willey House site and the cluster of log tourist buildings. Surmise for yourself what happened. Cross US 302 to reach a dammed pond with scenic views. Head down along the Saco River, with its rapids, pools, and wetlands at the base of the glacial valley. Wander among boulders then once again meet the Appalachian Trail. Here cross the Saco River and then make a short road walk back to the trailhead.

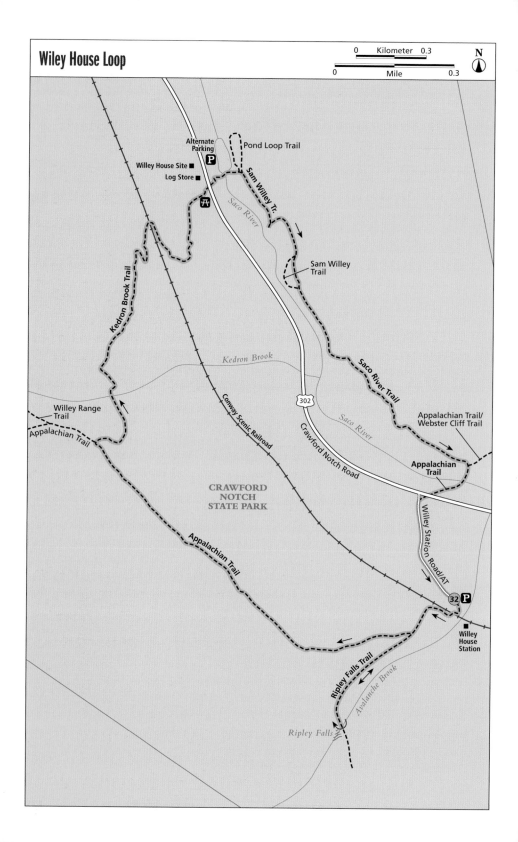

Wiley House Loop

0   Kilometer   0.3

0   Mile   0.3

N

Pond Loop Trail

Alternate Parking

P

Willey House Site ■

Log Store ■

Sam Willey Tr.

Saco River

Sam Willey Trail

Kedron Brook Trail

Kedron Brook

Saco River Trail

Willey Range Trail

Appalachian Trail

302

Saco River

Appalachian Trail/ Webster Cliff Trail

Appalachian Trail

Conway Scenic Railroad

Crawford Notch Road

CRAWFORD NOTCH STATE PARK

Appalachian Trail

Willey Station Road/AT

32 **P**

Willey House Station

Ripley Falls Trail

Avalanche Brook

Ripley Falls

Miles and Directions

0.0 Start from the Willey House Station parking area on a rocky path, the Appalachian Trail. Immediately cross the Conway Scenic Railroad and then walk left across the rail bridge over Avalanche Brook. View the stone remnants of the old Willey House Station railroad stop. Return to the AT and climb in woods.

0.2 Reach a trail intersection. Head left with the Ripley Falls Trail. Enter the Avalanche Brook valley on a rocky singletrack path.

0.5 Ripley Falls opens before you. Plenty of boulders present seating and photography opportunities. Backtrack to the AT from the 120-foot falls.

0.8 Return to the AT, also known here as the Ethan Pond Trail. Turn left, uphill, on a wide track on the slope of Mount Willey.

1.2 The ascent moderates after crossing a couple of intermittent streambeds. Keep uphill slightly.

1.9 Reach the Kedron Brook Trail. Head acutely right on this less-used path. The irregular track drops sharply, necessitating using your hands at times for balance. Cross some mucky spots. Views open of the slides on Mount Webster, across the Saco River valley.

2.1 Rock-hop Kedron Brook just above a waterfall. Briefly climb; then begin a moderate descent.

2.5 Make a pair of quick switchbacks.

2.7 Reach and cross the active Conway Scenic Railroad line. Continue descending.

3.0 Open onto a picnic area, log buildings, and the Willey House site. (**Note:** You will also find a restaurant, gift shop, and restroom here.) Explore the area, including behind the house site, then cross US 302 and take the wooden walkway across a pond dam. Enjoy mountain vistas.

3.1 Reach a trail intersection, just past a picnic area on the far side of the pond. Here the Pond Loop makes a short circuit left, but you turn right on the Sam Willey Trail, a level, easy path running parallel to the Saco River.

3.3 A dead-end spur leads right to the Saco River. Keep left on the Sam Willey Trail.

3.5 Stay left at the loop portion of the Sam Willey Trail.

3.6 Stay left at the second intersection with the Sam Willey Trail. Keep straight, now on the more primitive Saco River Trail. Enjoy watery views of the river and adjacent wetlands. Work around rocky mounds.

4.2 Meet the Webster Cliff/Appalachian Trail. Turn right and descend to bridge the Saco River, placid at this point.

4.5 Emerge onto US 302. Cross the road and begin walking up Willey House Station Road.

4.7 Arrive back at the trailhead.

33 Pondicherry Trail

This hike traces the old Maine Central Railroad grade, now a rail trail, into the heart of the Pondicherry wetland, regarded as the most important birding area in New Hampshire. Trace the rail line through lowland spruce-fir forest and then open onto Cherry Pond, where you meet the Presidential Range Rail Trail, another converted line. Soak in views of the Presidential Range before continuing through ecologically rich wetlands to Little Cherry Pond, where you just might see a moose.

Start: Hazen Road/Airport Road parking area
Distance: 5.0 miles out and back with mini-loops
Hiking time: 2.5–3.5 hours
Difficulty: Moderate
Trail surface: Natural
Best season: Year-round
Other trail users: Bicyclists, equestrians during warm season; snow machines in winter
Canine compatibility: Dogs allowed

Land status: National wildlife refuge
Fees and permits: No fees or permits required
Schedule: Open 30 minutes before sunrise to 30 minutes after sunset year-round
Maps: National Geographic #741, White Mountain National Forest East
Trail contact: Silvio O. Conte National Wildlife Refuge, US Fish and Wildlife Service, 300 Westgate Center Dr., Hadley, MA 01035-9589; (413) 253-8200; fws.gov/northeast

Finding the trailhead: From the intersection of US 2 and NH 16 on the west side of Gorham, New Hampshire, take US 2 west for 12.5 miles to NH 115. Turn left (west) on NH 115 and follow it for 5.3 miles to Hazen Road, alternately known as Airport Road. (There will be a sign for Mount Washington Regional Airport here.) Turn right onto Hazen/Airport Road and follow it for 1.4 miles to the trailhead on your right. **Trailhead GPS:** N44 21.526'/W71 32.368'

The Hike

This hike has a rare combination of history, natural beauty, incredible vistas, plus wildlife viewing opportunities. In addition, despite being in the White Mountains, your primary venue—the Pondicherry Rail Trail—is flat as a tabletop! Back in 1889 the Maine Central Railroad built this line linking New England to Quebec. Established in the pre-automobile era, it offered passenger and freight service, successfully too. However, the combination of the Great Depression and the establishment of the automobile for transportation caused the Maine Central to give up on the line's passenger service. Freight transportation continued until 1972. The rail link then went defunct.

But in the shadow of the Presidential Range, the line cut a path through a critical wetland, highlighted by two ponds that together form what has been called the most significant birding habitat in New Hampshire. More than 240 species have been identified here, including 130 breeding pairs here at Pondicherry.

Hiker balances past Cherry Pond.

The attention-grabbing name of Pondicherry was already appearing on maps in the late 1790s, in this area where the Johns River eventually feeds the Connecticut River at the Vermont border. The area was under dispute between the French and British and may have been dubbed Pondicherry by French interests for a French colony in India, of all places. Name aside, Pondicherry gained recognition as a birding hotspot back in 1911 when Horace Wright penned a birding guide to the White Mountains. Birders used the rail line to reach the ponds and wetlands. The more birding that went on, the more members of the New Hampshire Audubon Society regarded the tract as significant. Finally, in 1963 Audubon member Tudor Richards negotiated the purchase of 312 acres of land around Cherry Pond and Little Cherry Pond. But it wasn't until 2000 that the greater Pondicherry area came under the wing of the US Fish and Wildlife Service as the Pondicherry Division of the Silvio O. Conte National Wildlife Refuge. More land was purchased, and now the Pondicherry parcel comprises more than 6,500 acres of wildland, a critical wetland, and home to record trees at the base of the Presidential Range.

You can see not only avian life here but also bear and moose. Even if you don't find your favorite bird or beast, the views of the Presidential Range are spectacular, mirrored by Cherry Pond. The Pliny Range to the north and Cherry Mountain (shortened from Pondicherry Mountain) to the south stand out in bold relief.

One of only five national recreation trails in New Hampshire, the Pondicherry Trail is a four-season affair, though snow machines do use the path regularly in winter. The path begins its northeasterly tract very level and stays that way throughout. The wide, pea-gravel track is easy on the feet, allowing you to soak in the surroundings. A spruce-balsam forest lines the path. Somewhere to the right of the trail stands New Hampshire's record-size white spruce. You will pass by beaver bogs and marshes as you continue. Then the action heats up all at once. Here you meet the Presidential Range Rail Trail, an 18-mile path that leads east all the way to Gorham, New Hampshire. However, our hike leads only 0.2 mile on it to an observation deck overlooking 120-acre Cherry Pond, a glacial relic. Gaze east on the highest peaks in New England. The lower but still scenic Pliny Range forms a backdrop for the pond. In the near, the birds you see will depend on the season.

Beyond the observation deck, you span the Johns River, which flows from Cherry Pond to Little Cherry Pond. Come along the active New Hampshire & Vermont Railroad at a place known as Waumbeck Junction. Quickly diverge from the line to pick up the Shore Path. It runs along the west side of Cherry Pond and delivers arguably the best views the Presidentials. Wow! Beyond here, the hike travels a short distance along the active railroad line.

The hike then leaves left toward Little Cherry Pond and enters part of the original Audubon tract. The trails are singletrack here and come near the national champion-size black spruce tree. Bog bridges—narrow plank boardwalks—get you over sensitive wetlands. The forest morphs into boggier wetlands en route to Little Cherry Pond. Here you will find a small observation deck and bench. Moose are sometimes seen here. Maybe you will get lucky. Your return hike covers a little new ground exiting Little Cherry Pond, followed by a backtrack down the old railroad line that once connected New England to Quebec.

Miles and Directions

0.0 Start by walking around the pole gate and joining the Pondicherry Trail. The wide pea-gravel path aims northeast beside a mantle of spruce and balsam. Brush and flowers rise beside the trail in summer, including blackberries.

0.5 The trail makes a slight but noticeable bend to the left.

0.8 Bisect a segment of beaver bogs and wetlands. Just ahead, pass under a power line.

1.4 Reach a signed intersection. Here the Presidential Range Rail Trail leaves right. Follow it toward the observation deck on Cherry Pond.

1.5 The Presidential Range Rail Trail continues east. Head left here, stepping onto the observation deck. Worthwhile vistas reflect off Cherry Pond of the Pliny Range to the north and the Presidential Range to the east. Backtrack and then head right on the Waumbeck Link Trail.

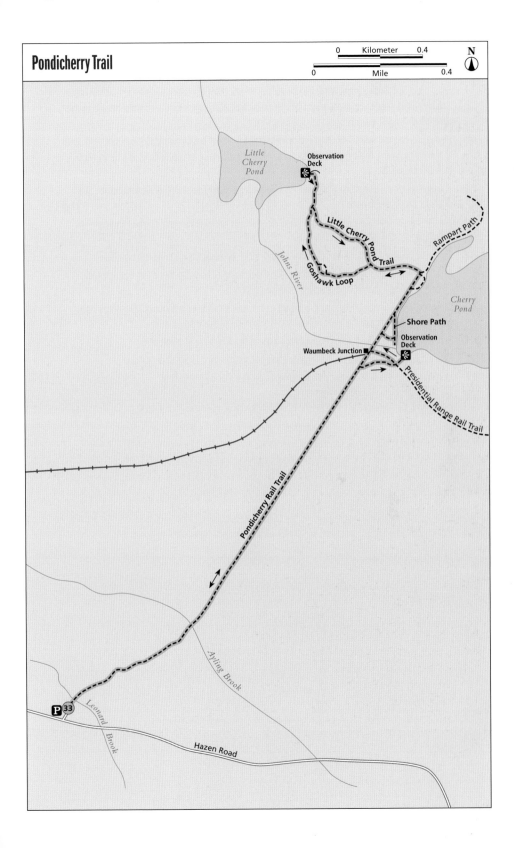

Pondicherry Trail

Little
Cherry
Pond

Observation
Deck

Little Cherry Pond Trail

Goshawk Loop

Rampart Path

Johns River

Cherry
Pond

Shore Path

Observation
Deck

Waumbeck Junction

Presidential Range Rail Trail

Pondicherry Rail Trail

Ayling Brook

P 33

Leonard Brook

Hazen Road

0   Kilometer   0.4

0   Mile   0.4

N

1.6 Reach Waumbeck Junction and the active Vermont & New Hampshire Railroad. Turn right here and bridge the Johns River. Walk a short distance beside the rail line and then split right onto the Shore Path. Walk the singletrack trail through evergreens to the west side of Cherry Pond. Inspiring vistas open of the Presidential Range. Pass a marker denoting this area as a registered national natural landmark.

1.9 Return to the rail line. Carefully walk along the tracks in a narrow part of the wetland, with the rail line being the only elevated spot. Multiple views open, including of Cherry Mountain to the south.

2.0 The sometimes-overgrown Rampart Path leaves right for the shore of Cherry Pond. Stay straight along the tracks.

2.1 Turn left onto the Little Cherry Pond Trail. The singletrack rocky path snakes through lowland forest.

2.2 Split left on the Goshawk Loop. Pass a mini-loop working through erratic boulders.

2.6 Reach a trail intersection. Rejoin the Little Cherry Pond Trail. Descend on boardwalks through spongy marsh and stunted trees.

2.7 Come to Little Cherry Pond, with a small observation deck and a bench. Sit a spell and watch for wildlife, maybe even a moose. Backtrack to the trail junction.

2.8 Stay left on the Little Cherry Pond Trail, looping back toward the railroad.

3.1 Stay straight at this intersection, having looped back from Little Cherry Pond.

3.2 Return to the rail line. Backtrack southwest on the Pondicherry Trail.

5.0 Arrive back at the trailhead.

34 CCC Perimeter Path

This hike takes you to a New Hampshire state park developed by the Civilian Conservation Corps (CCC), part of the 1930s work projects of President Franklin Delano Roosevelt, dubbed "Roosevelt's Tree Army." Explore a concentration of facilities erected by Moose Creek Camp #1129, then hike a path they built through upland woods. Join an old farm road; stop by a beaver bog and then return to the trailhead, stopping by the site of the farm that was changed by the CCC into the state park we see today.

Start: Berry Farm Road gate
Distance: 3.8-mile loop
Hiking time: 2–2.5 hours
Difficulty: Easy to moderate
Trail surface: Natural
Best season: Spring through fall
Other trail users: Mountain bikers in spots
Canine compatibility: Dogs allowed

Land status: New Hampshire state park
Fees and permits: No fees or permits required
Schedule: Mid-May through mid-Oct
Maps: Moose Brook State Park trails
Trail contact: Moose Brook State Park, 30 Jimtown Rd., Gorham, NH 03581; (603) 466-3860; nhstateparks.org

Finding the trailhead: From the intersection of US 2 and NH 16 on the west side of Gorham, take NH 16 west for 1.2 miles. Turn right onto Jim Foot Road; follow it for 0.7 mile and turn right into Moose Brook State Park. Follow the main road past the park office and then shortly turn right into the picnic area; park here. Walk up the main road you were on before turning into the picnic area, and start at the gate on Berry Farm Road. **Trailhead GPS:** N44 24.104' / W71 13.682'

The Hike

Moose Brook State Park stands on the edge of Gorham, New Hampshire, and is an excellent base camp for exploring the White Mountains. Mount Washington is within easy driving distance, as are man-made attractions, but don't overlook the small preserve that is Moose Brook, for this park is steeped in the legacy of the Civilian Conservation Corps. The federal works program developed local, state, and national parks and forests throughout the country, making history and an impact on many of the hikes detailed in this guide.

The imprint of the CCC is deep here at Moose Brook, a fine place to appreciate the work of these young men. Upon entering the park, you will immediately see the park office—a rustic wood structure still in use—crafted by the CCC boys. Visit the warming pond and the swimming pond, both dammed and lined by them. The warming pond was constructed upstream of the swimming pond to mitigate the chilly water of Moose and Perkins Brooks, flowing off Crescent Mountain to the north, before flowing into the swimming pond. A rustic bathhouse bordered by

The Civilian Conservation Corps

The Great Depression hit the United States in 1929 following a devastating stock market crash. At the time, no one knew how long the economic hard times would go on. In 1933, with the country still in the throes of economic malaise, President Franklin Delano Roosevelt initiated a government work program, the Civilian Conservation Corps, commonly known as the CCC. Under the program, men were hired for various projects throughout the United States, including transforming Moose Brook into the park we see today.

To qualify for the CCC, recruits had to be between the ages of 17 and 25, be out of school, and be unemployed. Workers were often shipped far from home to prevent desertion. They earned $30 per month, of which $25 went back home. They built hiking trails, scenic roads, cabins, dams, fish hatcheries, improved wildlife habitat, planted trees, and more at more than 800 parks in the United States. They also practiced fire management, building fire roads and erecting over 3,400 fire watch towers!

The CCC was organized into camps, generally of 100 to 300 men, using a military structure with an emphasis on discipline. New Hampshire had twenty-eight camps totaling more than 20,000 men. Over 2,600 camps containing a total half million men were spread across all forty-eight states.

Each camp had its specialists, from cooks to officers. Camp life was routine. The men generally rose around 6 a.m., ate a filling breakfast, and then worked until 4:30 in the afternoon, with a lunch break in the middle. Back at camp the men could do as they pleased, often writing letters home. These descriptive letters to loved ones helped build a historical record of life in the CCC camps.

Whether the CCC helped or hurt the nation's economy remains under debate. The CCC program continued until 1942, when for the most part potential enrollees instead entered the military to fight World War II. The CCC was never abolished, only defunded to extinction. Nearly all the CCC boys have passed away, but their legacy lives on in the buildings, ponds, campground, and trails of Moose Brook State Park.

A well-preserved chimney remains from the CCC camp at Moose Brook.

stonework overlooks the swimming pond. When was the last time you swam in a brook-fed, hand-lined, generations-old swimming pool? Head to the group camp area and see chimneys from the CCC camp, as well as the muster ground where the CCC gathered in mornings before setting off for the day's work. See stone and brick fireplaces at the campground they built.

The entire park was laid out by the CCC—the trails too. The hike traverses deep forest on the aptly named CCC Perimeter Path, with an eye for contour. Visualize these young men heading up the trail each morn, fashioning the pathway we see today with picks, shovels, and the sweat of their brow.

▶ Moose Brook Camp #1129 was in operation from 1933 to 1942.

Later in the hike you will join Berry Farm Road (closed to public vehicles), a track once used by the Berry family. Their farm was purchased to create Moose Brook State Park. Look for old grown-over fields beside the trail. At one point you will reach the Berry Farm site, now a group campsite. A walk around here will reveal a root cellar and other signs of the past. Remember to leave any artifacts you may find for others to discover.

The Berry Farm Road leads you back to the trailhead and the heart of the CCC legacy of Moose Brook. Walk around to find more signs of Roosevelt's Tree Army, which left its mark on this New Hampshire State Park—and beyond.

Miles and Directions

0.0 Start from the picnic area and walk up the road that you drove to reach the picnic area. Shortly reach a gate and Berry Farm Road. Pass around the gate and ascend piney woods on a doubletrack path.

0.1 Bear left on the CCC Link Trail and trace a level track up the Perkins Brook valley. Ignore the thread of mountain bike trails (not shown on the map) occasionally crossing the hiking trails. Traverse wet areas on boardwalks.

0.4 Meet the CCC Perimeter Path, built in the 1930s. The smooth trail makes for easy strolling. Streamlets flowing off the hillside to your right pass under concrete and rock culverts laid by the CCC.

0.9 The singletrack Perkins Path leaves left, crosses Perkins Brook, then returns to the park office. Stay right, still on the CCC Perimeter Path. Cross a small tributary and gently work up an incline.

1.5 The CCC Perimeter Trail curves east, hemmed in by the boundary of the small state park.

2.0 Reach an intersection. Here the Berry Farm Road goes right and left. Go left toward a beaver bog. The level track opens to a wetland with a water level determined by the season. Look for a beaver lodge in the pond. Backtrack to the Perimeter Path.

2.3 Bear left on the CCC Perimeter Path. Continue down Berry Farm Road in relatively young woods.

2.6 Walk by a former clearing—now growing over with pine, sumac, and aspen—a relic of the Berry Farm.

2.9 Pass a second former clearing on your left.

3.2 Come to a grassy clearing with a picnic table and fire ring. This group campsite marks the former Berry Farm site. Scan both left and right of the camp as you enter for relics. Continue the hike, making an extended curve to the left.

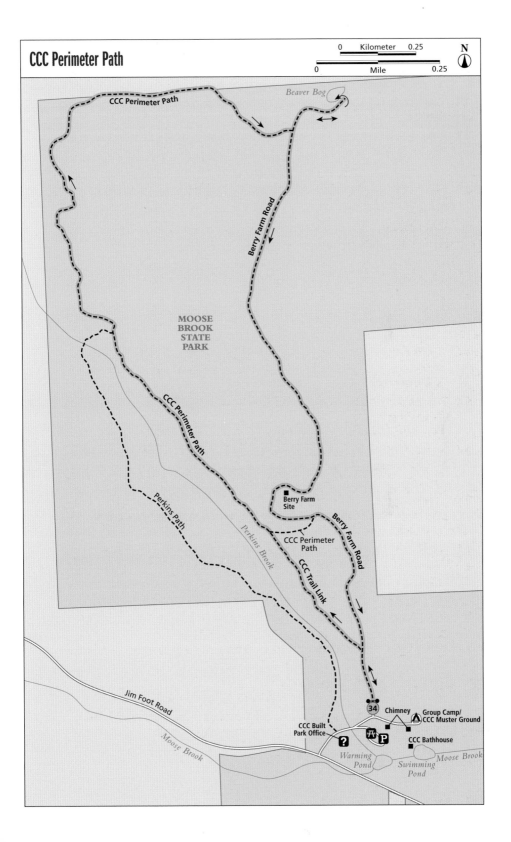

CCC Perimeter Path

CCC Perimeter Path

Beaver Bog

Berry Farm Road

MOOSE
BROOK
STATE
PARK

CCC Perimeter Path

Perkins Path

Perkins Brook

Berry Farm
Site

CCC Perimeter
Path

Berry Farm Road

CCC Trail Link

Jim Foot Road

Moose Brook

34

Chimney

Group Camp/
CCC Muster Ground

CCC Built
Park Office

CCC Bathhouse

Warming
Pond

Swimming
Pond

Moose Brook

Kilometer

Mile

N

0   0.25

0   0.25

3.3 Reach a trail intersection. Here the CCC Perimeter Path leaves acutely right. Stay straight on the Berry Farm Road. Descend past an elevated group campsite to your left, once the location of a barn. Pass more solitary group campsites.

3.7 Return to the CCC Link Trail, completing the loop portion of the hike. Backtrack to the trailhead.

3.8 Arrive back at the gate of Berry Farm Road. The park picnic area, the parking spot for this hike, is just down the road.

Maine

Crossing a granite slab on Dorr Mountain (hike 37).

35 Marginal Way

Walk an oceanside trail meandering along rocky cliffs above the Atlantic Ocean near Ogunquit, Maine. The walk starts by Ogunquit Beach and then heads south, working for a couple of blocks through the heart of touristy Ogunquit. Rejoin the coastline, savoring sweeping aquatic panoramas of the Atlantic beyond, with outcrops, coves, and small beaches in the foreground. The nearly century-old path ends where former fishing boat docks now harbor resort restaurants.

Start: Beach Street in Ogunquit
Distance: 2.8 miles out and back
Hiking time: 1.5–2 hours
Difficulty: Easy
Trail surface: Mostly asphalt
Best season: Summer for tourist watching
Other trail users: None
Canine compatibility: Dogs not allowed

Land status: City of Ogunquit, Maine property
Fees and permits: No fee for trail; parking fee almost certain
Schedule: Sunrise to sunset
Maps: Marginal Way
Trail contact: Town of Ogunquit, 23 School St., PO Box 875, Ogunquit, ME 03907; (207) 646-3032; townofogunquit.org

Finding the trailhead: From exit 19 on I-95 (Maine Turnpike) near Wells, Maine, take ME 109 east for 1.5 miles to a traffic light and US 1. Turn right onto US 1 south and follow it for 5.2 miles into the heart of Ogunquit. Make an acute left turn onto Beach Street. Follow Beach Street 0.3 mile, crossing a bridge to Ogunquit Beach and parking (fee). To pick up the Marginal Way, walk back across the bridge on Beach Street toward US 1 and pick up the gravel track leading left between two houses. **Trailhead GPS:** N43 14.998'/W70 35.823'

The Hike

When thinking of something as being marginal, you might conjure up something being minimal or barely making the grade. Well, the Marginal Way is anything but marginal in that context. The trail, in existence since 1925, presents spectacular far-reaching views of the Maine coastline as it arcs into the distance while delivering nearer looks to the rocks, beaches, coves, and crags that abut the Atlantic. So how did such an outstanding trail get such a name? The path curves along the edge of the Atlantic cliffs—the margin between the mainland and the chilly waters below—as the path links Ogunquit Beach to Perkins Cove.

Maine's coastline has always been something special. Ogunquit was settled in the 1640s and became a fishing village. The name in native Abenaki language translates to "beautiful place by the sea." And that certainly is true. However, Ogunquit's harbor was not very good—there wasn't one. Local fishermen tired of bringing their boats ashore nightly and took the matter into their own hands, forming the Fish Cove Harbor Association. The members dug a channel between the Atlantic and the unnavigable Josias River and then let the tide scour the passage. The anchorage became Perkins Cove, where this hike ends. Shipbuilding subsequently rose in Ogunquit, and the fishermen were a lot happier too.

Over time, visitors discovered the town's ocean scenery. Ogunquit began evolving from a fishing and shipbuilding village to a tourist and summer cottage destination. By the early 1900s folks were already building seasonal cottages all along the southern Maine coastline, enjoying the mild summer temperatures, the ocean breezes, the beaches, and the views. Raymond Brewster became alarmed at the speed at which the natural coastline was being altered, as well as the general public losing beach access. Raised in nearby York, Maine, Brewster had moved to Ogunquit, where he became civically involved.

Brewster's much older friend and neighbor from the York days, Josiah Chase, saw the value of the Maine coast as well. He began buying up coastline to sell to those wanting summer cottages. It was right here in Ogunquit where Chase had 20 prime acres along the elevated margin of land where the wild coastal habitat met the

Ogunquit Beach meets the Atlantic along the Marginal Way.

crashing foam of the Atlantic. It was a scenic spot, and there was a lot of money to be made by subdividing those 20 acres. Brewster petitioned Chase to instead donate his land to preserve its natural features and be enjoyed by the public in perpetuity. However, Chase had already filed a subdivision plan with the county.

Chase, who by this time was in his 80s, had served the public himself. Chase was a Union officer in the Civil War. He then practiced law and later represented York in the Maine legislature. He also directed York's water management body. Brewster continued appealing to his friend, who, at the age of 85, eventually deeded his 20 acres to the village of Ogunquit.

▶ The thirty-nine benches along the Marginal Way honor donors to the Marginal Way Preservation Fund.

Shortly thereafter, the trail that became the Marginal Way was constructed. Through the donations and easements of other property owners, the path was extended. Over the decades, the Marginal Way has been battered by storms, reconstructed, and paved with asphalt. To this day it is enjoyed by thousands of visitors every year. In order to maintain the path, a preservation fund was established in 2010. The Marginal Way Preservation Fund continues to solicit monies to maintain the Marginal Way, come what may.

The small lighthouse you see along the Marginal Way has its own story. In the 1940s Ogunquit was pumping its effluent directly into the Atlantic. The ocean waters off the town were less than clean, and beaches were closed due to health concerns. Ogunquit needed a water treatment plant, albeit a small one, to handle the town's needs, but no one wanted an ugly pumping plant marring the scene that so many came to see. In 1948 the seaside pump was built, disguised as a little lighthouse. That is how the Marginal Way Lighthouse came to be. Disguising the water treatment pump became a model for other coastal towns. The Marginal Way Lighthouse was rebuilt in the 1990s, making the replica more in line with authentic New England lighthouses.

When you walk the Marginal Way, remember the persistence of Raymond Brewster and the generosity of Josiah Chase, because now we can enjoy some very valuable Maine coastline via the far-from-marginal Marginal Way.

Miles and Directions

0.0 Start on the first gravel path leading left (south) from the west side of the bridge between the town of Ogunquit and Ogunquit Beach. Walk between a house to your left and the Marginal Way House & Motel. Soon the gravel track crosses a wooden bridge with excellent views of Ogunquit Beach and the tidal Ogunquit River.

0.1 Reach Wharf Lane. Turn right and then come to busy Shore Road. Turn left here, walking south through tourist central.

0.3 Turn left onto the balance of the Marginal Way, an asphalt track, after passing the Anchorage by the Sea resort. After you turn left onto the Marginal Way, the Sparhouse will be to your right. The narrow passage quickly reaches the Atlantic Ocean. Turn right, walking the edge above rocky cliffs to your left. Enjoy fantastic views of the coastline and beyond.

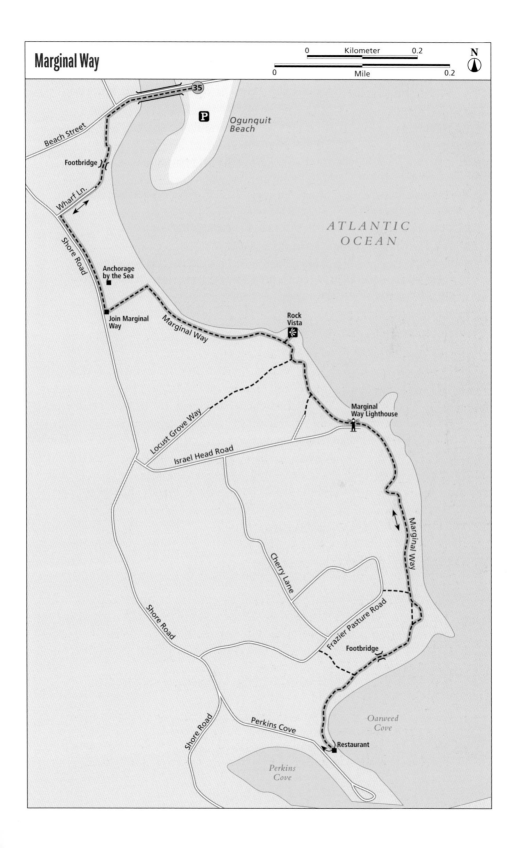

Marginal Way

0   Kilometer   0.2

0   Mile   0.2

N

Beach Street

35

P

Ogunquit
Beach

ATLANTIC
OCEAN

Footbridge

Wharf Ln.

Shore Road

Anchorage
by the Sea

Join Marginal
Way

Marginal Way

Rock
Vista

Locust Grove Way

Marginal
Way Lighthouse

Israel Head Road

Cherry Lane

Shore Road

Marginal Way

Frazier Pasture Road

Footbridge

Shore Road

Perkins Cove

Oarweed
Cove

Restaurant

Perkins
Cove

0.6 Come to a rocky outcrop to your left, near the outlet of the Ogunquit River. Walk out for stellar panoramas. Ogunquit Beach is across the river. Look north as the coastline recedes into the mist of the Atlantic. A small beach is below the outcrop. Stone steps lead to the mini-beach and a few other sandy spots betwixt the rocks. Rejoin the Marginal Way.

0.7 An asphalt spur trail leads right to Locust Grove Way. Stay straight on the Marginal Way.

0.8 Pass a spur trail leading right to Briar Bank Way.

0.9 Reach Israel Head Road and the Marginal Way Lighthouse. Keep south along the coastline. Ahead, work around a deeply cut inlet.

1.1 Pass a spur to Frazier Pasture Road. Just ahead, the trail briefly splits at a point and then comes together again. Turn into Oarweed Cove.

1.2 Cross over a bridge. Ahead, cedars shade benches overlooking the water.

1.3 Pass a second spur leading to Frazier Pasture Road.

1.4 The Marginal Way ends at a restaurant overlooking Oarweed Cove, with Perkins Cove across the way. Backtrack or turn right onto Perkins Cove Road, then right on Shore Road, then right again on Beach Street, walking past shops and restaurants galore.

2.8 Arrive back at the trailhead.

36 Salt Bay Preserve

Take a walk to one of the oldest archaeological sites in Maine—the Glidden Shell Midden on the banks of the Damariscotta River. Here prehistoric tribes piled oyster shells along the shore after consuming their meats. Your hike starts along boardwalks astride Great Salt Bay. Wind through pine and hardwood forests, gaining views of the estuarine waters. View an old sheep tunnel and then reach the Glidden Midden. View the shells and complete your loop, passing a tidal marsh and a freshwater pond.

Start: Across from Loudon County Publishing on ME 215
Distance: 2.8-mile loop
Hiking time: 2–2.5 hours
Difficulty: Easy to moderate
Trail surface: Natural
Best season: Year-round
Other trail users: None
Canine compatibility: Dogs not allowed

Land status: Damariscotta River Association property
Fees and permits: No fees or permits required
Schedule: Open sunrise to sunset
Maps: Salt Bay Preserve Heritage Trail
Trail contact: Damariscotta River Association, PO Box 333, Damariscotta, ME 04543; (207) 563-1393; damariscottariver.org

Finding the trailhead: From the intersection of US 1 and ME 215 in Newcastle, Maine, take ME 215 (Mills Road) north 0.2 mile to Lincoln County Publishing Company, just north of the Newcastle post office. Trailhead parking is at Lincoln County Publishing, which they allow. However, park as far from the business building as possible, closer to the road and trailhead. The trailhead is directly across the street, on the east side of ME 215. The Lincoln County Publishing Company address is 116 Mills Rd., Newcastle, ME. **Trailhead GPS:** N44 2.539' / W69 31.982'

The Hike

The human history of what became Maine goes back a long time—to a period after the glaciers receded, to a time when ancient peoples settled on the shores of the shellfish-rich Damariscotta River, feasting on oysters that thrived in the warmer waters of the tidal waterway. Over time, perhaps 1,000 years, the ancient peoples piled mounds of shells on both sides of the Damariscotta. Later, European settlers found these enormous shell heaps, known to archaeologists as middens. Middens are more than just shells. They are garbage piles of sorts, containing not only shell remains but also tools, pottery, and bones of anything the ancients were using—then discarding—at the time.

On this hike we visit the Glidden Midden. Just across the Damariscotta stands the Whaleback Midden, which was once much larger than it is today. That story comes later. These two middens are the largest shell heaps on the East Coast north of Florida, and together they comprise a significant archaeological site.

Damariscotta River Association

The Damariscotta River Association is a private philanthropic organization formed in 1973. They "promote the natural, cultural, and historical heritage of the Damariscotta River and surrounding areas for the benefit of all." The organization protects and maintains over 2,900 land acres that include 22 miles of mainland and island shoreline. You can join their group or simply make a donation. For more information visit damariscottariver.org.

There is a reason the oysters thrived here on the Damariscotta. After the glaciers receded thousands of years ago, the oceans were quite cold as they rose with the new ice melt. However, on the Damariscotta just downstream of these midden sites, the tides passed back and forth over a shallow rocky area known as the Johnny Orr Rapids—likely caused by glacial debris. These rocky shallows warmed and trapped waters of the river and Great Salt Bay, making them better suited for oysters. And the prehistoric peoples thrived along with the oyster beds, leaving a record of their presence in the form of the Whaleback and Glidden Middens.

Johnny Orr, for whom the water-warming rapids were named, settled hereabouts in the 1790s. Orr paid a high price to leave his name on these rocky shoals: His boat capsized, and he drowned floating through them. These rapids are also known as the Damariscotta Reversing Falls, since the river flows both ways due to the tides.

You will see plenty of tidal influence along this hike. After starting at the signed ME 215, bisect a small forest and then enter grassy flats on Great Salt Bay, pulsing with the flow of the Damariscotta River. Plank boardwalks lead through the flats. The Salt Bay Preserve Heritage Trail then rejoins pine-oak-evergreen forests, skirting the shore. Pass a tidal inlet to visit a pair of rocky points delivering excellent views of Great Salt Bay. Bring your lunch and dine at aptly named Picnic Point. More woodsy walking leads to Lookout Point, a narrows where the tides rush between two rocky peninsulas.

▶ It is theorized that Glidden and Whaleback Middens were built up over several hundred years, starting around 2,400 years ago.

Upon reaching US 1, you will find the sheep tunnel—a metal culvert running under the highway. As its name suggests, sheep could once safely access grazing tracts on either side of this watery peninsula via this underpass. Next visit the Glidden Midden, on the National Register of Historic Places. The Glidden Midden is a waterside shell heap cut vertically by the flowing Damariscotta, making it easy to see the layers of shells marking the passage of time, much as the rings of a tree do. You can stand along the shore and see the midden rise from the water.

What is left of the Whaleback Midden is across the river and is a Maine state historic site. A 0.5-mile trail leads from the historic site parking area to the midden. The Whaleback Midden was once much larger than the Glidden Midden. However, the shell heap was seen as a valuable resource to be ground down and turned into lime. Ultimately that is what happened—the remarkable midden was literally turned into fertilizer and chicken feed! Back in 1886 the Damariscotta Shell and Fertilizer Company was formed, shipping more than 200 tons of ground shells in the first year. The Whaleback Midden was already considerably reduced. Even as the midden was mined, the excavators noted that they discovered ". . . charcoal, bones

Layers of shells represent the passage of thousands of years at Glidden Midden.

of fish and animals, and of the human frame; stone hatchets, chisels, and deep sea sinkers; bone stilettos, and tools of art and the chase; pottery, sometimes ornamented; and even lumps of clay." What once was 15 feet high, over 1,500 feet long, and extended 400 feet back from the river was reduced to a mere "shell" of its former grandeur. The operation ceased within a few years; the business buildings burned. Think of all the lost archaeological artifacts and knowledge!

At least we still have the Glidden Midden, thanks to the Damariscotta River Association. Without them we couldn't take this historic hike.

Miles and Directions

0.0   Start from the Lincoln County Publishing Company parking lot. Cross ME 215 and join the signed Salt Bay Preserve Heritage Trail. Enter woods and quickly open into a cove of Great Salt Bay. Join a long segmented plank boardwalk spanning a grassy wetland. Come near US 1. Wild roses grow on the mainland.

0.2   Leave the boardwalk and enter oaks, pines, spruce, and balsam. Great Salt Bay extends to your left.

0.5   Cross a small tidal stream on a metal bridge. Peer into the water, looking for saltwater life such as horseshoe crabs. Reenter woods.

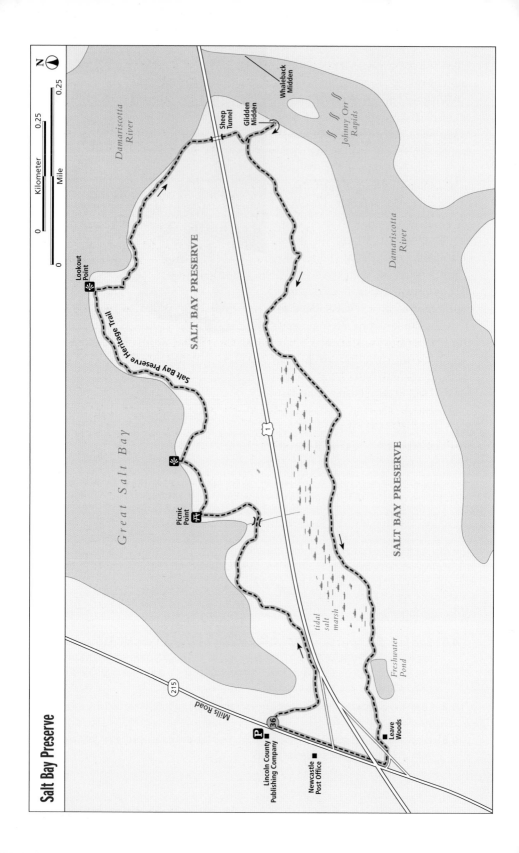

Salt Bay Preserve

N

Kilometer
0   0.25   0.25

Mile
0   0.25

Damariscotta River

Whaleback Midden

Sheep Tunnel

Glidden Midden

Johnny Orr Rapids

Damariscotta River

Lookout Point

Salt Bay Preserve Heritage Trail

SALT BAY PRESERVE

Great Salt Bay

Picnic Point

1

SALT BAY PRESERVE

tidal salt marsh

Freshwater Pond

Leave Woods

215

Mills Road

36

P

Lincoln County Publishing Company

Newcastle Post Office

0.6 Reach Picnic Point. The pine-shaded locale looks north on Great Salt Bay and has a stone protrusion extending into the water. Resume the loop after your break.

0.7 Come to a second, unnamed point. This one also looks north into Great Salt Bay. Begin curving past a hill to your right as the path continues to parallel the shore.

1.1 Emerge at Lookout Point. This spot presents a good opportunity to see the tidal action of the Damariscotta River squeezing through a narrows. From here turn southeast, walking along a bluff. Look for broken shells along the trail.

1.4 Come to US 1. The metal culvert ahead of you is the sheep tunnel, once used by flocks to access grazing plots across US 1. Cross the highway and rejoin the Salt Bay Preserve Heritage Trail. Cross a wetland on a boardwalk.

1.5 Split left at an intersection and descend to the Damariscotta River and the Glidden Midden. Once at the shore, head left and come along the vertically cut mound, tide permitting. What is left of the Whaleback Midden stands across the river. Johnny Orr Rapids are downriver to your right. Backtrack and continue the loop, heading west on faded woods roads. A meadow stretches to your left.

1.9 The trail gets mushy in places as you travel between a tidal marsh to your right and seeping hillside to your left.

2.1 Come to a turn. Here a woods road you have been following keeps straight and uphill for a private home, while the trail splits right and descends. Ahead, the trail can be brushy where open to the sun.

2.4 Come along a freshwater pond to your left.

2.6 Emerge onto an on ramp for US 1. Walk left along the ramp and join ME 215, heading north. Walk under the US 1 bridge.

2.8 Arrive back at the trailhead and Lincoln County Publishing.

37 Cadillac Mountain

Start this view-heavy hike at historic Sieur de Monts Spring. Visit the Abbe Museum of American Antiquities, then hike century-old paths to Cadillac Mountain, Acadia National Park's high point. En route, pass The Tarn, then climb the Ladder Trail. Surmount the open slopes of Dorr Mountain, named for the man who helped the park come to be. Make a final push for Cadillac Mountain, where vistas of the adjacent hills, Atlantic Ocean, and the isles of Maine make this a classic New England hike.

Start: Nature Center at Sieur de Monts
Distance: 4.7-mile loop with spur
Hiking time: 4–5.5 hours
Difficulty: Moderate to difficult due to elevation gains and rocky trails
Trail surface: Natural
Best season: Whenever skies are clear
Other trail users: None
Canine compatibility: Dogs allowed
Land status: National park
Fees and permits: Entrance fee required
Schedule: Park open 24 hours per day year-round

Maps: Acadia National Park
Trail contact: Acadia National Park, PO Box 177, Bar Harbor, ME 04609-0177; (207) 288-3338; nps.gov/acad/index.htm
Special considerations: Much of this hike is open to the sun—bring a hat and sunscreen. Sections are steep, involving ladders and irregular granite boulders as well as precisely laid steps. Do the hike on a clear day and be prepared to take pictures aplenty. Free bus shuttles run through the park, enabling you to hike point to point. Check the park's website for schedules.

Finding the trailhead: From the village green in Bar Harbor, Maine, take ME 3 south toward Northeast Harbor/Seal Harbor. Drive for 2.2 miles to the Sieur de Monts entrance into Acadia National Park. Turn right on the entrance road and then quickly left into the Wild Gardens/Abbe Museum area. The hike starts at the back of the nature center. **Trailhead GPS:** N44 21.711'/W68 12.444'

The Hike

Acadia National Park proudly boasts being the first national park east of the Mississippi River. The park story took many different turns and involved many different people. The starting point is Mount Desert Island, that spectacular granite parcel just off mainland Maine, a place with a picture postcard coastline and the objective of our hike—Cadillac Mountain—at 1,530 feet the highest point on the North American Atlantic coast. You have to go south all the way to Brazil to find a peak rising higher from the Atlantic Ocean.

From the iconic summit of Cadillac, appreciate the national park level scenery—granite-topped peaks rising above an island-dotted ocean; ponds and streams adding an inland aquatic component; and more than 165 species of plants and 60 mammal species calling the park home. Also, see the villages of Mount Desert Island, where

Climbing a ladder on the Ladder Trail

lobstermen, summer cottage owners, and tourists like us live, work, and play. Your view from atop Cadillac Mountain shows why Maine is known as "Vacationland."

This story starts with the Wabanaki peoples. You can learn about them at the Abbe Museum, seeing artifacts from their days on Mount Desert Island. They worked Somes Sound, hunting, fishing, and gathering berries (you too can gather berries on

The view from atop Cadillac Mountain draws in the crowds.

this hike starting midsummer). Then came the French and British, battling for the coast of Maine, when Frenchman Antoine de la Mothe, Sieur de Cadillac, claimed Mount Desert Island but only left a name (thankfully only his last name). Ultimately the British kept claim to Maine, and a sailor named Abraham Somes liked that harbor on Mount Desert Island so much he moved his family here, establishing the first permanent English settlement on the island. Other harbors came to be, each supporting small fishing and shipbuilding villages.

Two artists, Frederic Church and Thomas Cole, visited Mount Desert Island, tired of painting the Adirondacks and Catskills. Their unrestrained landscapes of this truly picturesque place drew art admirers to see if the coast of Maine matched the images these painters created on their easels. Mount Desert Island was even better in person. These early visitors weren't called tourists yet, they became known as "rusticators." Since there wasn't anywhere to stay on the island, local families took them in as they explored the mountains, ponds, and shoreline.

Mainers quickly saw dollars could be made by catering to the rusticators. Hotels, restaurants, and entertainment options rose around Mount Desert Island. The village of Bar Harbor came out on top, becoming a nationally recognized tourist destination. Coastal Maine's mild summer weather sure beat the stifling cities of the pre−air conditioned Northeast.

Then came the elites of the Gilded Age. People with names like Ford, Astor, Pulitzer, Morgan, Vanderbilt, and Rockefeller built incredible summer residences they called cottages. Mount Desert Island was changed forever—or at least until the national park came. These moneyed folk saw that as natural resources (read: wood for building) were extracted and more facilities were built for tourists, especially with the advent of the automobile, the unspoiled landscape would become, well, spoiled. Summer resident and president of Harvard University, Charles Eliot, formed a public land trust to halt the despoliation. Eliot hired Charles Dorr to spearhead the effort. The mountain we climb en route to Cadillac Mountain is named for Dorr.

It took Dorr a little while to get going, but he purchased a signature feature near Bar Harbor known as "The Beehive," a cliffy coastal headland that is popular with hikers to this day. He then obtained Cadillac Mountain. More land was acquired. Just about this time, pressure was being put on the federal government to create some national parks in the East. Dorr got national monument status for the land in 1916, and Congress created the national park in 1919. George Dorr was the first park superintendent and stayed in that position until 1943. The park wasn't called Acadia in those early days. It went by Lafayette National Park, for the Frenchman who aided the Patriots in the American Revolution.

Name aside, the park grew with more acquisitions, especially when John D. Rockefeller donated more than 10,000 acres to the park, as well as his famous carriage roads. And about that park name . . . A family on the Schoodic Peninsula wanted to donate 2,000 mainland acres to the park but didn't like the idea of the preserve being named for a Frenchman. Their piece of land would come only if the park's name was changed. It took a lot of arm-twisting by George Dorr—and an act of Congress—but the additional land was secured and the park renamed Acadia.

All was well until 1947, when a dry Maine summer got worse. A fire erupted near the Bar Harbor dump, spreading over 10,000 acres of the island. It burned much of the park and also the summer homes of Bar Harbor's elite, the millionaires who bankrolled the purchase of Acadia National Park, the first park ever to be bought entirely with private funds. Mount Desert Island was changed yet again. Hardwoods replaced conifers, and tourism for the masses replaced the exclusive playground of the elite (who are now primarily ensconced in Seal Harbor and Northeast Harbor on Mount Desert Island).

Our hike examines the legacy left by those park founders and uses trails they laid out, pathways of granite. After examining the springs, wild gardens, museum, and nature center, take off for The Tarn. Walk amid waterside boulders and then ascend the Ladder Trail, where metal ladders make the hike fun and challenging. After gaining elevation and the first of dozens of vistas, reach the crest of Dorr Mountain. Descend to a deeply wooded gorge and then climb Cadillac Mountain. Your return trip takes you past more vistas of land and sea.

Cadillac Mountain

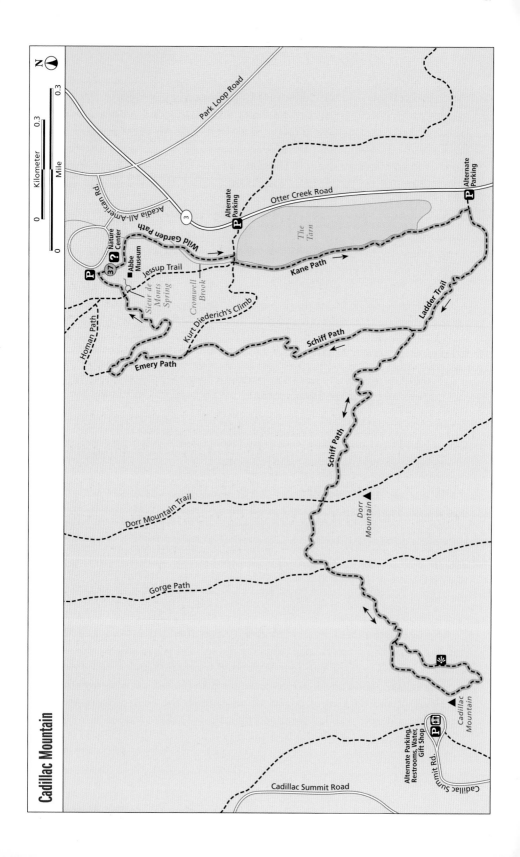

Park Loop Road

Acadia All-American Rd.

Nature Center
Abbe Museum
Jessup Trail
Sieur de Monts Spring
Kurt Diederich's Climb
Cromwell Brook
Wild Garden Path

Otter Creek Road
Alternate Parking

The Tarn

Kane Path

Alternate Parking

Homan Path
Emery Path
Schiff Path

Ladder Trail

Schiff Path

Dorr Mountain Trail

Dorr Mountain

Gorge Path

Schiff Path

Cadillac Mountain

Alternate Parking, Restrooms, Water, Gift Shop

Cadillac Summit Rd.

Cadillac Summit Road

N

Kilometer
0   0.3
Mile
0   0.3

37

Miles and Directions

0.0   Start from the rear of the nature center. Walk south and join the Wild Garden Path, not the actual Wild Gardens set of interconnected pathways. Traverse a natural-surface path east through hardwoods. Come alongside Cromwell Brook.

0.2   Bridge Cromwell Brook.

0.4   Ascend granite steps to reach The Tarn. Turn right here, cross Cromwell Brook, then turn left onto the Kane Path. Walk south along the west side of The Tarn among boulders.

0.8   Turn right here on the Ladder Trail, ascending granite steps.

1.0   Reach the first of three metal ladders ascending granite slopes. Views open in exposed rock areas.

1.2   The Ladder Trail ends. Head left on the Schiff Path. Walk over open view-laden slabs between stunted pines.

1.7   Meet the Dorr Mountain Trail. It is 0.1 mile left to the peak. This hike descends a bouldery path into a rift between Dorr and Cadillac Mountains.

1.9   Reach a four-way intersection with the Gorge Path deep in evergreen woods. Keep straight here for Cadillac Mountain. Quickly emerge into open bouldery slopes.

2.1   Come to a popular outcrop used by those who drive to the top of Cadillac Mountain. Amazing panoramas open of Frenchman Bay and beyond. Continue to the mountain peak, reaching a pebble-and-concrete loop path. Restrooms, water, and a gift shop are atop the mountain. Backtrack toward Dorr Mountain.

2.9   Return to the four-way intersection and ascend the west side of Dorr Mountain.

3.1   Meet the Dorr Mountain Trail a second time. Continue backtracking.

3.6   Reach the Ladder Trail and Schiff Path. Now turn left, joining a new segment of the Schiff Path. Walk north on the east slope of Dorr Mountain.

4.1   Head left on the Emery Path. Incredible views open ahead. A side trail heads right toward The Tarn.

4.3   The Homan Path leaves left. Stay with the Emery Path, slicing between cliffs, over open slopes on a steep slope.

4.7   Pass the Jessup Trail and Sieur de Monts Spring and arrive back at the nature center.

38 Jordan Pond House

This Acadia National Park hike is long on beauty and history. Start at the Jordan Pond House, where social gatherings based on popovers and tea became legendary. From there walk around Jordan Pond, as visitors have done for more than a century. Climb South Bubble for a fantastic view of Jordan Pond and Atlantic Ocean beyond. On your return trip, walk a section of the historic carriage roads that lace the park.

Start: Jordan Pond House parking area
Distance: 4.2-mile loop
Hiking time: 2.5–3.5 hours
Difficulty: Moderate due to 480-foot climb
Trail surface: Natural, some pea gravel
Best season: Mid-May through Columbus Day for popovers
Other trail users: None
Canine compatibility: Dogs not allowed in Jordan Pond House

Land status: National park
Fees and permits: Entrance fee required
Schedule: Trails open year-round, Jordan Pond House open mid-May through Columbus Day
Maps: Acadia National Park
Trail contact: Acadia National Park, PO Box 177, Bar Harbor, ME 04609-0177; (207) 288-3338, nps.gov/acad

Finding the trailhead: From the intersection of ME 3 and the Stanley Brook entrance to Acadia National Park in Seal Harbor, Maine, take the park road from the Stanley Brook entrance north for 1.2 miles to reach Park Loop Road. Turn left onto Park Loop Road and continue for 0.5 mile to the Jordan Pond House entrance on your left. The hiking trails start at the rear of the building, near the restrooms. **Trailhead GPS:** N41 40.539' / W73 30.494'

The Hike

Jordan Pond lies within the boundaries of Acadia National Park, on Mount Desert Island, with national park–worthy scenery. Jordan Pond is a deep, clear tarn walled in by Penobscot and Pemetic Mountains, as well as a pair of rounded peaks known as The Bubbles. Jordan Pond is no doubt alluring. This is where George and John Jordan, from nearby Seal Harbor, built a farmhouse and sawmill back in 1847 to tap the verdant woodlands that rose all around them. Along came Melvan Tibbetts, who saw the scenic beauty of Jordan Pond and its enveloping mountains differently. After purchasing the Jordan farm in 1864, Tibbetts began renting boats for the budding Mount Desert Island tourist trade. He then saw another need and began serving food to visitors who came to boat, picnic, and hike; he even added a dining room to his place.

Tibbetts's food idea was improved upon—some say perfected—by Mr. and Mrs. Thomas McIntire, who bought the Jordan Pond House in 1895. Mrs. McIntire began baking a hollow muffin known as a popover, serving it to guests, who loved to slather it with savory butter and preserves! A tradition was born. The island's wealthy elite came to dine on these popovers while recreating at Jordan Pond.

A local family peers down on Jordan Pond from South Bubble.

The McIntires ran the Jordan Pond House for a full fifty years, establishing it as a must-visit destination for Acadia National Park visitors. It was during the last half of the McIntires' running of the Jordan Pond House that one of Mount Desert Island's elite part-time residents, John D. Rockefeller, bought the Jordan Pond House and its surrounding property and later donated the land as an addition to Acadia National Park.

The Jordan Pond House was eventually taken over by a park-endorsed concessionaire. Tragedy struck in 1979 when the Jordan Pond House was consumed by fire. A new structure was built, and visitors can still enjoy dining on the Tea Lawn overlooking Jordan Pond, with The Bubbles rising in the background, framed by Penobscot Mountain to the west and Pemetic Mountain to the east. The rebuilt Jordan Pond House may not have the charm of the old structure, but the setting remains spectacular.

In his nearly thirty-year involvement with Mount Desert Island and Acadia National Park, John D. Rockefeller built over 45 miles of rustic carriage roads that wind through the park. Mr. Rockefeller, a skilled horseman, wanted auto-free roads upon which he could ride. The carriage roads, now an integral part of the Acadia National Park experience, were laid out with the landscape in mind, integrating the trails into the contours of the mountains and traversing places where the scenery can be best appreciated. Large blocks of granite lining the road serve as guardrails and are affectionately known as "Rockefeller's teeth." Cedar signposts are installed at carriage road intersections. There are seventeen rustic stone-faced bridges, each uniquely designed with the date of construction placed somewhere on it. Each bridge is named and adds to the impressive trail system of not only the carriage roads but also the hiking trails here at Acadia National Park.

You will hike a portion of these carriage roads, constructed between 1913 and 1940, and see a couple of the bridges. First the walk leaves Jordan Pond House, where you should ignore temptation for a popover until after your hike, and joins the Jordan Pond Path. Views of the pond and the adjacent hills are immediate and inspiring. Skirt around the edge of the lake on a level path, stabilized with elaborate rockwork, especially where intermittent streambeds flow down from the lands above. The hike parallels the eastern shore then reaches South Bubble Trail. Gaze back across the pond and then take the bouldery South Bubble Trail. It is a short, steep, fun scramble up the south face of South Bubble. Open onto outcrops affording magnificent views. Look back on Jordan Pond, Jordan Pond House, Seal Harbor, and the Atlantic Ocean, dotted by the Cranberry Isles. Take a side trail to view Bubble Rock, a balanced boulder seemingly about to topple. Capture vistas of Cadillac Mountain and Eagle

What Is a Popover?

Made with eggs, flour, and milk, popovers are baked in muffin tins in a very hot oven. Air trapped in the batter makes the inside of the popover hollow and doughy, while the outside is baked to a crispy, flaky perfection. Popovers have been served at Jordan Pond House for more than a century. They are traditionally eaten with butter and jam. The best part is that after your hike, you can eat them guilt free!

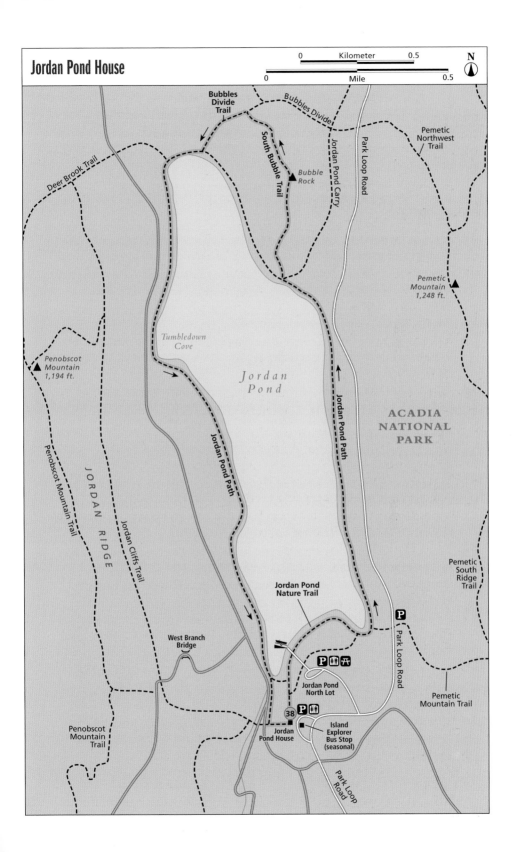

Jordan Pond House

0 | Kilometer | 0.5
0 | Mile | 0.5

N

Bubbles
Divide
Trail

Bubbles Divide

Deer Brook Trail

South Bubble Trail

Bubble
Rock

Jordan Pond Carry

Park Loop Road

Pemetic
Northwest
Trail

Pemetic
Mountain
1,248 ft.

*Tumbledown
Cove*

*Jordan
Pond*

Penobscot
Mountain
1,194 ft.

ACADIA
NATIONAL
PARK

Penobscot Mountain Trail

JORDAN RIDGE

Jordan Cliffs Trail

Jordan Pond Path

Jordan Pond Path

Pemetic
South
Ridge
Trail

**Jordan Pond
Nature Trail**

West Branch
Bridge

P

Park Loop Road

Pemetic
Mountain Trail

P 🚻 ⛲

Jordan Pond
North Lot

Penobscot
Mountain
Trail

38 **P** 🚻

Jordan
Pond House

Island
Explorer
Bus Stop
(seasonal)

Park Loop Road

Lake before dropping off South Bubble back to Jordan Pond. Walk alongside a sandy beach and then turn toward Jordan Pond House, walking the pond's edge. Open onto boulder fields as you pass through Tumbledown Cove, named for the boulders fallen from Penobscot Mountain above. Next comes a fun-to-hike extended boardwalk along the pond. Reach one of Rockefeller's historic carriage roads and cross a rustic bridge, tracing the carriage road a short distance before making a final jaunt back to the Jordan House.

And then you can have a popover.

Miles and Directions

0.0 Start from the rear of the Jordan Pond House, near the restrooms. Look for a gravel path heading right and descending toward Jordan Pond. Pass the Tea Lawn on your right.

0.1 Reach the pond and the Jordan Pond Path. Head right, counterclockwise around the pond. Soon pass a spur leading back to the Jordan Pond House. Views open of The Bubbles. Walk by the boat ramp.

0.4 Pass the last access back to the Jordan Pond area.

0.5 The Pemetic Mountain Trail leaves right. Keep straight on the Jordan Pond Path. Walk north along the scenic tarn, stepping over rock-lined intermittent drainages flowing into Jordan Pond.

1.3 Come to a trail intersection. Here the Jordan Pond Path continues along the water and Jordan Pond Carry Trail leads to Park Loop Road. You take the rocky South Bubble Trail. Begin scrambling up boulders on a marked path. Stone steps are integrated into the rock. The path steepens and becomes less wooded.

1.6 Open onto an outcrop and a view. Gaze upon Jordan Pond, the Jordan Pond House, and the Atlantic beyond. What a view! Continue up South Bubble. Ropes cordon off revegetating areas. Take the spur path leading right to Bubble Rock, also known as Balanced Rock.

1.7 Reach Bubble Rock. Views open of Cadillac Mountain, Eagle Lake, and territory northwest of Cadillac Mountain. Backtrack, pass over the crest of South Bubble, and leave the outcrop, entering a mix of forest and rock. Descend.

2.0 Come to an intersection. Turn left on the Bubbles Divide Trail. Descend an irregular boulder garden beneath thin woods.

2.2 Return to the Jordan Pond Path. Go right here on level trail, walking alongside a little beach. Bridge a stream.

2.3 The Deer Brook Trail leaves right and could be used to access a parallel carriage road. Stay left on the Jordan Pond Path. Ahead, pass through boulder fields along Tumbledown Cove.

2.8 Begin the long boardwalk running parallel to the shore.

3.4 Leave the boardwalk and join a gravel track.

3.7 Reach the southwest corner of the lake and emerge onto a carriage road. Cross the stone bridge here and turn right on the carriage road.

3.8 Come to a major intersection. Most paths go right over a bridge, but you take a left, uphill, on a singletrack trail.

4.2 Arrive back at the rear of the Jordan Pond House.

39 West Quoddy Head Lighthouse

This is one ultra-scenic hike. Start at the easternmost point in the entire United States, then curve along the rugged Maine coast to reach historic West Quoddy Head Lighthouse, its current incarnation in operation since 1857. Continue walking along cliffs above the Atlantic, viewing crashing waves in the near, with island and big water panoramas in the far. Return to the trailhead via deep woods inland paths.

Start: West Quoddy Head Lighthouse parking area
Distance: 4.4-mile loop
Hiking time: 3–3.5 hours
Difficulty: Moderate
Trail surface: Gravel and natural
Best season: Summer to access visitor center
Other trail users: None
Canine compatibility: Dogs allowed

Land status: Maine state park
Fees and permits: Parking fee required
Schedule: Open sunrise to sunset
Maps: Quoddy Head State Park
Trail Contact: Quoddy Head State Park, 973 South Lubec Rd., Lubec, ME 04652; (207) 733-0911 (Apr–Oct); (207) 941-4014 (Nov–Mar); maine.gov

Finding the trailhead: From ME 189 in downtown Lubec, Maine, turn right onto South Lubec Road and continue 2 miles to a fork. Bear left and continue 2 miles to the park entrance. **Trailhead GPS:** N44 48.966' / W66 57.158'

The Hike

This part of Downeast Maine is also known as the Bold Coast, where high cliffs and rock shores give way to sporadic cobble beaches facing the crashing Atlantic Ocean head on, where slow but sure weathering has carved a landscape that is inspiration for painters and photographers alike. Then there's West Quoddy Head Lighthouse, the historic red-and-white-striped beacon with its caretaker's house complementing the natural splendor. Finally, add the distinction of using the easternmost trail system in the United States at the easternmost point in the entire nation!

This hike of superlatives will deliver exceptional scenery, even if the area is blanketed by one of the fogs for which it is famous. The mist will add an air of otherworldliness to the trek. But first, let's go back in time to 1800, twenty years before Maine was admitted to the Union, to when mariners operating out of nearby ports petitioned the US government to put a lighthouse hereabouts, assisting passage through these waters. In 1808 the first beacon at Quoddy Head was lit, and lighthouse keeper Thomas Dexter began earning his $250 annual salary.

Yet the original octagonal wooden structure was headed for darker times. During the War of 1812, nearby Eastport was occupied by the British. They also commandeered the lighthouse, giving it the dubious distinction of being the only lighthouse in

The striped West Quoddy Head Lighthouse stands in the fog.

Maine to be foreign-occupied, albeit for a brief period. We Americans have a penchant for making things bigger and better; thus, in 1830 a second lighthouse was built here. The white, circular structure of stone was an improvement over the wooden original.

However, that wasn't good enough. In 1857 the circular brick structure you see today was constructed. (These three increasingly strong towers recall the childhood story of "The Three Little Pigs.") This newest model cost $15,000. The structure was not only sturdier but also had a Fresnel lens—a magnifying complex of mirrors that vastly improved the distance from which the light could be seen. That same lens is still in use today.

A lighthouse keeper's employ was a unique sort of job and life, the type of job Hollywood would have a reality show about today if lighthouses weren't automated. That first light keeper, Thomas Dexter, was a Revolutionary War veteran who "hauled oil, lit lamps, rang foghorn bells and endured bad weather." His house doesn't remain. The keeper's house currently on-site was also built in 1857 and now serves as the lighthouse visitor center. Inside, there is all sort of fascinating information about life here at the easternmost tip of the United States. Originally built for one family, the house was added onto in 1899 and then divided into a duplex, whereby the lighthouse keeper and the assistant lighthouse keeper—and their families—could reside here at Quoddy Head. The structure was returned to a one-family dwelling in the 1950s. The last light keeper lived here until 1988, when the light became automated.

The lighthouse is still an important beacon, helping boaters navigate the island-and-rock-studded Bay of Fundy, also known for its enormous tides and the biggest whirlpool in the Western Hemisphere. Nevertheless, this part of the Atlantic Coast is best recognized for its fog. An important function of the West Quoddy Head Lighthouse was to sound out during fogs. This process also underwent an evolution much as the lighthouse itself did. Cannons, bells, triangular bars, even compact air trumpets were used, all with limited effect. Even at that, the soundings did decrease shipwrecks. As time went on, steam-powered whistles were used. Things changed by 1900, when the first incarnation of the foghorn was invented. Its deep sounds carried well in the mist. In the 1930s the foghorn was fully developed and remains in use today.

Don't be surprised if your hike here is in the fog. If so, the coast will have an ethereal effect. However, clear days will deliver stunning views of Canada's Grand

A hiker treks on, undaunted by a coastal storm.

Manan Island, among other coastal features. Fog or sun, the immediate shore will make you want to stop and snap shot after shot. The trek starts on the Coast Guard Trail, where it heads north and stops by a vista point on an elevated wooded deck. You can see across to big Campobello Island and the balance of Passamaquoddy Bay. Turn back along the coast and reach the West Quoddy Head Lighthouse, very near your starting point. Stop in the visitor center and appreciate this brick beauty as it shines for passing mariners. From there, head south along the coastline, passing the park picnic area and an accessible cobblestone beach. Ahead, visit places like Gullivers Hole and High Ledge. Look for freshwater cascades spilling from the cliffs below. Green Point and other outcrops will beckon you. The trail turns into quiet Carrying Place Cove, where Indians portaged the peninsula to avoid the swift tides and dangerous whirlpools of the Bay of Fundy. The hike then enters inland forest on the Thompson Trail, where you travel under rich, mossy, evergreen maritime forests. Take the optional spur to an arctic bog and grab one more look at the lighthouse before ending the scenic walk.

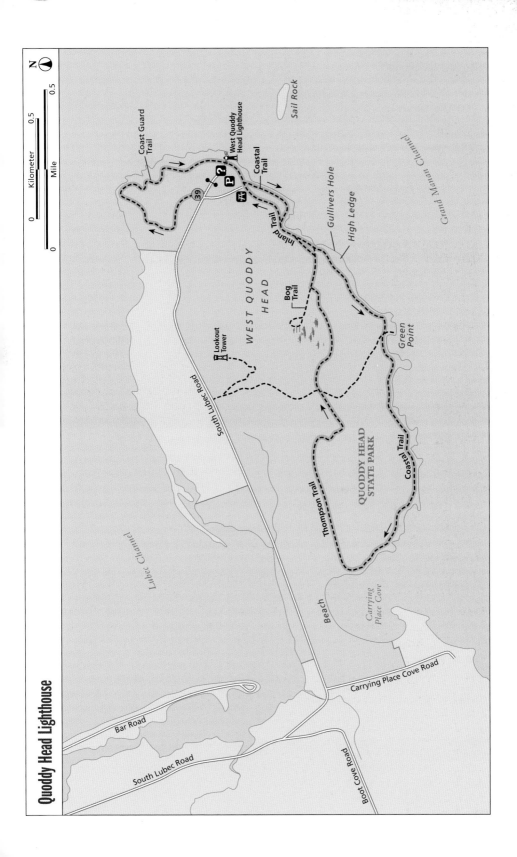

Quoddy Head Lighthouse

N

Kilometer
0   0.5   0.5

Mile
0   0.5

Bar Road

South Lubec Road

Lubec Channel

South Lubec Road

Boot Cove Road

Carrying Place Cove Road

Beach

Carrying Place Cove

Lookout Tower

WEST QUODDY HEAD

QUODDY HEAD STATE PARK

Thompson Trail

Coastal Trail

Green Point

Bog Trail

Inland Trail

Coast Guard Trail

West Quoddy Head Lighthouse

Coastal Trail

High Ledge

Gullivers Hole

Grand Manan Channel

Sail Rock

39

P

?

Miles and Directions

0.0 Start on the Coast Guard Trail, a gravel path heading north from the parking area and away from the lighthouse. Enter rich evergreen woods of spruce and fir, below which spreads spongy moss.

0.4 Reach an observation bench looking north toward Canada. A wooden observation deck is reached by forty-four steps. From this perch, the view widens to the east. After leaving the observation deck, resume the Coast Guard Trail, now a primitive, rooty, rocky track. Keep along the coastline. Great views lie ahead. Occasional spurs head to vistas.

0.8 Emerge at the West Quoddy Head Lighthouse, with its additional outbuildings. Enter the visitor center to absorb in-depth local history. From there walk south along the coast and pick up the signed trail indicating "To Beach."

1.0 Come to the park picnic area. Keep straight on the Coastal Trail and soon pass wooden steps leading down to a cobblestone beach.

1.2 Reach an intersection. Stay left here; the path leading acutely right heads back to the picnic area.

1.3 The trail splits again. Stay left as the trail heading right, the Inland Trail, goes toward the bog. (This is your return route.) Ahead, a shortcut leads right to the Inland Trail. Pass by steep cliffs and Gullivers Hole, an eroded, nearly enclosed cliff.

1.7 A short spur leads left to Green Point. Continue working along the coast through woods and brush, over undulating terrain. The views continue to amaze. Use occasional bridges, wooden steps, and boardwalks to make your way among dramatic headlands.

2.7 Meet the Thompson Trail after turning into Carrying Place Cove. Turn right onto the Thompson Trail as a user-created path keeps straight. Head inland on a slight uphill.

3.8 Reach the Bog Trail. (**Option:** To explore it, leave left and circle through an arctic bog.) To continue, stay right, now on a gravel path.

3.9 Pass a shortcut leading right to the Coastal Trail.

4.0 Meet the Coastal Trail. Keep straight.

4.1 Take the Inland Trail spur leading left to the picnic area.

4.2 Emerge at the picnic area. Rejoin the Coastal Trail, returning to the West Quoddy Head Lighthouse.

4.4 From the lighthouse, take the short, gated road back to the trailhead.

40 Katahdin

This is the most difficult hike in this guide, to arguably the most significant peak in all of New England. Katahdin is the northern terminus of the Appalachian Trail and is a good place to contemplate the historic nature of the AT. The route to the peak uses a long-traveled path within the confines of equally historic and wild Baxter State Park.

Start: Katahdin Stream Campground
Distance: 9.6 miles out and back
Hiking time: 8–11 hours
Difficulty: Very difficult due to 4,188-foot climb
Trail surface: Natural
Best season: Summer for long hours of daylight for hiking
Other trail users: None

Canine compatibility: Dogs not allowed in Baxter State Park
Land status: Maine state park
Fees and permits: Park entrance fee required
Schedule: Park open 6 a.m. to sunset during the warm season
Maps: Baxter State Park, Abol Trailhead map
Trail contact: Baxter State Park, 64 Balsam Dr., Millinocket, ME 04462; (207) 723-5140; http://baxterstateparkauthority.com

Finding the trailhead: From exit 244 on I-95 near Medway, Maine, take ME 157 west through Medway, East Millinocket, and Millinocket. Proceed through both traffic lights in Millinocket. Bear right at the three-way intersection after the second traffic light in downtown Millinocket. Bear left at the next Y intersection, staying on the main road. (ME 157 ends in Millinocket; the road to the park is unnumbered and has many names—Baxter State Park Road, Lake Road, and Millinocket Lake Road.) Eight miles from Millinocket, pass buildings and the Northwoods Trading Post on the right. Continue another 8 miles on the blacktop road to Togue Pond Gatehouse. All the major turns are signed for Baxter State Park. **Trailhead GPS:** N45 53.240' / W68 59.993'

The Hike

You just never know where a hike may lead you. In the case of Percival Baxter, hiking, fishing, and camping in the Maine woods led the one-time Maine governor to purchase lands for and create Baxter State Park, the entity that encompasses Mount Katahdin—Maine's highest peak at 5,268 feet, as well as the northern terminus of the Appalachian Trail. And it is to the top of Mount Katahdin where this hike leads us. After all, Baxter's idea was to create a park "for those who love nature and are willing to walk and make an effort to get close to nature."

Baxter's foresightedness inspired. And it was at that same time and in the same vein that the Appalachian Trail was conceived and routed end to end. However, let's start with the year 1930. Baxter's three-year term as governor had ended six years prior. In 1930 he made his initial purchase of 6,000 acres, acreage that included Mount Katahdin. The next year he donated the land to the State of Maine. And so it

A hiker scales an open rock ridge on Katahdin as Baxter State Park spreads below.

went—purchase land, give it to Maine, purchase land, give it to Maine—for a stunning thirty-two years!

But that wasn't all. Baxter had a specific vision for this state park. To execute his directives, which included having wilderness, logging, and hunting areas, the land needed to be managed. And that cost money. To that end, Percival Baxter left $7 million in a trust to endow the park with operating funds, rather than burdening the taxpayers of Maine. To this day, nary a dime comes from the state. Monies to staff and operate the park originate from the endowment, timber sales, and fees paid by park users.

Baxter State Park comprises a whopping 209,644 acres, one of the largest state parks in the nation. It contains not only the Katahdin massif but also rolling lower elevation forests, streams, ponds, wetlands, and trails galore to explore in this year-round home to moose, black bear, deer, and lesser mammals. The richness of life moves down the chain, even to annoying bugs such as mosquitoes and blackflies. Flora ranges from the unique and fragile alpine tundra atop Katahdin down to the hardwood and evergreen forests carpeting the lower reaches.

The massif held sway with aboriginal Mainers. The Penobscot Indians dubbed it Katahdin, which means "greatest mountain." However, in 1931 the US Geological Survey named the actual high point, the summit, the tiptop, Baxter Peak—a nod to Percival Baxter. So don't let that confuse you. Besides, almost everyone refers to climbing Katahdin rather than Baxter Peak.

In the twentieth century, Mount Katahdin's fame spread nationwide. It started with Benton MacKaye conceiving the idea for an "Appalachian Trail" extending the entirety of the eastern mountains, a destination to which man could break off from the grind of modern life. The first mile of the Appalachian Trail was laid out in 1922, and by 1937 the first end-to-end route was completed.

▶ Charles Turner made the first recorded ascent of Katahdin in 1804.

Katahdin's place in AT lore came to be when another proud Mainer named Myron Avery, who happened to be the chairman of the Appalachian Trail Conference, put forth the idea of making Mount Katahdin the trail's northern terminus. It was made so. And today, among AT enthusiasts, the name Katahdin is spoken with a reverence unlike any other peak on the trail.

Traditionally, the Appalachian Trail has been thru-hiked from south to north—from Springer Mountain, Georgia, to Mount Katahdin, Maine. Thru-hikers normally begin in spring, ending up in the shadow of Katahdin anywhere from four to six months later. You may see some thru-hikers in late summer/early fall, making that final ascent. Even after covering roughly 2,180 miles (the exact mileage continually changes due to trail reroutes), they still have 4.8 miles and 4,188 feet to climb. Once they get to the top, they have to get back down.

The Glory of Katahdin

Percival Baxter realized the revitalizing qualities of time spent in nature and that Mount Katahdin was one of those special places. Being a Mainer, the peak was dear to his heart. When Baxter gave the mountain away, he penned the following words. They are inscribed on a plaque embedded into granite at the base of the mountain, where this hike starts.

Man is born to die,
His works are short-lived.
Buildings crumble,
Monuments decay,
Wealth vanishes.
But Katahdin in all its glory,
Forever shall remain
The Mountain
Of the People of Maine.

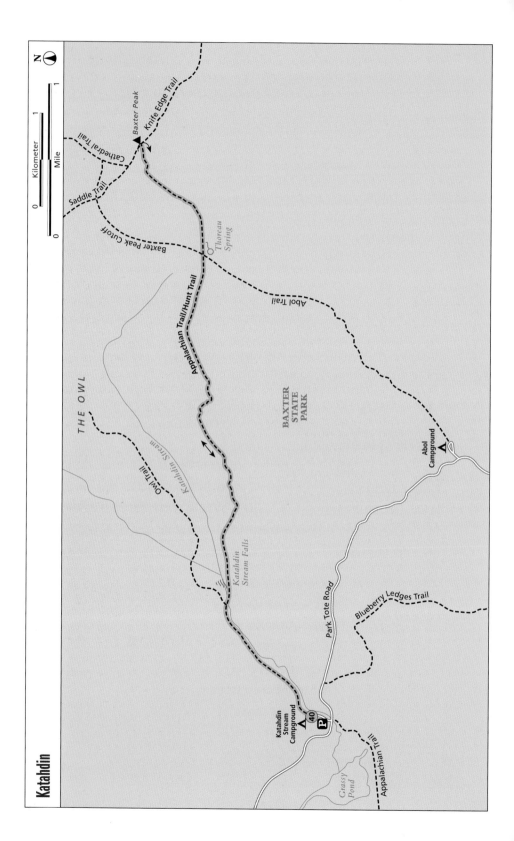

Katahdin

THE OWL

Owl Trail

Katahdin Stream

BAXTER STATE PARK

Appalachian Trail/Hunt Trail

Baxter Peak Cutoff

Thoreau Spring

Abol Trail

Cathedral Trail

Saddle Trail

Baxter Peak

Knife Edge Trail

Katahdin Stream Falls

Katahdin Stream Campground

40

P

Park Tote Road

Blueberry Ledges Trail

Grassy Pond

Appalachian Trail

Abol Campground

N

Kilometer

0   1

Mile

0   1

This route to Katahdin follows the AT/Hunt Trail, leaving Katahdin Stream Campground. You will follow Katahdin Stream, crossing it just before arriving at Katahdin Stream Falls, a crashing 60-foot cataract. The ascent sharpens and you begin working up boulders. The route later joins an all-rock ridge, where you are working over boulders most of the time. The going is extremely slow. Pass through the Gateway, the upper part of the boulder ridge, before opening onto the aptly named Tablelands, an above–tree line windswept plain of rock and fragile alpine plants. Pass Thoreau Spring, named for the renowned New England naturalist who climbed Katahdin in 1846. The AT winds upward through continual rock gardens, topping out on Baxter Peak, marked with an oft-photographed sign. It is well worth the challenges to scale Katahdin.

Here is some important advice: Start early, very early. It usually takes longer to get down than up, due to fatigue, the trail's steepness, and irregular terrain. Be prepared for weather extremities of wind, temperature, and precipitation atop the mountain. The hike requires using all fours, and at times it is more bouldering than hiking. This is a hike not be taken lightly. That being said, thousands of trekkers do it every year. Be prepared.

Miles and Directions

0.0 Start on the Appalachian Trail/Hunt Trail at the upper end of the day-use parking area at Katahdin Stream Campground. Walk through the upper campsites, with Katahdin Stream to your right. Pass campsite #16, then pick up a bona fide hiking path. Sign the trail register.

1.0 The Owl Trail leaves left. Stay straight with the AT/Hunt Trail. Ahead, bridge Katahdin Stream. There is a restroom after the crossing.

1.2 Reach Katahdin Stream Falls. A spur trail leads left to the crashing stair-step froth of whitewater. Continue up, clambering over stone steps among low shrubs. The trail steepens.

1.9 Cross a streamlet. This is a good place to rest before the climb ahead.

2.2 Pass an overhanging boulder to your left. Big boulders become more common.

2.6 Emerge onto an open boulder field among stunted trees. Views open of the lands below. Begin the prolonged boulder ascent, at times using metal rungs hammered into rock. Take your time, and make every move count.

3.3 Emerge onto the Tablelands after passing through the Gateway, the final maze of boulders. You are above tree line. Follow the blazes across a surprisingly level plain of rocks and fragile alpine flora. Stay on the trail.

3.8 Reach a four-way trail intersection at signed Thoreau Spring. Keep straight on the AT/Hunt Trail. A moderate but steady ascent soon resumes. The ridgeline narrows. Expect strong winds.

4.8 Reach Baxter Peak, the apex of Mount Katahdin, marked by a sign. Other trails spur from here. Backtrack, giving yourself more time to make it down than up as you descend the boulder fields.

9.6 Arrive back at the trailhead.

The Art of Hiking

When standing nose to nose with a mountain lion, you're probably not too concerned with the issue of ethical behavior in the wild. No doubt you're just terrified. But let's be honest. How often are you nose to nose with a mountain lion? For most of us a hike into the "wild" means loading up the SUV with expensive gear and driving to a toileted trailhead. Sure, you can mourn how civilized we've become—how GPS units have replaced natural instinct and Gore-Tex stands in for true grit—but the silly gadgets of civilization aside, we have plenty of reason to take pride in how we've matured. With survival now on the back burner, we've begun to understand that we have a responsibility to protect, no longer just conquer, our wild places: that they, not we, are at risk. So please, do what you can. The following section will help you understand better what it means to "do what you can" while still making the most of your hiking experience. Anyone can take a hike, but hiking safely and well is an art requiring preparation and proper equipment.

TRAIL ETIQUETTE

Leave No Trace. Always leave an area just like you found it—if not better than you found it. For more information visit LNT.org.

Avoid camping in fragile, alpine meadows and along the banks of streams and lakes. Use a camp stove versus building a wood fire. Pack up all of your trash and extra food. Bury human waste at least 100 feet from water sources under 6 to 8 inches of topsoil or 3 to 4 inches in a desert environment. Don't bathe with soap in a lake, stream, or river—use prepackaged moistened towels to wipe sweat and dirt, or bathe in the water without soap.

Stay on the trail. It's true, a path anywhere leads nowhere new, but purists will just have to get over it. Paths serve an important purpose; they limit impact on natural areas. Straying from a designated trail may seem innocent, but it can cause damage to sensitive areas—damage that may take years to recover, if it can recover at all. Even simple shortcuts can be destructive. So, please, stay on the trail.

Leave no weeds. Noxious weeds tend to overtake other plants, which in turn affects animals and birds that depend on them for food. To minimize the spread of noxious weeds, hikers should regularly clean their boots, tents, packs, and hiking poles of mud and seeds. Also brush your dog to remove any weed seeds before heading out into a new area.

Keep your dog under control. You can buy a flexi-lead that allows your dog to go exploring along the trail, while allowing you the ability to reel him in should another hiker approach or should he decide to chase a rabbit. Always obey leash laws and be sure to bury your dog's waste or pack it in resealable plastic bags.

Respect other trail users. Often you're not the only one on the trail. With the rise in popularity of multiuse trails, you'll have to learn a new kind of respect, beyond the nod and "hello" approach you may be used to. First, investigate whether you're on a multiuse trail, and assume the appropriate precautions. When you encounter motorized vehicles (ATVs, motorcycles, and 4WDs), be alert. Though they should always yield to the hiker, often they're going too fast or are too lost in the buzz of their engine to react to your presence. If you hear activity ahead, step off the trail just to be safe. Note that you're not likely to hear a mountain biker coming, so be prepared and know ahead of time whether you share the trail with them. Cyclists should always yield to hikers, but that's little comfort to the hiker. Be aware. When you approach horses or pack animals on the trail, always step quietly off the trail, preferably on the downhill side, and let them pass. If you're wearing a large backpack, it's often a good idea to sit down. To some animals, a hiker wearing a large backpack might appear threatening. Many national forests allow domesticated grazing, usually for sheep and cattle. Make sure your dog doesn't harass these animals, and respect ranchers' rights while you're enjoying yours.

GETTING INTO SHAPE

Unless you want to be sore—and possibly have to shorten your trip or vacation—be sure to get in shape before a big hike. If you're terribly out of shape, start a walking program early, preferably 8 weeks in advance. Start with a 15-minute walk during your lunch hour or after work and gradually increase your walking time to an hour. You should also increase your elevation gain. Walking briskly up hills really strengthens your leg muscles and gets your heart rate up. If you work in a storied office building, take the stairs instead of the elevator. If you prefer going to a gym, walk the treadmill or use a stair machine. You can further increase your strength and endurance by walking with a loaded backpack. Stationary exercises you might consider are squats, leg lifts, sit-ups, and push-ups. Other good ways to get in shape include biking, running, aerobics, and, of course, short hikes. Stretching before and after a hike keeps muscles flexible and helps avoid injuries.

PREPAREDNESS

It's been said that failing to plan means planning to fail. So do take the necessary time to plan your trip. Whether going on a short day hike or an extended backpack trip, always prepare for the worst. Simply remembering to pack a copy of the *U.S. Army Survival Manual* is not preparedness. Although it's not a bad idea if you plan on entering truly wild places, it's merely the tourniquet answer to a problem. You need to do your best to prevent the problem from arising in the first place. In order to survive—and to stay reasonably comfortable—you need to concern yourself with the basics: water, food, and shelter. Don't go on a hike without having these bases covered. And don't go on a hike expecting to find these items in the wilderness.

Water. Even in frigid conditions you need at least two quarts of water a day to function efficiently. Add heat and taxing terrain and you can bump that figure up to one gallon. That's simply a base to work from—your metabolism and your level of conditioning can raise or lower that amount. Unless you know your level, assume that you need one gallon of water a day. Now, where do you plan on getting the water? Preferably not from natural water sources. These sources can be loaded with intestinal disturbers, such as bacteria, viruses, and fertilizers. Giardia, the most common of these disturbers, is a protozoan parasite that lives part of its life cycle as a cyst in water sources. The parasite spreads when mammals defecate in water sources. Once ingested, Giardia can induce cramping, diarrhea, vomiting, and fatigue within two days to two weeks after ingestion. Giardiasis is treatable with prescription drugs. If you believe you've contracted giardiasis, see a doctor immediately.

Treating water. The best and easiest solution to avoid polluted water is to carry your water with you. Yet, depending on the nature of your hike and the duration, this may not be an option—one gallon of water weighs eight-and-a-half pounds. In that case you'll need to look into treating water. Regardless of which method you choose, you should always carry some water with you in case of an emergency. Save this reserve until you absolutely need it.

There are three methods of treating water: boiling, chemical treatment, and filtering. If you boil water, it's recommended that you do so for 10 to 15 minutes. This is often impractical because you're forced to exhaust a great deal of your fuel supply. You can opt for chemical treatment, which will kill Giardia but will not take care of other chemical pollutants. Another drawback to chemical treatments is the unpleasant taste of the water after it's treated. You can remedy this by adding powdered drink mix to the water. Filters are the preferred method for treating water. Many filters remove Giardia, organic and inorganic contaminants, and don't leave an aftertaste. Water filters are far from perfect as they can easily become clogged or leak if a gasket wears out. It's always a good idea to carry a backup supply of chemical treatment tablets in case your filter decides to quit on you.

Food. If we're talking about survival, you can go days without food, as long as you have water. But we're also talking about comfort. Try to avoid foods that are high in sugar and fat like candy bars and potato chips. These food types are harder to digest and are low in nutritional value. Instead, bring along foods that are easy to pack, nutritious, and high in energy (e.g., bagels, nutrition bars, dehydrated fruit, gorp, and jerky). If you are on an overnight trip, easy-to-fix dinners include rice mixes with dehydrated potatoes, corn, pasta with cheese sauce, and soup mixes.

For a tasty breakfast you can fix hot oatmeal with brown sugar and reconstituted milk powder topped off with banana chips. If you like a hot drink in the morning, bring along herbal tea bags or hot chocolate. If you are a coffee junkie, you can purchase coffee that is packaged like tea bags. You can prepackage all of your meals in heavy-duty resealable plastic bags to keep food from spilling in your pack. These bags can be reused to pack out trash.

Shelter. The type of shelter you choose depends less on the conditions than on your tolerance for discomfort. Shelter comes in many forms—tent, tarp, lean-to, bivy sack, cabin, cave, etc. If you're camping in the desert, a bivy sack may suffice, but if you're above the tree line and a storm is approaching, a better choice is a three- or four-season tent. Tents are the logical and most popular choice for most backpackers as they're lightweight and packable—and you can rest assured that you always have shelter from the elements. Before you leave on your trip, anticipate what the weather and terrain will be like and plan for the type of shelter that will work best for your comfort level (see Equipment later in this section).

Finding a campsite. If there are established campsites, stick to those. If not, start looking for a campsite early—around 3:30 or 4 p.m. Stop at the first decent site you see. Depending on the area, it could be a long time before you find another suitable location. Pitch your camp in an area that's level. Make sure the area is at least 200 feet from fragile areas like lakeshores, meadows, and stream banks. And try to avoid areas thick in underbrush, as they can harbor insects and provide cover for approaching animals.

If you are camping in stormy, rainy weather, look for a rock outcrop or a shelter in the trees to keep the wind from blowing your tent all night. Be sure that you don't camp under trees with dead limbs that might break off on top of you. Also, try to find an area that has an absorbent surface, such as sandy soil or forest duff. This, in addition to camping on a surface with a slight angle, will provide better drainage. By all means, don't dig trenches to provide drainage around your tent—remember you're practicing zero-impact camping.

If you're in bear country, steer clear of creekbeds or animal paths. If you see any signs of a bear's presence (e.g., scat, footprints), relocate. You'll need to find a campsite near a tall tree where you can hang your food and other items that may attract bears such as deodorant, toothpaste, or soap. Carry a lightweight nylon rope with which to hang your food. As a rule, you should hang your food at least 20 feet from the ground and 5 feet away from the tree trunk. You can put food and other items in a waterproof stuff sack and tie one end of the rope to the stuff sack. To get the other end of the rope over the tree branch, tie a good-size rock to it and gently toss the rock over the tree branch. Pull the stuff sack up to the top of the branch and tie it off. Don't hang food near your tent! Try to hang it at least 100 feet away from your campsite. Alternatives to hanging your food are bear-proof plastic tubes and metal bear boxes.

Lastly, think of comfort. Lie down on the ground where you intend to sleep and see if it's a good fit. For morning warmth (and a nice view to wake up to), have your tent face east.

FIRST AID

If you develop a blister on your hike, you'll wish you had that first-aid kit. Face it, it's just plain good sense. Many companies produce lightweight, compact first-aid kits. Just make sure yours contains at least the following:

- ❑ adhesive bandages
- ❑ moleskin or duct tape
- ❑ various sterile gauze and dressings
- ❑ white surgical tape
- ❑ an Ace bandage
- ❑ an antihistamine
- ❑ aspirin
- ❑ Betadine solution
- ❑ a first-aid book
- ❑ antacid tablets
- ❑ tweezers
- ❑ scissors
- ❑ antibacterial wipes
- ❑ triple-antibiotic ointment
- ❑ plastic gloves
- ❑ sterile cotton tip applicators
- ❑ syrup of ipecac (to induce vomiting)
- ❑ thermometer
- ❑ wire splint

Here are a few tips for dealing with and hopefully preventing certain ailments.

Sunburn. Take along sunscreen or sun block, protective clothing, and a wide-brimmed hat. If you do get a sunburn, treat the area with aloe vera gel and protect it from further sun exposure. At higher elevations the sun's radiation can be particularly damaging to skin. Remember that your eyes are vulnerable to this radiation as well. Sunglasses can help prevent headaches and permanent eye damage from the sun, especially in places where light-colored rock or patches of snow reflect light up onto your face.

Blisters. Be prepared to take care of these hike-spoilers by carrying moleskin (a lightly padded adhesive), gauze and tape, or adhesive bandages. An effective way to apply moleskin is to cut out a circle of moleskin and remove the center—like a doughnut—and place it over the blistered area. Cutting the center out will reduce the pressure applied to the sensitive skin. Other products can help you combat blisters. Some are applied to suspicious hot spots before a blister forms to help decrease friction to that area, while others are applied to the blister after it has popped to help prevent further irritation.

Insect bites and stings. You can treat most insect bites and stings by applying hydrocortisone 1 percent cream topically and taking a pain medication such as ibuprofen or acetaminophen to reduce swelling. If you forgot to pack these items, a cold compress or a paste of mud and ashes can sometimes assuage the itching and discomfort. Remove any stingers by using tweezers or scraping the area with your fingernail or a knife blade. Don't pinch the area as you'll only spread the venom.

Some hikers are highly sensitive to bites and stings and may have a serious allergic reaction that can be life-threatening. Symptoms of such a reaction can include difficulty breathing, wheezing, tightness or swelling in the throat, trouble speaking, or swollen lips or tongue. The treatment for this severe type of reaction is epinephrine. If you know that you are sensitive to bites and stings, carry a prepackaged kit of epinephrine, which can be obtained only by prescription from your doctor.

Ticks. Ticks can carry diseases such as Rocky Mountain spotted fever and Lyme disease. The best defense is, of course, prevention. If you know you're going to be hiking through an area littered with ticks, wear long pants and a long-sleeved shirt. You can apply a permethrin repellent to your clothing and a Deet repellent to exposed skin. At the end of your hike, do a spot check for ticks (and insects in general). If you do find a tick, grab the head of the tick firmly—with a pair of tweezers if you have them—and gently pull it away from the skin with a twisting motion. Sometimes the mouthparts linger, embedded in your skin. If this happens, try to remove them with a disinfected needle. Clean the affected area with an antibacterial cleanser and then apply triple-antibiotic ointment. Monitor the area for a few days. If irritation persists or a white spot develops, see a doctor for possible infection.

Poison ivy, oak, and sumac. These skin irritants can be found most anywhere in North America and come in the form of a bush or a vine, having leaflets in groups of three, five, seven, or nine. Learn how to spot the plants. The oil they secrete can cause an allergic reaction in the form of blisters, usually about 12 hours after exposure. The itchy rash can last from 10 days to several weeks. The best defense against these irritants is to wear clothing that covers the arms, legs, and torso. For summer zip-off cargo pants come in handy. There are also nonprescription lotions you can apply to exposed skin that guard against the effects of poison ivy/oak/sumac and can be washed off with soap and water. If you think you were in contact with the plants, after hiking (or even on the trail during longer hikes) wash with soap and water. Taking a hot shower with soap after you return home from your hike will also help to remove any lingering oil from your skin. Should you contract a rash from any of these plants, use an antihistamine to reduce the itching. If the rash is localized, create a light bleach/water wash to dry up the area. If the rash has spread, either tough it out or see your doctor about getting a dose of cortisone (available both orally and by injection).

Dehydration. Have you ever hiked in hot weather and had a roaring headache and felt fatigued after only a few miles? More than likely you were dehydrated. Symptoms of dehydration include fatigue, headache, and decreased coordination and judgment. When you are hiking, your body's rate of fluid loss depends on the outside temperature, humidity, altitude, and your activity level. On average, a hiker walking in warm weather will lose four liters of fluid a day. That fluid loss is easily replaced by normal consumption of liquids and food. However, if a hiker is walking briskly in hot, dry weather and hauling a heavy pack, he or she can lose one to three liters of water an hour. It's important to always carry plenty of water and to stop often and drink fluids regularly, even if you aren't thirsty.

Heat exhaustion is the result of a loss of large amounts of electrolytes and often occurs if a hiker is dehydrated and has been under heavy exertion. Common symptoms of heat exhaustion include cramping, exhaustion, fatigue, lightheadedness, and nausea. You can treat heat exhaustion by getting out of the sun and drinking an electrolyte solution made up of one teaspoon of salt and one tablespoon of sugar dissolved in a liter of water. Drink this solution slowly over a period of one hour. Drinking plenty of fluids (preferably an electrolyte solution/sports drink) can prevent heat exhaustion. Avoid hiking during the hottest parts of the day, and wear breathable clothing, a wide-brimmed hat, and sunglasses.

Hypothermia is one of the biggest dangers in the backcountry, especially for day hikers in the summertime. That may sound strange, but imagine starting out on a hike in midsummer when it's sunny and 80°F out. You're clad in nylon shorts and a cotton T-shirt. About halfway through your hike, the sky begins to cloud up, and in the next hour a light drizzle begins to fall and the wind starts to pick up. Before you know it you are soaking wet and shivering—the perfect recipe for hypothermia. More advanced signs include decreased coordination, slurred speech, and blurred vision. When a victim's temperature falls below 92°F, the blood pressure and pulse plummet, possibly leading to coma and death.

To avoid hypothermia always bring a windproof/rainproof shell; a fleece jacket; long underwear made of a breathable, synthetic fiber; gloves; and hat when you are hiking in the mountains. Learn to adjust your clothing layers based on the temperature. If you are climbing uphill at a moderate pace, you will stay warm, but when you stop for a break, you'll become cold quickly, unless you add more layers of clothing. If a hiker is showing advanced signs of hypothermia, dress him or her in dry clothes and make sure he or she is wearing a hat and gloves. Place the person in a sleeping bag in a tent or shelter that will protect him or her from the wind and other elements. Give the person warm fluids to drink and keep him awake.

Frostbite. When the mercury dips below 32°F, your extremities begin to chill. If a persistent chill attacks a localized area, say, your hands or your toes, the circulatory system reacts by cutting off blood flow to the affected area—the idea being to protect and preserve the body's overall temperature. And so it's death by attrition for the affected area. Ice crystals start to form from the water in the cells of the neglected tissue. Deprived of heat, nourishment, and now water, the tissue literally starves. This is frostbite. Prevention is your best defense against this situation. Most prone to frostbite are your face, hands, and feet, so protect these areas well. Wool is the traditional material of choice because it provides ample air space for insulation and draws moisture away from the skin. Synthetic fabrics, however, have made great strides in the cold-weather clothing market. Do your research. A pair of light silk liners under your regular gloves is a good trick for keeping warm. They afford some additional warmth, but more importantly they'll allow you to remove your mitts for tedious work without exposing the skin. If your feet or hands start to feel cold or numb due to the elements, warm them as quickly as possible. Place cold hands under your armpits or bury them in your crotch. If your feet are cold, change your socks. If there's plenty of room in your boots, add another pair of socks. Do remember, though, that constricting your feet in tight boots can restrict blood flow and actually make your feet colder more quickly. Your socks need to have breathing room if they're going to be effective. Dead air provides insulation. If your face is cold, place your warm hands over your face, or simply wear a head stocking. Should your skin go numb and start to appear white and waxy, chances are you've got or are developing frostbite. Don't try to thaw the area unless you can maintain the warmth. In other words don't stop to warm up your frostbitten feet only to head back on the trail. You'll do more damage than good. Tests have shown that hikers who walked on thawed feet did more harm, and endured more pain, than hikers who left the affected areas alone. Do your best to get out of the cold entirely and seek medical attention—which usually consists of performing a rapid rewarming in water for 20 to 30 minutes.

The overall objective in preventing both hypothermia and frostbite is to keep the body's core warm. Protect key areas where heat escapes, like the top of the head, and maintain the proper nutrition level. Foods that are high in calories aid the body in producing heat. Never smoke or drink when you're in situations where the cold is threatening. By affecting blood flow these activities ultimately cool the body's core temperature.

Hantavirus Pulmonary Syndrome (HPS). Deer mice spread the virus that causes HPS, and humans contract it from breathing it in, usually when they've disturbed an area with dust and mice feces from nests or surfaces with mice droppings or urine. Exposure to large numbers of rodents and their feces or urine presents the greatest risk. As hikers, we sometimes enter old buildings, and often deer mice live in these places. We may not be around long enough to be exposed, but do be aware of this disease. About half the people who develop HPS die. Symptoms are flulike and appear about 2 to 3 weeks after exposure. After initial symptoms a dry cough and shortness of breath follow. Breathing is difficult. If you even think you might have HPS, see a doctor immediately!

NATURAL HAZARDS

Besides tripping over a rock or tree root on the trail, there are some real hazards to be aware of while hiking. Even if where you're hiking doesn't have the plethora of poisonous snakes and plants, insects, and grizzly bears found in other parts of the United States, there are a few weather conditions and predators you may need to take into account.

Lightning. Thunderstorms are prevalent during the summer, especially at higher altitudes. Lightning is generated by thunderheads and can strike without warning, even several miles away from the nearest overhead cloud. The best rule of thumb is to start leaving exposed areas by about noon. This time can vary a little depending on storm buildup. Keep an eye on cloud formation, and don't underestimate how fast a storm can build. The bigger the clouds get, the more likely a thunderstorm will happen. Lightning takes the path of least resistance, so if you're the high point, it might choose you. Ducking under a rock overhang is dangerous as you form the shortest path between the rock and ground. If you dash below tree line, avoid standing under the only or the tallest tree. If you are caught above tree line, stay away from anything metal you might be carrying, Move down off the ridge slightly to a low, treeless point, and squat until the storm passes. If you have an insulating pad, squat on it. Avoid having both your hands and feet touching the ground at once and never lay flat. If you hear a buzzing sound or feel your hair standing on end, move quickly as an electrical charge is building up.

Flash floods. Flash floods pose a threat to those hiking near many of the creeks described in this guide. Keep an eye on the weather and always climb to safety if danger threatens. Flash floods usually subside quickly, so be patient and don't cross a swollen stream.

Bears. Most of the United States (outside of the Pacific Northwest and parts of the Northern Rockies) does not have a grizzly bear population, although some rumors exist about sightings where there should be none. Black bears are plentiful, however. There are black bears in New England. Here are some tips in case you and a bear scare each other. Most of all, avoid surprising a bear. Talk or sing where visibility or hearing are limited, such as along a rushing creek or in thick brush. While hiking, watch for bear tracks (five toes), droppings (sizable with leaves, partly digested berries, seeds, and/ or animal fur), or rocks and roots along the trail that show signs of being dug up (this could be a bear looking for bugs to eat). Keep a clean camp, hang food or use bear-proof storage containers, and don't sleep in the clothes you wore while cooking. Be especially careful to avoid getting between a mother and her cubs. In late summer and fall, bears are busy eating to fatten up for winter, so be extra careful around berry bushes. If you do encounter a bear, move away slowly while facing the bear, talk softly, and avoid direct eye contact. Give the bear room to escape. Since bears are very curious, it might stand upright to get a better whiff of you, and it may even charge you to try to intimidate you. Try to stay calm. If a black bear attacks you, fight back with anything you have handy. Unleashed dogs have been known to come running back to their owners with a bear close behind. Keep your dog on a leash or within view at all times.

Mountain lions. It is extremely unlikely that you will see a mountain lion while hiking. With that being said, mountain lion sightings in New England do happen.

Mountain lions appear to be getting more comfortable around humans as long as deer (their favorite prey) are in an area with adequate cover. Usually elusive and quiet, lions rarely attack people. If you meet a lion, give it a chance to escape. Stay calm and talk firmly to it. Back away slowly while facing the lion. If you run, you'll only encourage the cat to chase you. Make yourself look large by opening a jacket, if you have one, or waving your hiking poles. If the lion behaves aggressively, throw stones, sticks, or whatever you can while remaining tall. If a lion does attack, fight for your life with anything you can grab.

Other considerations. Hunting is a popular sport in the United States, especially during rise season in October and November. Hiking is still enjoyable in those months in many areas, so just take a few precautions. First, learn when the different hunting seasons start and end in the area in which you'll be hiking. During this time frame be sure to at least wear a blaze orange hat and possibly put an orange vest over your pack. Don't be surprised to see hunters in camo outfits carrying bows or rifles around during their season. If you would feel more comfortable without hunters around, hike in national parks and monuments or state and local parks where hunting is not allowed.

NAVIGATION

Whether you are going on a short hike in a familiar area or planning a weeklong backpack trip, you should always be equipped with the proper navigational equipment—at the very least a detailed map and a sturdy compass.

Maps. There are many different types of maps available to help you find your way on the trail. Easiest to find are Forest Service maps and BLM (Bureau of Land Management) maps. These maps tend to cover large areas, so be sure they are detailed enough for your particular trip. You can also obtain national park maps as well as high-quality maps from private companies and trail groups. These maps can be obtained either from outdoor stores or ranger stations.

US Geological Survey topographic maps are particularly popular with hikers—especially serious backcountry hikers. These maps contain the standard map symbols such as roads, lakes, and rivers, as well as contour lines that show the details of the trail terrain like ridges, valleys, passes, and mountain peaks. The 7.5-minute series (1 inch on the map equals approximately 0.4 mile on the ground) provides the closest inspection available. USGS maps are available by mail (U.S. Geological Survey, Map Distribution Branch, PO Box 25286, Denver, CO 80225) or at mapping.usgs.gov/esic/to_order.html.

If you want to check out the high-tech world of maps, you can purchase topographic maps on CD-ROM. These software-mapping programs let you select a route on your computer, print it out, then take it with you on the trail. Some software mapping programs let you insert symbols and labels, download waypoints from a GPS unit, and export the maps to other software programs.

The art of map reading is a skill you can develop by first practicing in an area you are familiar with. To begin, orient the map so the map is lined up in the correct direction (i.e., north on the map is lined up with true north). Next, familiarize yourself with the map symbols and try and match them up with terrain features around you such as a high ridge, mountain peak, river, or lake. If you are practicing with a USGS map, notice the contour lines. On gentler terrain these contour lines are spaced farther apart, and on steeper terrain they are closer together. Pick a short loop trail, and stop frequently to check your position on the map. As you practice map reading, you'll learn how to anticipate a steep section on the trail, a good place to take a rest break, and so on.

Compasses. First off, the sun is not a substitute for a compass. So, what kind of compass should you have? Here are some characteristics you should look for: a rectangular base with detailed scales, a liquid-filled housing, protective housing, a sighting line on the mirror, luminous alignment and back-bearing arrows, a luminous north-seeking arrow, and a well-defined bezel ring.

You can learn compass basics by reading the detailed instructions included with your compass. If you want to fine-tune your compass skills, sign up for an orienteering class or purchase a book on compass reading. Once you've learned the basic skills of using a compass, remember to practice these skills before you head into the backcountry.

If you are a klutz at using a compass, you may be interested in checking out the technical wizardry of the GPS (Global Positioning System) device. The GPS was developed by the Pentagon and works off twenty-four NAVSTAR satellites, which were designed to guide missiles to their targets. A GPS device is a handheld unit that calculates your latitude and longitude with the easy press of a button. The Department of Defense used to scramble the satellite signals a bit to prevent civilians (and spies!) from getting extremely accurate readings, but that practice was discontinued in May 2000, and GPS units now provide nearly pinpoint accuracy (within 30 to 60 feet).

There are many different types of GPS units available, and they range in price from $100 to $400. In general, all GPS units have a display screen and keypad where you input information. In addition to acting as a compass, the unit allows you to plot your route, easily retrace your path, track your traveling speed, find the mileage between waypoints, and calculate the total mileage of your route. Before you purchase a GPS unit, keep in mind that these devices don't pick up signals indoors, in heavily wooded areas, on mountain peaks, or in deep valleys. Also, batteries can wear out or other technical problems can develop. A GPS unit should be used in conjunction with a map and compass, not in place of those items.

TRIP PLANNING

Planning your hiking adventure begins with letting a friend or relative know your trip itinerary so she can call for help if you don't return at your scheduled time. Your next task is to make sure you are outfitted to experience the risks and rewards of the trail. This section highlights gear and clothing you may want to take with you to get the most out of your hike.

Day Hike

- ❏ camera
- ❏ compass/GPS unit
- ❏ daypack
- ❏ first-aid kit
- ❏ fleece jacket
- ❏ food
- ❏ guidebook
- ❏ headlamp/flashlight with extra batteries and bulbs
- ❏ hat
- ❏ insect repellent
- ❏ knife/multipurpose tool

- ❏ map
- ❏ matches in waterproof container and fire starter
- ❏ pedometer
- ❏ rain gear
- ❏ space blanket
- ❏ sunglasses
- ❏ sunscreen
- ❏ swimsuit and/or fishing gear (if hiking to a lake)
- ❏ watch
- ❏ water
- ❏ water bottles/water hydration system

Overnight Trip

- ❏ backpack and waterproof rain cover
- ❏ backpacker's trowel
- ❏ bandanna
- ❏ bear canister or rope to hang food
- ❏ biodegradable soap
- ❏ collapsible water container (two- to three-gallon capacity)
- ❏ clothing—extra wool socks, shirts, and shorts
- ❏ cook set/utensils
- ❏ ditty bags to store gear
- ❏ extra plastic resealable bags
- ❏ gaiters
- ❏ garbage bag
- ❏ ground cloth
- ❏ journal/pen

- ❏ long underwear
- ❏ nylon rope to hang food
- ❏ permit (if required)
- ❏ pot scrubber
- ❏ rain jacket and pants
- ❏ sandals to wear around camp and to ford streams
- ❏ sleeping bag
- ❏ sleeping pad
- ❏ small bath towel
- ❏ stove and fuel
- ❏ tent
- ❏ toiletry items
- ❏ waterproof stuff sack
- ❏ water filter
- ❏ whistle

EQUIPMENT

With the outdoor market currently flooded with products, many of which are pure gimmickry, it seems impossible to both differentiate and choose. Do I really need a tropical-fish-lined collapsible shower? (No, you don't.) The only defense against the maddening quantity of items thrust in your face is to think practically—and to do so before you go shopping. The worst buys are impulsive buys. Since most name brands will differ only slightly in quality, it's best to know what you're looking for in terms of function. Buy only what you need. You will, don't forget, be carrying what you've bought on your back. Here are some things to keep in mind before you go shopping.

Clothes. Clothing is your armor against Mother Nature's little surprises. Hikers should be prepared for any possibility, especially when hiking in mountainous areas. Adequate rain protection and extra layers of clothing are a good idea. In summer a wide-brimmed hat can help keep the sun at bay. In the winter months the first layer you'll want to wear is a "wicking" layer of long underwear that keeps perspiration away from your skin. Wear long underwear made from synthetic fibers that wick moisture away from the skin and draw it toward the next layer of clothing, where it then evaporates. Avoid wearing long underwear made of cotton as it is slow to dry and keeps moisture next to your skin.

The second layer you'll wear is the "insulating" layer. Aside from keeping you warm, this layer needs to "breathe" so you stay dry while hiking. A fabric that provides insulation and dries quickly is fleece. It's interesting to note that this one-of-a-kind fabric is made out of recycled plastic. Purchasing a zip-up jacket made of this material is highly recommended.

The last line of layering defense is the "shell" layer. You'll need some type of waterproof, windproof, breathable jacket that will fit over all of your other layers. It should have a large hood that fits over a hat. You'll also need a good pair of rain pants made from a similar waterproof, breathable fabric. Some Gore-Tex jackets cost as much as $500, but you should know that there are more affordable fabrics out there that work just as well.

Now that you've learned the basics of layering, you can't forget to protect your hands and face. In cold, windy, or rainy weather, you'll need a hat made of wool or fleece and insulated, waterproof gloves that will keep your hands warm and toasty. As mentioned earlier, buying an additional pair of light silk liners to wear under your regular gloves is a good idea.

Footwear. If you have any extra money to spend on your trip, put that money into boots or trail shoes. Poor shoes will bring a hike to a halt faster than anything else. To avoid this annoyance, buy shoes that provide support and are lightweight and flexible. A lightweight hiking boot is better than a heavy, leather mountaineering boot for most day hikes and backpacking. Trail running shoes provide a little extra cushion that many people wear for hiking.

These running shoes are lighter, more flexible, and more breathable than hiking boots. If you know you'll be hiking in wet weather often, purchase boots or shoes with a Gore-Tex liner, which will help keep your feet dry.

When buying your boots, be sure to wear the same type of socks you'll be wearing on the trail. If the boots you're buying are for cold-weather hiking, try the boots on while wearing two pairs of socks. Speaking of socks, a good cold-weather sock combination is a thinner sock made of wool or polypropylene covered by a heavier outer sock made of wool or a synthetic/wool mix. The inner sock protects the foot from the rubbing effects of the outer sock and prevents blisters. Many outdoor stores have some type of ramp to simulate hiking uphill and downhill. Be sure to take advantage of this test, as toe-jamming boot fronts can be very painful and debilitating on the downhill trek.

Once you've purchased your footwear, be sure to break it in before you hit the trail. New footwear is often stiff and needs to be stretched and molded to your foot.

Trekking poles. Trekking poles help with balance, and more importantly take pressure off your knees. The ones with shock absorbers are easier on your elbows and knees. Some poles even come with a camera attachment to be used as a monopod. And heaven forbid you meet a mountain lion, bear, or unfriendly dog—the poles can make you look a lot bigger.

Backpacks. No matter what type of hiking you do, you'll need a pack of some sort to carry the basic trail essentials. There are a variety of backpacks on the market, but let's first discuss what you intend to use it for. Day hikes or overnight trips?

If you plan on doing a day hike, a daypack should have some of the following characteristics: a padded hip belt that's at least 2 inches in diameter (avoid packs with only a small nylon piece of webbing for a hip belt); a chest strap (the chest strap helps stabilize the pack against your body); external pockets to carry water and other items that you want easy access to; an internal pocket to hold keys, a knife, a wallet, and other miscellaneous items; an external lashing system to hold a jacket; and, if you so desire, a hydration pocket for carrying a hydration system (which consists of a water bladder with an attachable drinking hose).

For short hikes some hikers like to use small, lightweight daypacks to store just a camera, food, a compass, a map, and other trail essentials. Most of these light-weight daypacks have pockets for two water bottles and areas to store cell phones, snacks, and other items you will want to access easily.

If you intend to do an extended overnight trip, there are multiple considerations. First off, you need to decide what kind of framed pack you want. There are two backpack types for backpacking: the internal frame and the external frame. An internal frame pack rests closer to your body, making it more stable and easier to balance when hiking over rough terrain. An external frame pack is just that, an aluminum frame attached to the exterior of the pack. Some hikers consider an external frame pack to be better for long backpack trips because it distributes the pack weight better and allows you to carry heavier loads. It's often easier to pack, and your gear is more accessible. It also offers better back ventilation in hot weather.

The most critical measurement for fitting a pack is torso length. The pack needs to rest evenly on your hips without sagging. A good pack will come in two or three sizes and have straps and hip belts that are adjustable according to your body size and characteristics.

When you purchase a backpack, go to an outdoor store with salespeople who are knowledgeable in how to properly fit a pack. Once the pack is fitted for you, load the pack with the amount of weight you plan on taking on the trail. The weight of the pack should be distributed evenly, and you should be able to swing your arms and walk briskly without feeling out of balance. Another good technique for evaluating a pack is to walk up and down stairs and make quick turns to the right and to the left to be sure the pack doesn't feel out of balance. Other features that are nice to have on a backpack include a removable day pack or fanny pack, external pockets for extra water, and extra lash points to attach a jacket or other items.

Sleeping bags and pads. Sleeping bags are rated by temperature. You can purchase a bag made with synthetic insulation, or you can buy a goose down bag. Goose down bags are more expensive, but they have a higher insulating capacity by weight and will keep their loft longer. You'll want to purchase a bag with a temperature rating that fits the time of year and conditions you are most likely to camp in.

One caveat: The techno-standard for temperature ratings is far from perfect. Ratings vary from manufacturer to manufacturer, so to protect yourself you should purchase a bag rated 10° to 15° below the temperature you expect to be camping in. Synthetic bags are more resistant to water than down bags, but many down bags are now made with a Gore-Tex shell that helps to repel water. Down bags are also more compressible than synthetic bags and take up less room in your pack, which is an important consideration if you are planning a multiday backpack trip. Features to look for in a sleeping bag include a mummy-style bag, a hood you can cinch down around your head in cold weather, and draft tubes along the zippers that help keep heat in and drafts out.

You'll also want a sleeping pad to provide insulation and padding from the cold ground. There are different types of sleeping pads available, from the more expensive self-inflating air mattresses to the less expensive closed-cell foam pads. Self-inflating air mattresses are usually heavier than closed-cell foam mattresses and are prone to punctures.

Tents. The tent is your home away from home while on the trail. It provides protection from wind, rain, snow, and insects. A three-season tent is a good choice for backpacking and can range in price from $100 to $500 and more. These lightweight and versatile tents provide protection in all types of weather, except heavy snowstorms or high winds, and range in weight from 4 to 8 pounds. Look for a tent that's easy to set up and will easily fit two people with gear. Dome-type tents usually offer more headroom and places to store gear. Other handy tent features include a vestibule where you can store wet boots and backpacks. Some nice-to-have items in a tent include interior pockets to store small items and lashing points to hang a clothesline. Most three-season tents also come with stakes so you can secure the tent in high winds. Before you purchase a tent, set it up and take it down a few times to be sure it is easy to handle. Also, sit inside the tent and make sure it has enough room for you and your gear.

Cell phones. Many hikers are carrying their cell phones into the backcountry these days in case of emergency. That's fine and good, but please know that cell phone coverage is often poor to nonexistent in valleys, canyons, and thick forest. More important, people have started to call for help because they're tired or lost. Let's go back to being prepared. You are responsible for yourself in the backcountry. Use your brain to avoid problems, and if you do encounter one, first use your brain to try to correct the situation. Only use your cell phone, if it works, in true emergencies. If it doesn't work down low in a valley, try hiking to a high point where you might get reception.

HIKING WITH CHILDREN

Hiking with children isn't a matter of how many miles you can cover or how much elevation gain you make in a day; it's about seeing and experiencing nature through their eyes.

Kids like to explore and have fun. They like to stop and point out bugs and plants, look under rocks, jump in puddles, and throw sticks. If you're taking a toddler or young child on a hike, start with a trail you're familiar with. Trails that have interesting things for kids, like piles of leaves to play in or a small stream to wade through during the summer, will make the hike much more enjoyable for them and will keep them from getting bored.

You can keep your child's attention if you have a strategy before starting on the trail. Using games is not only an effective way to keep a child's attention, it's also a great way to teach him or her about nature. Quiz children on the names of plants and animals. Pick up a family-friendly outdoor hobby like Geocaching (geocaching .com) or Letterboxing (atlasquest.com), both of which combine the outdoors, clue solving, and treasure hunting. If your children are old enough, let them carry their own daypack filled with snacks and water. So that you are sure to go at their pace and not yours, let them lead the way. Playing follow the leader works particularly well when you have a group of children. Have each child take a turn at being the leader.

With children a lot of clothing is key. The only thing predictable about weather is that it will change. Especially in mountainous areas, weather can change dramatically in a very short time. Always bring extra clothing for children, regardless of the season. In the winter have your children wear wool socks and warm layers such as long underwear, a fleece jacket and hat, wool mittens, and good rain gear. It's not a bad idea to have these along in late fall and early spring as well. Good footwear is also important. A sturdy pair of high-top tennis shoes or lightweight hiking boots is the best bet for little ones. If you're hiking in the summer near a lake or stream, bring along a pair of old sneakers that your child can put on when he wants to go exploring in the water. Remember that when you're near any type of water, always watch your child at all times. Also, keep a close eye on teething toddlers who may decide a rock or leaf of poison oak is an interesting item to put in their mouth.

From spring through fall you'll want your kids to wear a wide-brimmed hat to keep their face, head, and ears protected from the hot sun. Also, make sure your children wear sunscreen at all times. Choose a brand without PABA—children have sensitive skin and may have an allergic reaction to sunscreen that contains PABA. If you are hiking with a child younger than 6 months, don't use sunscreen or insect repellent. Instead, be sure that his or her head, face, neck, and ears are protected from the sun with a wide-brimmed hat and that all other skin exposed to the sun is protected with the appropriate clothing.

Remember that food is fun. Kids like snacks, so it's important to bring a lot of munchies for the trail. Stopping often for snack breaks is a fun way to keep the trail interesting. Raisins, apples, granola bars, crackers and cheese, cereal, and trail mix all make great snacks. Also, a few of their favorite candy treats can go a long way toward heading off a fit of fussing. If your child is old enough to carry her own backpack, let her fill it with some lightweight "comfort" items such as a doll, a small stuffed animal, or a little toy (you'll have to draw the line at bringing the 10-pound Tonka truck). If your kids don't like drinking water, you can bring some powdered drink mix or a juice box.

Avoid poorly designed child-carrying packs—you don't want to break your back carrying your child. Most child-carrying backpacks designed to hold a 40-pound child will contain a large carrying pocket to hold diapers and other items. Some have an optional rain/sun hood.

HIKING WITH YOUR DOG

Bringing your furry friend with you is always more fun than leaving him behind. Our canine pals make great trail buddies because they never complain and always make good company. Hiking with your dog can be a rewarding experience, especially if you plan ahead.

Getting your dog in shape. Before you plan outdoor adventures with your dog, make sure he's in shape for the trail. Getting your dog into shape takes the same discipline as getting yourself into shape, but luckily, your dog can get in shape with you. Take your dog with you on your daily runs or walks. If there is a park near your house, hit a tennis ball or play Frisbee with your dog.

Swimming is also an excellent way to get your dog into shape. If there is a lake or river near where you live and your dog likes the water, have him retrieve a tennis ball or stick. Gradually build your dog's stamina up over a 2- to 3-month period. A good rule of thumb is to assume that your dog will travel twice as far as you will on the trail. If you plan on doing a 5-mile hike, be sure your dog is in shape for a 10-mile hike.

Training your dog for the trail. Before you go on your first hiking adventure with your dog, be sure he has a firm grasp on the basics of canine etiquette and behavior. Make sure he can sit, lie down, stay, and come. One of the most important commands you can teach your canine pal is to "come" under any situation. It's easy for your friend's nose to lead him astray or possibly get him lost. Another helpful command is the "get behind" command. When you're on a hiking trail that's narrow, you can have your dog follow behind you when other trail users approach. Nothing is more bothersome than an enthusiastic dog that runs back and forth on the trail and disrupts the peace of the trail for others—or, worse, jumps up on other hikers and gets them muddy. When you see other trail users approaching you on the trail, give them the right of way by quietly stepping off the trail and making your dog lie down and stay until they pass.

Equipment. The most critical pieces of equipment you can invest in for your dog are proper identification and a sturdy leash. Flexi-leads work well for hiking because they give your dog more freedom to explore but still leave you in control. Make sure your dog has identification that includes your name and address and a number for your veterinarian. Other forms of identification for your dog include a tattoo or a microchip. You should consult your veterinarian for more information on these last two options.

The next piece of equipment you'll want to consider is a pack for your dog. By no means should you hold all of your dog's essentials in your pack—let him carry his own gear! Dogs that are in good shape can carry 30 to 40 percent of their own weight.

Most packs are fitted by a dog's weight and girth measurement. Companies that make dog packs generally include guidelines to help you pick out the size that's right for your dog. Some characteristics to look for when purchasing a pack for your dog include a harness that contains two padded girth straps, a padded chest strap, leash attachments, removable saddlebags, internal water bladders, and external gear cords.

You can introduce your dog to the pack by first placing the empty pack on his back and letting him wear it around the yard. Keep an eye on him during this first introduction in case he decides to chew through the straps. Once he learns to treat the pack as an object of fun and not a foreign enemy, fill the pack evenly on both sides with a few ounces of dog food in resealable plastic bags. Have your dog wear his pack on your daily walks for a period of 2 to 3 weeks. Each week add a little more weight to the pack until your dog will accept carrying the maximum amount of weight he can carry.

You can also purchase collapsible water and dog food bowls for your dog. These bowls are lightweight and can easily be stashed into your pack or your dog's. If you are hiking on rocky terrain or in the snow, you can purchase footwear for your dog that will protect his feet from cuts and bruises.

Always carry plastic bags to remove feces from the trail. It is a courtesy to other trail users and helps protect local wildlife.

The following is a list of items to bring when you take your dog hiking: collapsible water bowls, a comb, a collar and a leash, dog food, plastic bags for feces, a dog pack, flea/tick powder, paw protection, water, and a first-aid kit that contains eye ointment, tweezers, scissors, stretchy foot wrap, gauze, antibacterial wash, sterile cotton tip applicators, antibiotic ointment, and cotton wrap. Your dog is just as prone—if not more prone—to getting in trouble on the trail as you are, so be prepared. Here's a rundown of the more likely misfortunes that might befall your canine friend.

Bees and wasps. If a bee or wasp stings your dog, remove the stinger with a pair of tweezers and place a mudpack or a cloth dipped in cold water over the affected area.

Porcupines. One good reason to keep your dog on a leash is to prevent it from getting a nose full of porcupine quills. You may be able to remove the quills with pliers, but a veterinarian is the best person to do this nasty job because most dogs need to be sedated.

Heat stroke. Avoid hiking with your dog in really hot weather. Dogs with heat stroke will pant excessively, lie down and refuse to get up, and become lethargic and disoriented. If your dog shows any of these signs on the trail, have him lie down in the shade. If you are near a stream, pour cool water over your dog's entire body to help bring his body temperature back to normal.

Heartworm. Dogs get heartworms from mosquitoes, which carry the disease in the prime mosquito months of July and August. Giving your dog a monthly pill prescribed by your veterinarian easily prevents this condition.

Plant pitfalls. If you have a long-haired dog, consider trimming the hair between his toes and giving him a summer haircut to help prevent plants from becoming tangled in his fur. After every hike always look over your dog for burs and other seeds—especially between his toes and his ears.

Plant hazards include burs, thorns, thistles, and poison ivy. If you find any burs or thistles on your dog, remove them as soon as possible before they become an unmanageable mat. Thorns can pierce a dog's foot and cause a great deal of pain. If you see that your dog is lame, stop and check his feet for thorns. Dogs are not immune to poison ivy, and they can pick up the sticky, oily substance from the plant and transfer it to you.

Protect those paws. Be sure to keep your dog's nails trimmed so he avoids getting soft tissue or joint injuries. If your dog slows and refuses to go on, check to see that his paws aren't torn or worn. You can protect your dog's paws from trail hazards such as sharp gravel and thorns by purchasing dog boots. Ruff Wear makes an excellent pair that is both sturdy and stays on dogs' feet.

Sunburn. If your dog has light skin, he is an easy target for sunburn on his nose and other exposed skin areas. You can apply a nontoxic sunscreen to exposed skin areas that will help protect him from overexposure to the sun.

Ticks and fleas. Ticks can easily give your dog Lyme disease, as well as other diseases. Before you hit the trail, treat your dog with a flea and tick spray or powder. You can also ask your veterinarian about a once-a-month pour-on treatment that repels fleas and ticks.

Mosquitoes and deer flies. These little flying machines can do a job on your dog's snout and ears. Best bet is to spray your dog with fly repellent for horses to discourage both pests.

Giardia. Dogs can get Giardia, which results in diarrhea. It is usually not debilitating, but it's definitely messy. A vaccine against Giardia is available.

Mushrooms. Make sure your dog doesn't sample mushrooms along the trail. They could be poisonous to him, but he doesn't know that.

When you are finally ready to hit the trail with your dog, keep in mind that national parks and many wilderness areas do not allow dogs on trails. Your best bet is to hike in national forests, BLM lands, and state parks. Always call ahead to see what the restrictions are.

Hike Index

About the Author

Johnny Molloy is a writer and adventurer who has penned over fifty outdoor hiking, camping, and paddling guides, as well as true outdoor adventure stories. His nonfiction passion started after reading *In Cold Blood* by Truman Capote, which his father had left lying around. After that, he delved into all manner of nonfiction reading, from *Strange But True Football Stories* to books about the Mississippi River, Lewis and Clark, and the Civil War. He has since focused his reading on early American history.

His outdoor passion started on a backpacking trip in Great Smoky Mountains National Park while attending the University of Tennessee. That first foray unleashed a love of the outdoors that has led Molloy to spend most of his time hiking, backpacking, canoe camping, and tent camping for the past three decades. Friends enjoyed his outdoor adventure stories, and one even suggested he write a book. He pursued his friend's idea and soon parlayed his love of the outdoors into an occupation.

Molloy writes for various magazines, websites, and newspapers. He continues writing and traveling extensively throughout the United States, engaging in a variety of outdoor pursuits. His non-outdoor interests include serving God as a Gideon and University of Tennessee sports. For the latest on Johnny, visit johnnymolloy.com.

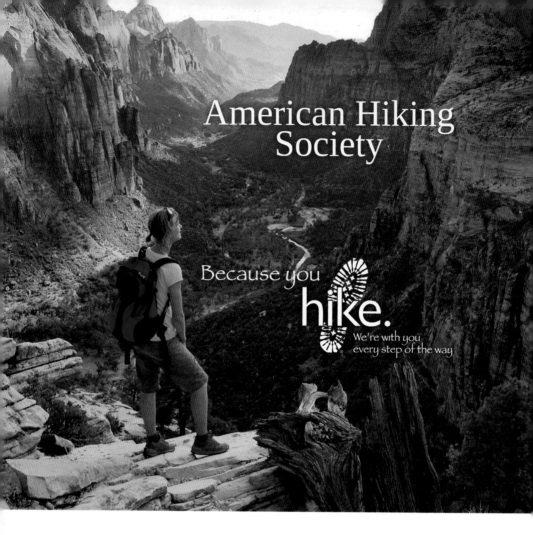

American Hiking Society

Because you
hike.
We're with you
every step of the way

As a national voice for hikers, **American Hiking Society** works every day:

- Building and maintaining hiking trails
- Educating and supporting hikers by providing information and resources
- Supporting hiking and trail organizations nationwide
- Speaking for hikers in the halls of Congress and with federal land managers

Whether you're a casual hiker or a seasoned backpacker, become a member of American Hiking Society and join the national hiking community! You'll enjoy great member benefits and help preserve the nation's hiking trails, so tomorrow's hike is even better than today's. We invite you to join us now!

American Hiking Society